THE NINE DAYS OF DUNKIRK

David Divine was born at Cape Town, South Africa, in 1904. He began work in the Anthropological Department of the South African Museum but then went to work on the staff of the *Cape Times* in 1923. After three years he left the paper to travel and later married in England. In 1931 he returned to South Africa to originate the daily column in the *Cape Times* entitled 'The World Goes By', which he edited for four years. He returned to England and soon became established as the author of a long series of thrillers. During the war he served in the navy and was awarded the DSM. He received the OBE in 1946. He has subsequently written many books on the work of the navy and on themes of war. He is currently Defence Correspondent on the *Sunday Times*.

The Nine Days of Dunkirk

by David Divine

WHITE LION PUBLISHERS LIMITED
London, New York, Sydney and Toronto

First published in Great Britain
by Faber and Faber Ltd 1959

Copyright © David Divine 1959

White Lion edition 1976

ISBN 7274 0195 5

Made and printed in Great Britain
for White Lion Publishers Limited,
138 Park Lane, London W1Y 3DD
by Hendington Limited,
Deadbrook Lane, Aldershot, Hampshire

Contents

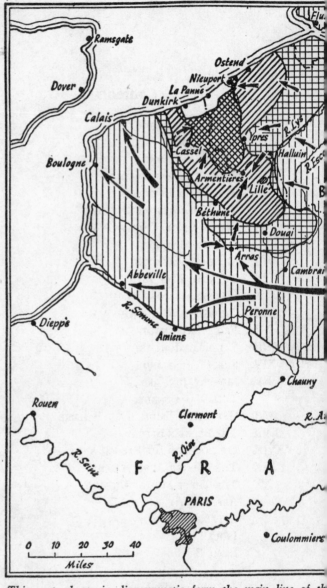

This map shows in diagrammatic form the main line of the
Armies of the North and the rest of France, and the progressi
Dunkirk perimeter. It illustrates graphically the speed and th
of the Armies of th

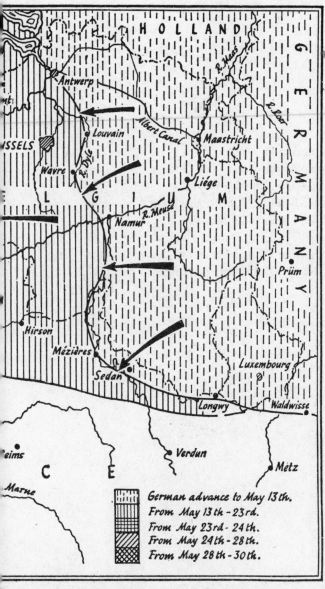

German advance to May 13th.
From May 13th – 23rd.
From May 23rd – 24th.
From May 24th – 28th.
From May 28th – 30th.

German advance, the severance of communication between the
shrinking of the Allied pocket until the establishment of the
ficiency with which von Manstein's plan for the elimination
North was executed.

Maps

ILLUSTRATIONS

are between pages 160 and 161

The photographs in this book appear
by permission of The Imperial War
Museum, and the Hulton Picture Library

Acknowledgments

Acknowledgments are made to the following for the use of quotations from the books listed below:

Cassell & Co. Ltd.
THEIR FINEST HOUR by Winston S. Churchill
SEA WARFARE, 1939–1945 by Vice-Admiral Friedrich Ruge
IN THE THICK OF THE FIGHT by Paul Reynaud

Chatto & Windus Ltd.
MY FIRST WAR by Sir Basil Bartlett, Bt.

Wm. Collins Sons & Co. Ltd.
THE ROMMEL PAPERS by Captain B. H. Liddell Hart
THE TURN OF THE TIDE by Arthur Bryant

H.M. Stationery Office
THE WAR IN FRANCE AND FLANDERS by Major L. F. Ellis
THE DEFENCE OF THE UNITED KINGDOM by Basil Collier
Vice-Admiral Sir Bertram Ramsay's Dispatch (No. 38017)
General the Viscount Gort's Dispatch (No. 35305)

Hodder & Stoughton Ltd.
RETURN VIA DUNKIRK by 'Gun Buster'

Hutchinson & Co. (Publishers) Ltd.
THE BUSINESS OF WAR by Major-General Sir John Kennedy

Michael Joseph Ltd.
PANZER LEADER by General Heinz Guderian

William Kimber & Co. Ltd.
THE MEMOIRS OF FIELD-MARSHAL KESSELRING

Methuen & Co. Ltd.
LOST VICTORIES by Field-Marshal Erich von Manstein

John Murray (Publishers) Ltd.
SPITFIRE! by Squadron Leader 'B. J. Ellan'

Foreword

THIS is not the whole story of Dunkirk. The nature of the campaign, the character of the evacuation make it inevitable that much escaped the record. A million men, if those of our Allies and those of the enemy are included, had their share in it. A thousand ships, British, Belgian, French – and German – took part. So far as the official documentation of the operation is concerned orders were not always written, minutes of meetings were not always kept, signals were frequently not received, logs were often unentered. In addition to these purely Service considerations there has been no military and naval operation in historic times in which civilian enterprise has played so wide a part. For all these reasons the official record of Dunkirk lacks the shape and the definition of more formal operations.

Through the very generous help of many of those who took a leading part in the campaign and the evacuation I have been given access to unpublished diaries, letters, signals, orders and private papers, which cover every major facet of this most complex period. With this assistance I have been able to construct what I believe to be a just account of the operations in their failure as well as in their triumph.

On the side of the British Expeditionary Force my thanks are due to Lieutenant-General Sir Henry Pownall, Lord Gort's Chief of General Staff throughout the campaign, to Viscount Bridgeman, who prepared the first general plan for the retreat to the beaches, to the Earl of Munster, who was Gort's Military Assistant, to Viscount De L'Isle, to Major-General Gordon Lennox, and to many other officers and men.

On the naval side I had the privilege of discussing the operation with Admiral Sir Bertram Ramsay shortly before his untimely death, and with the late Admiral Sir James Somerville. My thanks are due also to Admiral Sir Vaughan Morgan, who was Ramsay's Chief of Staff at Dover, to Admiral Sir William Tennant, who was Senior Naval Officer ashore at Dunkirk, and to Lady Wake-Walker, who gave me access to her late husband's unpublished account of the proceedings offshore.

On the side of the 'little ships' I am grateful to Admiral Sir Lionel Preston and Captain Wharton of the Small Vessels Pool, to Mr Bellamy and Mr Riggs of the Ministry of War Transport, to Rear-Admiral Taylor, and to His Honour J. D. Casswell, Q.C., who collected the logs of the civilian craft on which my war-time book *Dunkirk* was based and which have in some part been used again in this volume.

On the side of the Allies I have had invaluable information from M. Jacques Mordal, the French naval historian, and from Lord Keyes with regard to the work of his father with King Leopold of the Belgians.

I must acknowledge also much assistance from the German Official Historians, and, finally, from the numerous authors of all nations upon whose work I have drawn for fact, for opinion, or for criticism.

CHAPTER I

The Legends

I feared it would be my hard lot to announce from this box the greatest military disaster in our long history.

WINSTON CHURCHILL,
House of Commons, June 4th, 1940

IN THE EARLY morning of June 4th HMS *Albury* lay stopped off the North Foreland picking up the survivors of the French minesweeper *Emile Deschamps*. At Ramsgate the fast motor-boats crept in between the curving piers of the harbour at the end of their last crossing. At Dover Admiral Ramsay greeted Admiral Abrial – the *Amiral Nord* – and the evacuation of Dunkirk came in triumph to its end. 338,226 men of the Allied armies had been brought to safety on the English shore, and in the House of Commons that afternoon Mr Churchill rose to make the second of the great Dunkirk speeches.

'When a week ago I asked the House to fix this afternoon for a statement,' he said, 'I feared it would be my hard lot to announce from this box the greatest military disaster in our long history.'

In measured and memorable words he outlined the story of the miracle of the week that had passed, and when that was done he said with a deep humility:

'We must be very careful not to assign to this deliverance the attributes of a victory. Wars are not won by evacuations.'

No one will challenge that assertion. Wars are not won by evacuations, yet in innumerable campaigns in the long military history of Britain they have played their part. It is not necessary to search far for an explanation. Properly considered, evacuation is an exercise in the application of sea-power. The history of Britain rests upon sea-power. The great land campaigns that have been fought in the past by British armies have depended ultimately upon the strength of the ships of the Royal Navy. The recognition of that fact has led by simple logic to an interdependence between the Services, so that in crises British armies have fallen back naturally upon the sea in the assurance of assistance or of rescue.

Oddly, that fact has not been acknowledged in formal military or naval thinking. There has never been a department for the study of the technique of evacuation at Greenwich or at Camberley. It would not be difficult to make out a case for one; for though wars are not won by evacuations, time can be. Again and again in the record well-judged evacuation has given to British armies a flexibility that has never been possible to Continental forces. It is not a simple matter of saving an army from annihilation or even from defeat. Correctly used, the technique can give to armies the opportunity to fight again, and to fight at a time and in the place of their own choosing.

This is the real significance of Dunkirk. Its apparent triumph in the early days of June was that it had saved a quarter of a million men of the British Expeditionary Force from death or from a German prison camp. Its real triumph is that it brought back to England the core of the professional army.

War weariness following upon 1918, financial crises, and the peace moves between the wars had brought the British Army by way of disarmament to a dangerous level of inadequacy. The decision to send an expeditionary force to France, taken hastily and too late, had drawn from Britain almost the whole of the trained and equipped formations that existed. The equipment was abandoned in Flanders, the men came back, and from that fact sprang two consequences. The first is that when Britain woke to the danger of invasion there was a sound foundation for public confidence in the knowledge that, even if equipment were desperately short, the trained men were there to use it. The second is infinitely more important. Without the leaders, without the trained NCOs and the battle-tried men who came back through Dunkirk, the task of constructing the armies of the future must have been indefinitely delayed – may well have been wholly impossible. Most of the senior commanders of the later war fought in Flanders and in France. From the BEF came the cadres of the armies of victory. The invasion of Normandy was made possible in the nine days of Dunkirk.

Because of the scale of the operation, because of its illimitable consequences, it is hardly possible to find parallels for it.

Yet the history of evacuation is an ancient one. It goes back at least to the French Wars. It was used endlessly in the Colonial campaigns. In the Napoleonic Wars alone nineteen British forces were evacuated from various points along the Continental coasts. The most important of these withdrawals was that of the army of Sir John Moore from Corunna, and for more than a hundred years it stood as the model and the measure of evasive action.

Moore, it will be remembered, had disrupted Napoleon's expedition against Lisbon by a bold thrust at Burgos. Attacked by an army three times the size of his own, he fell back, fighting, towards Corunna. A final desperate march of seventeen days brought him to the port to find that the fleet which he had been promised had not arrived. On the ridge of the Monte Mero he established a perimeter of defence. Soult attacked that perimeter on January 16th, 1808, but in a great defensive action Moore held his position, and though, mortally wounded, he died before the battle ended, the ships had come and the French, fought to a standstill, watched his army go. Twenty thousand men went out from Corunna to the sanctuary of the sea.

Until Gallipoli there was no match for it. The Gallipoli evacuation in turn stood for twenty years as the masterpiece of military deception, the pinnacle of naval organisation. It is the yardstick by which we can measure Operation 'Dynamo', by which we may assess something of the magnitude, something of the astonishing stature of the nine days of the beaches.

The problem at Gallipoli was to move from two shallow positions served by the main landing places two forces of men, the first (from Anzac and Suvla) numbering 83,000, the second (from Helles) numbering approximately 42,000. These men were deployed in perimeters securely held, admirably defended with trench systems, wire and artillery, that had stood the test of eight months of bitter fighting. Transport difficulties were insignificant, every man, even in the forward observation posts, fought within walking distance of the embarkation points. On the beaches there were piers and quays. These were rough and improvised, but they had served to put an army ashore and to keep it supplied through the long months of the campaign. Everywhere along the perimeters the enemy lines were within reach of naval guns which could give – and did give – an astonishing covering fire. General Monro had two months after the decision was taken in which to prepare for the operation, he had sufficient ships, and he had nothing to fear from the primitive aircraft of the time.

Yet of Gallipoli Lord Kitchener could say in a telegram to General Birdwood:

'I absolutely refuse to sign order for evacuation, which I think would be greatest disaster, and would condemn a large percentage of our men to death or imprisonment.'

It is not necessary to examine the unhappy history of the decision for the abandonment of Gallipoli. It was an evacuation of policy, not of necessity. Monro selected his own moment for withdrawal. Before that moment there was time to practise every artifice, every device that might mislead the enemy.

The withdrawal from Suvla and Anzac was fixed for the night of December 19th, 1915. By the afternoon of December 18th 44,000 men, 130 guns and several thousand animals had already been embarked by an intensification of the normal traffic from the beaches. There remained something under 40,000 men ashore. It was considered impossible to lift more than 20,000 of these in a single night. In the darkness of the 18th the first 20,000 were embarked. On the night of the 19th, without interference from the enemy, the last men left the beaches, the dumps were fired and the mines exploded. There were no casualties and no losses.

The German military correspondent of the *Vossiche Zeitung* wrote:

'As long as wars last this evacuation of Suvla and Anzac will stand before the eyes of all strategists as a hitherto unattained masterpiece.'

Three weeks later the 'masterpiece' was surpassed at Helles. Once again a meticulously prepared operation was carried out – despite this time the intervention of the Turks – with complete success. On the night of January 8th the last 17,000 men were brought away.

There have been evacuations since Dunkirk. Norway, Greece, Crete, each had its epic. The Korean War witnessed the tremendous story of Hungnam, when under the cover of overwhelming seaborne air support a fleet of deep-sea ships brought away 105,000 men of the US Army, the Royal Marines and the South Korean Army, together with 100,000 refugees, in the face of numerically superior Chinese and North Korean forces.

Equally there have been failures since Dunkirk. There was no possibility of evacuation at Singapore; there was no time for it at Tobruk; there was no intention at Hong Kong. On the enemy's side the Germans and Italians failed utterly at Tunis, and it is in the surrender of von Arnim's and Rommel's armies that it is most instructive to search for the alternatives to Dunkirk. To begin with, the channel which separated the North African coast from Sicily was hardly wider than the channel between Dover and the beaches of La Panne by what came to be known as Route Y. In addition, the Italians and the Germans had had infinitely longer to prepare in planning and in practical measures for what was clearly an inescapable necessity. Yet a quarter of a million men surrendered at Tunis; fewer than 200 crossed to Sicily by sea. The explanation lies in the strength of Allied sea-power coupled with the superiority of the Allied air. When on May 8th, 1943, Admiral Cunningham sent out the signal 'Sink, burn and destroy. Let nothing pass!' which set in motion Operation 'Retribution', the destruction of the armies of North Africa was certain. The capitulation at Tunis is the measure of failure. Dunkirk stands – it may stand, in the light of the development of modern war, for ever – as the ultimate measure of success.

Great episodes of war attract legends. Dunkirk, because of its size, perhaps because of its success, has attracted more than its share. Much of the world still believes that it was executed by vast fleets of small craft spontaneously setting out from the English ports, unorganised and uncontrolled, to the rescue of the Army. Most of the German generals still hold that the BEF won clear because Hitler stopped the panzer divisions on the line of the Aa Canal. An important section of French opinion still believes the Vichy assertions of 'desertion'. Much of Britain even now considers that Leopold betrayed the British Army. The RAF still claims that it won qualitative superiority over the Luftwaffe above the beaches.

There are innumerable lesser legends. Insufficient credit has been given to the French Navy for its share in liftings. Insufficient credit has been given to the French Army for certain aspects of the fighting. Too much credit has been given to the battle of the left flank in an attempt to set up General Brooke as 'the man who saved the British Army at Dunkirk'.

Dunkirk has two aspects. In the retreat to the beaches Lord Gort fought a campaign of extraordinary complexity with desperately limited resources. Above him the French High Command dissolved in impotence. To his right the French centre broke and opened France to the power of Rundstedt's panzer divisions. To his left the Belgian Army, slowly battered into submission, capitulated and opened the way to the coast for the infantry of Bock. Between them Gort brought back the British Expeditionary Force unbroken to the beaches of Dunkirk. There he was met by the armada of a fantastic improvisation. Controlled by Admiral Ramsay from Dover Castle, 848 ships carried out a plan, brilliantly conceived and infinitely flexible, to a triumphant conclusion. The story of Dunkirk is the story of the achievement of these two men.

CHAPTER II

The *Schwerpunkt*

11 May 1940

Dearest Lu,

I've come up for breath for the first time today and have a moment to write. Everything wonderful so far. Am way ahead of my neighbours. I'm completely hoarse from orders and shouting. Had a bare three hours' sleep and an occasional meal. Otherwise I'm absolutely fine. Make do with this, please, I'm too tired for more.

GENERAL ROMMEL to his wife

A LITTLE AFTER half-past two in the darkness of the morning of May 10th, 1940, sixty-four men of the German Army, disguised as Dutch soldiers or wearing the 'overalls of working men, crossed the frontier between Roermond and Maastricht charged with the task of capturing the bridges across the Maas. Twenty-five days later in the same darkness before the dawn the destroyer *Shikari* slipped from the East Mole at Dunkirk for the last time, and·at his headquarters in the subterranean workings under Dover Castle Admiral Ramsay wrote out the signal which brought Operation 'Dynamo' to an end.

To understand 'the nine days' miracle' of Dunkirk it is essential to understand at least in outline the sixteen days of the fighting which preceded it, the fighting that broke Holland, shattered Belgium, and swept like a high wind across the fields of France.

The first phase of the German campaign against the Western Powers is a military masterpiece. Wars have been won in the past by the exploitation of new weapons and new methods. Seldom before has nation after nation fallen so swiftly, so completely before the remorseless application of a new technique.

The Germans had experimented with the blitzkrieg in

Spain and developed it in Poland. For nine months, while Britain and France painstakingly built up traditional forces, they had perfected it. For nine months, while the jest was current that the blitzkrieg was 'a lightning war that never struck in the same place once', the French High Command had perfected its traditional strategy. On May 10th the blitzkrieg struck.

By May 14th Holland was overwhelmed. By May 20th the German armour had reached the Channel coast at Abbeville. By May 27th the Belgian forces, fought to exhaustion on the left flank of the British Army, had surrendered. In the pocket that remained were trapped the British Expeditionary Force, the French First Army with the remnants of the French Seventh Army, and France was at the nadir of her fortune.

It was the triumph of the dynamic against the static, the triumph of a moving force – of tanks, of aircraft, of mechanised infantry – against the defensive principles which produced the Maginot Line.

*   *   *

The British Expeditionary Force began its movement to France on September 4th, 1939. By the end of that month 160,000 men, 25,000 vehicles and 100,000 tons of stores, fuel, and ammunition had reached France in safety. The nature of that achievement is perhaps not wholly understood. As late as April 1938 the Government intention was that in the event of war with Germany the British contribution to the Allied effort should be confined to naval and air forces. Not until March 1939 was the decision taken to commit more than a token force to fight with the French Army. The years of disarmament inevitably limited the size of that force. The figure of 160,000 men must not be accepted as a figure of fighting troops. It covered base structure, lines of communication, airfield, and technical personnel as well.

The French mobilisation had called up 2,000,000 men. For logical reasons the part played by the British Army in the field was a minor one. The part played by its Command in council was scaled to its strength in the field. The major decisions on strategy, then, were French. Broadly, the French intention was to establish an effective defence of the frontiers of France and to maintain it until some indeterminate time when the Allied forces could be built up to a scale sufficient for an offensive against Germany. To that policy Britain agreed, and the BEF

20

was tied to the French strategic plan.

The Maginot Line is one of the great illusions of history. Long before André Maginot, as Minister of War, secured the first appropriation of 2,900,000,000 francs towards its construction it had become an article of faith with the French High Command. The experience of the First World War, with its long-drawn struggle between fixed positions, projected itself into the period between the wars. In the middle of that struggle the tank had been born. The very nature of the war, however, had masked its qualities. In England, in France and, later, in Germany small groups of far-seeing men looked beyond that masking and saw the possibilities of the tank in movement, but only in Germany was a section of the newly re-created Army flexible enough to develop what those groups visualised. Even there it had to fight endlessly against the conservatism of the High Command. It fought, however, with success.

The German Army, if not the German High Command, believed in 1939 that tanks could thrust fast and far into the hinterland of an enemy country, that they could be supported – and, if necessary, supplied – by aircraft, that mechanised artillery could move with them, and that motorised infantry could co-operate and could hold the ground that they had won. It seems a commonplace today. It was an idea of genius then.

The French believed that a line of fortifications, constructed according to modern engineering principles, with all its personnel deep underground, with its guns commanding every possible line of approach, could hold an enemy indefinitely at bay. André Maginot, incidentally, had been a sergeant in the French Army in the First World War and his personal experience unquestionably induced him to throw his weight on the side of this belief.

The Maginot Line proper was, in fact, astonishingly strong. It was not broken in the battle that broke France. It was not broken for precisely the reason that made it an illusion – the Maginot Line ended in mid air. From Longuyon, where it ended, to the North Sea coast 200 miles away there was no defence. Once already in the lifetime of the men who made French policy the neutrality of Belgium had been brushed aside.

*   *   *

The Flanders plain is the natural approach to France. Except for the canal and river lines – none of them impassable to modern armies – there lie across it no strong defensive positions. It was the area of the Schlieffen Plan.

Count Alfred von Schlieffen, Chief of the German General Staff from 1891–1906, was the author of the plan which, in its broad outlines, was followed in 1914. Essentially it proposed that the German Army should ignore the fortified eastern frontier of France, should remain on the defensive in the area of the Rhine, and should swing through Belgium to attack the undefended Franco-Belgian frontier. If it had been pushed to its logical conclusions, the Schlieffen Plan would have succeeded then. It was to form the essential part of the first plan for the attack in the West a quarter of a century later. As a by-product the plan had the advantage of threatening at the very beginning of hostilities the dense industrial area of northern France, which held a high proportion of France's productive capacity for war.

Despite the Maginot Line no French General Staff could remain blind to the possibility of an attack across the Flanders plain, and equally no Staff could remain blind to the fact that a war fought with Lille, Roubaix, Tourcoing, Halluin, Tournai, and Armentières concentrated in a deep salient of a frontier battle line might result in the collapse of much of France's war industry in the first weeks. If the Staff had been blind to it, no politician could have been deaf to the political clamour of the representatives of that industry.

To guard against the possibility the frontier was manned. Along it lay five armies: the French Second Army from the end of the Maginot Line roughly to Sedan, the Ninth Army from Sedan to the valley of the Oise, the First Army from there to Maulde, the British Expeditionary Force from Maulde to Bailleul, and the French Seventh Army from there to the sea. Though some degree of fortification of the frontier line was carried out, the French General Staff never at any time had any real intention of fighting on it. The plan was to swing forward into Belgium and to carry the battle to the advancing enemy. This depended, firstly, on the strength of the Belgian frontier line – glibly spoken of at the time as a 'continuation' of the Maginot Line. It depended, secondly, on the ability of the four armies principally involved to swing into position without loss of time.

Two plans were in actual fact prepared. The first provided

22

for a limited advance to the Escaut (the River Scheldt) and was called Plan E. The second proposed an advance to the line of the River Dyle, which would cover Brussels and Antwerp: this was called Plan D.

The vital factor in the whole conception was the *Schwerpunkt* – the point at which the weight of the German blow would fall. In October 1939 General Sir Edmund Ironside, Chief of the Imperial General Staff, visited General Gamelin, Supreme Commander of the Allied Forces. General Gamelin stated that he 'expected a pinning-down attack on the Maginot Line . . . accompanied by an attack across the western frontier of Luxembourg into the Ardennes, sweeping south of the Meuse . . .'[1] But when in the first months of 1940 the final decisions as to planning were made General Gamelin had changed his mind. He now declared that 'an attack with large forces through the Ardennes is impracticable'.[2]

It was on the basis of his second thought that the final disposition of the armies was established. The requirement for speed and mobility dictated logically the position of the three armies nearest the sea – the French Seventh Army, the British Expeditionary Force and the French First Army. These three were mechanised and could cover the distances necessary to fulfil Plan D without difficulty. Connecting them with the Maginot Line was, first, General Corap's Ninth Army, which had to carry out a relatively short 'wheel' to the defile of the Meuse facing the Ardennes, and the French Second Army, which occupied the comparatively strong extension of the Maginot Line in the Sedan area. These two armies were amongst the weakest in the French order of battle. General Gamelin's estimate of the enemy's point of attack is one of the great errors in the history of strategic thinking.

Just after dawn on May 10th a heavy air raid developed over Arras – the headquarters of the British Expeditionary Force – and on the airfields, railways, and supply bases of the area. At 5.30 am a message was received by General the Viscount Gort, commanding the British Expeditionary Force, ordering 'Alertes 1, 2 and 3'. The effect of the alerts was to bring the British Expeditionary Force to immediate readiness to cross into Belgium. At 6.15 am Lord Gort was ordered to put Plan D into effect. At 1 pm the 12th Royal Lancers crossed the Belgian frontier.

*　　　*　　　*

[1] *The War in France and Flanders* by Major L. F. Ellis.　[2] Ibid.

23

By 10.30 that night the 12th Lancers had reached the line of the Dyle unopposed. The advance into Belgium was carried out with complete success. There was virtually no interference from the German air. The only real difficulty was with the Belgian road system. On the left the French Seventh Army,

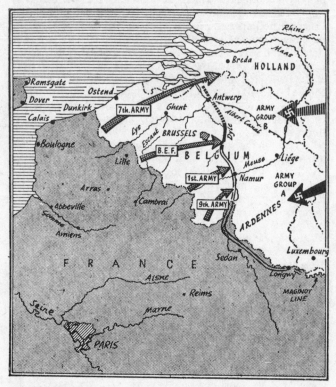

This diagram illustrates the swing forward of the four armies from the frontier positions to the line of the Meuse and the Dyle.

under General Giraud, swept across the plain to the estuary of the Scheldt and beyond it into Holland. On the right the French First Army, under General Blanchard, moved towards its assigned position across the Gembloux gap, the area of high ground between the Dyle and the Meuse, its cavalry taking up its line on schedule, its main body slower and less certain.

Below it the Ninth Army failed to carry out its time-table.

The Ninth Army was composed of what were called Series B divisions. It lacked transport and equipment, it had virtually no regular officers, and it had not been blooded to war. It was charged with holding a front of fifty miles with seven infantry divisions and two light cavalry divisions, still horsed and supported only by a few light tanks.

By May 12th the main outline of Plan D was complete except for the positioning of the Ninth Army, and on that day Lord Gort in his dispatch says:

'Disquieting news was received from the Ardennes, where a German thrust was reported as developing on the front of the French 9th Army, with at least two armoured divisions.'

* * *

The German plan for the offensive against the West dates from September 27th. Warsaw had fallen; the triumph of the new German technique had been proved. Hitler judged that the moment was ready for attack. The whole weight of the German General Staff was opposed to him, but on October 9th a formal directive ordering preparations for an offensive against the West was issued and on October 19th *Fall Gelb* – Plan Yellow – was complete.

Plan Yellow was the Schlieffen Plan in everything except name. Thirty-seven divisions, eight of them armoured and two motorised, were to smash across Holland and the Belgian plain, crash through the area of Brussels and shatter the Franco-Belgian frontier on the level flats of Flanders. A secondary attack was to be made through Luxembourg, principally to pin down the French reserves and to threaten the Maginot Line. As the plan developed Army Group B, the Northern German force, under Colonel-General von Bock, was strengthened. At the time when Gamelin was sure that the thrust would come through the Ardennes forty-three divisions, nine of them armoured and four motorised, were concentrated for the attack over the Belgian plain.

A comparison of the plans of the two sides in any war is a fruitful and fascinating study: in no war is it more fascinating than in this last. As General Gamelin altered his mind and accepted the advice of his experts that the Ardennes was an impossible country for a major armoured assault and that the attack must inevitably come across the open Flanders plain, the Germans abandoned the first version of Plan Yellow.

25

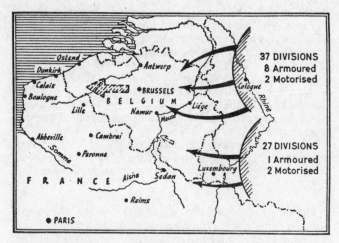

1. *Plan Yellow in its original form, showing the direction of the main weight of the German advance across the Flanders Plain with supplementary attacks in the area of the Maginot Line and Sedan.*

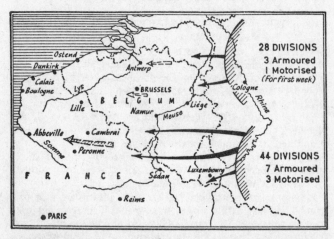

2. *Plan Yellow in the revised form evolved by von Manstein, showing the main weight directed across the Meuse between Sedan and Namur to take the Armies of the North in rear, with supplementary attacks across the Flanders Plain.*

The story of the change begins as early as October 31st when Colonel-General von Rundstedt, commanding Army Group A (the Southern force), wrote to Colonel-General von Brauchitsch, Commander-in-Chief of the German Army, to advocate that the main effort of the operation should be made on the southern wing. It is not possible to apportion exactly the credit between Rundstedt and his Chief of Staff, Lieutenant-General von Manstein, despite the latter's detailed account in *Lost Victories*, nor is it necessary to follow the long move and counter-move of the revisions of the plan.

Had the assault begun on November 5th, as was originally intended, it would have been unchanged but, largely owing to weather conditions, it was postponed. The second date was fixed for January 17th. On January 10th an aircraft of the German Air Fleet II was forced down in Belgium. One of the two officers on board endeavoured to burn papers which were in his possession, but the flames were put out while much of the material was still legible. It proved to be the orders for Air Fleet II for the offensive. The incident provoked one of the more remarkable of Hitler's explosions. None the less it was again weather that caused a second postponement of the attack and that continued to make it impossible. The accident – since information as to the contents of the paper was immediately transmitted to the French – had an important consequence for the Allied side, for it finally confirmed Gamelin's view that the Schlieffen Plan was to be used.

In the respite won by these postponements Rundstedt secured important concessions. Manstein, however, by his enthusiasm made himself obnoxious to the High Command and he was translated from his post to the command of the 38th Infantry Corps at Liegnitz. Lieutenant-Colonel von Tresckow, a colleague on Rundstedt's staff, apparently induced Colonel Schmudt, Hitler's Military Assistant, to arrange an opportunity for Manstein to talk to Hitler personally. On February 17th he was summoned to Berlin to lunch with the Führer, with other new corps commanders, and, following the luncheon, Hitler took him to his study and asked him to outline his views on the Western offensive.

'I found him surprisingly quick to grasp the points which our Army Group had been advocating for many months past, and he entirely agreed with what I had to say.'[1]

It is one of the fascinating little side issues of history that

[1] *Lost Victories* by Field-Marshal Erich von Manstein.

Manstein's virtual 'banishment' was used to convert the Führer. Three days later, on February 20th, the final operations order was sent out.

Plan Yellow was wholly altered: the emphasis of the attack was moved to the south, and its character was changed to give full rein to the possibilities of speed and armour in conjunction; Army Group B, advancing over the plain of Holland and Belgium, was cut down to twenty-eight divisions (three armoured and one motorised) and the main weight of the German armour was concentrated on the hill country of the Ardennes. As Corap's Ninth Army, with its horse-drawn trans-

The breaching of the Allied line. This diagram illustrates the crossing of the Meuse on May 13th and the first stage of the collapse of Plan D.

port, its exiguous armour and its jingling squadrons of cavalry, moved up to cover the roads through the Ardennes which run to the bridges of the River Meuse, forty-four divisions, seven of them armoured and three motorised, were already thundering down the defiles of the Ardennes towards them. General von Kleist's panzer group, in the van of Colonel-General List's Twelfth Army, led the attack. It had two prongs: one made up of three panzer divisions under General Guderian, the other of two under General Hoth. Smashing their way through felled tree trunks and undefended road blocks, the panzers overwhelmed the thin Belgian resistance. As they swept on through the 'impassable Ardennes' they met and brushed aside or drove back the cavalry of the Ninth Army, and on May 13th, barely three days from the start of operations, Major-General Erwin Rommel with the 7th Panzer Divisions crossed the Meuse on pontoons built by his engineers. On the afternoon of the same day two other crossings of the Meuse were made. Corap's Army, not yet in position, far too weak even had it reached and prepared its ground, was shattered.

On May 16th Rommel received orders to advance on the defensive positions that formed the continuation of the Maginot Line. As he moved forward in the middle of the morning, Lord Gort, far to the north, his own front holding firm against all German attacks, received orders to withdraw to the line of the River Scheldt. The front of the French First Army, on his immediate right flank, had been pierced over a width of 5,000 yards. Because of the confused and broken situation to the south there was no hope of reinforcement. It was urgently necessary for the French First Army to find a shorter and a better defensive position. On his left flank the Belgians, beaten back from their own front line, were endeavouring to form a firm front between Louvain and Antwerp. On their left in turn, Giraud, with the French Seventh Army, was falling back to Antwerp with much of his strength lost in the débâcle of Holland.

On the night of the 16th Lord Gort began his withdrawal to the River Senne, the first stage of the retreat to the Scheldt. In the same clear moonlight that eased the problems of retreat Rommel smashed through the defences of the French line and, as the moon rose, he wrote: 'The way to the West is open.' From the moment of that moonrise the evacuation at Dunkirk became as inevitable as the climax of a Greek tragedy.

CHAPTER III

Ramsay's Appointment

*About half-past seven on the morning of the 15th
I was woken up with the news that M. Reynaud was
on the telephone at my bedside. He spoke in English,
and evidently under stress. 'We have been defeated.'
As I did not immediately respond he said again: 'We
are beaten; we have lost the battle.'*

WINSTON CHURCHILL

ON MAY 15th the War Office informed the Ministry of
Shipping that changing circumstances might make necessary the reorganisation of the supply lines of the British
Expeditionary Force. For the first time the sea comes into the
picture of the battle of the Low Countries.

The British Expeditionary Force, because of the threat of
enemy air activity, had been landed at the western French
ports – Cherbourg, Brest, St Nazaire, and Nantes. As the
period of preparation continued Le Havre and Rouen and,
later, Dieppe were used; the main supply lines of the British
Army still ran north-east through Amiens and Arras to the
British sector of the front, though arrangements for a change
of base to make full use of the Channel ports were being considered before May 10th. The German thrust across the Meuse
was a direct threat to Amiens, a threat made infinitely more
dangerous by the dissolution of the Ninth Army. Officially the
thrust was spoken of as the 'bulge'. In fact it was a breach, a
breach that spread for fifty miles across almost the whole
width of the Ninth Army front, and all the efforts of elements
of Giraud's Seventh Army, withdrawn piecemeal for this purpose across the rear of the Belgians and the British, could not
hope to plug it. The reorganisation of the supply lines of the
British Army was not so much 'necessary' as vital.

From Dieppe the coast of France runs north-east and then
north to Cap Gris Nez at the narrows of the Straits of Dover.
From Gris Nez it trends east-north-easterly to the coast of

Holland. Five of the Channel ports lie on that stretch – Boulogne, Calais, Dunkirk, Ostend, and Zeebrugge. Beyond them, far up the Scheldt, lies Antwerp, but already Antwerp was at the point of surrender.

The first plan for the reorganisation of the supply of the BEF was based on the Channel ports. The area involved in the fighting lay within the limits of two naval commands. The southern part of the North Sea down to a line drawn from the North Foreland to the island of Walcheren was covered by the Nore Command under Admiral Sir Reginald Plunkett-Ernle-Erle-Drax. From the Foreland almost to Beachy Head the narrows of the Straits were the responsibility of the Dover Command under Vice-Admiral Bertram Ramsay; the Channel ports through which it was hoped to supply the BEF lay entirely within the limits of his command. As disaster overwhelmed the Armies of the North it became inevitable that Bertram Ramsay should be selected to command the operations for the attempt to evacuate the British Army.

Much, then, devolved on the personality and the capacity of Ramsay. He was a man of medium height, spare, with a face clean cut after a fashion that is almost a naval tradition. His voice was quiet and his manner unemotional. It was widely held amongst his contemporaries that he had little human sympathy. It was also held against him that he had an impatience of detail. Yet in the nine days of Dunkirk he was the architect and the inspiration of one of the greatest operations in the history of sea warfare; and, as the war progressed, he was the organiser, first, of the tremendous achievement of the landings in North Africa and in Sicily, and, finally, of the masterstroke of Normandy.

His career is a curious one. He was a naval failure – retired before his time with the rank of Rear-Admiral as a consequence of his refusal to accommodate himself to his Commander-in-Chief. His early career was undistinguished; his first experience of war was in 1903 when, as a Sub-Lieutenant in HMS *Hyacinth*, he took an assault party in through the surf of the Somali coast to a landing on the open African beaches. In the First World War his principal service, after a short period as Flag Lieutenant in HMS *Dreadnought*, was in the Straits of Dover, first, in command of a monitor and, subsequently, in command of HMS *Broke* of the Dover patrol.

In the difficult post-war years he moved steadily up the

ladder until in 1935 his efficiency as Captain of the *Royal Sovereign* brought him the appointment of Chief of Staff to the Home Fleet with the rank of Rear-Admiral. The appointment was foredoomed to failure. The Commander-in-Chief of the Home Fleet, Sir Roger Backhouse, brilliant academically, had no hobby except his work and rarely went ashore. He chose to keep everything in his own hands. Ramsay believed in a proper delegation of staff duties. The methods and the temperaments clashed. After a single cruise Ramsay asked to be relieved, throwing up an appointment that was one of the plums of the Service and a certain step to future promotion, and was placed on half-pay. After a short while he was offered the command of the Yangtse gun-boats. It was a 'retirement' appointment; moreover, it would take him out of the main current of naval development. Ramsay refused the offer and, in the opinion of the Navy, broke himself. In 1938 he was automatically placed on the Retired list on reaching the top of the Rear-Admiral's list.

The demands of the time and his unquestioned ability brought him almost immediately, however, a fresh employment. Because of his previous wartime experience of the area he was appointed, as the Munich crisis began, to make an examination of the state of Dover and its defences in the light of a possible war. His report was a devastating analysis of neglect. Dover had been allowed to run to seed: the harbour was silted up, the port facilities were inadequate, the defences and communications deplorable. By the time the report was complete Munich was over; Mr Chamberlain had brought back 'peace with honour', and Ramsay's services were dispensed with.

Two things, however, emerged from the report. The first was a £750,000 programme for the rehabilitation of Dover as a naval base and the second was a 'dormant appointment' for Ramsay himself to command at Dover in the event of hostilities or on orders from the Board of Admiralty. At the outbreak of war in September 1939, therefore, he became automatically 'Flag Officer in Charge, Dover'. The area was subsidiary to the Nore Command, but in a very short while it was obvious that it ought to be independent and Ramsay's title was changed to 'Flag Officer Commanding Dover' or, more shortly, 'Vice-Admiral, Dover', with responsibility direct to the Board of Admiralty.

Ramsay's first task was to safeguard the left flank of the

British Expeditionary Force in its movement to France. The Straits of Dover had a primary importance as a U-boat block. Ramsay brought to it the accumulated experience of the Dover Patrol in the First World War. But, as the 'quiet period' of the war developed, it achieved a painful importance as one of the principal areas of the magnetic-mine campaign. That the Navy should have expected and prepared for the magnetic mine before the outbreak of war is accepted. Its neutralisation, none the less, is one of the most brilliant stories of the work of the naval scientists, and because of their success the Command in May 1940 was again relatively quite. Adequate measures for the protection of ships against the mine had been put into operation, the U-boat had ceased to be of practical importance in the area, aircraft had not yet become a vital issue, and there was no surface activity.

*   *   *

The possibility of the loss of Holland and the ports of the Low Countries had been considered at the outbreak of the war. As early as October 1939 plans were completed for the blocking of the ports in the area if a German advance made this necessary, and reinforcements for the Nore Command were, in principle, decided upon.

On May 8th intelligence reports of enemy movements indicated that the time had come for the second of these plans to be put into active preparation, and reinforcements of cruisers and destroyers were ordered to the Nore and Harwich. The laying of a minefield off Ijmuiden, the sending of demolition parties to that port, the Hook of Holland, Flushing, and Antwerp were the responsibility of the Nore Command. Operations off the Belgian coast were made the responsibility of Vice-Admiral Abrial, the French *Amiral Nord*, who was lent, first four, and later another two, British destroyers. In the speed and confusion of the time the command areas overlapped, and Ramsay took over the demolitions.

On the morning of May 10th four destroyers left Dover with demolition parties while the Nore Command cruisers covered the operation and other ships sailed to lay minefields. In a series of remarkable exploits the Dutch gold reserve, the Crown Princess and her family, and, finally, the Dutch Queen and the Cabinet were brought from Holland before the resistance of the Dutch Army finally collapsed. It is not necessary – indeed, it is hardly possible – to separate the responsibilities for individual exploits here, but under tremendous pressure demolitions were carried out wherever the co-operation of the Dutch could be secured, and Dutch naval vessels and merchantmen were successfully convoyed back to England.

On May 14th in the nine o'clock news from London the BBC broadcast the following announcement:

'The Admiralty have made an order requesting all owners of self-propelled pleasure craft between 30 and 100 feet in length, to send all particulars to the Admiralty within 14 days from today, if they have not already been offered or requisitioned.'

This announcement has been considered by some commentators as the starting point of the naval preparations which led to the evacuation. In particular the French have advanced it as one of the 'proofs' that evacuation was decided upon early and without consultation.

It had, in fact, nothing whatever to do with Dunkirk. It was a perfectly normal administrative step initiated by an Admiralty department known as the Small Vessels Pool, in view of the fact that requirements for small craft were increasing rapidly everywhere at that time. The Small Vessels Pool was under the command of Admiral Sir Lionel Preston, and it controlled the supply of small craft for harbour work and auxiliary purposes. Though it had begun a considerable programme of boat building, the urgent necessity for wooden minesweepers which arose out of the magnetic-mine campaign had absorbed most of the effort of the boat yards, and the department considered that its immediate needs could best be met by requisition. The order had passed through normal Admiralty channels and had been initiated long before the attack opened on May 10th, nor were its terms urgent, owners being given fourteen days in which to send particulars of their ships. None the less it was to play an important part when the desperate need for small craft arose.

On the evening of May 16th demolition work in the port of Antwerp began. Twenty-six Allied ships, fifty tugs, 600 barges, dredgers, and floating cranes had already got clear of the port. On this evening 150,000 tons of oil were destroyed and the entrances to the docks and the basins blocked. The enemy reaction to these operations was confined mainly to the air – the German Navy was still licking its wounds after the losses of the Norwegian campaign – but to German bombers

Britain lost the destroyer *Valentine*, and the *Winchester* and the *Westminster* were both badly damaged.

As Lord Gort gave the orders for the retreat to the Senne to begin, the small forces of the Nore and the Dover Commands were already hard worked and hard pressed.

CHAPTER IV

The Three Blunders

I then asked: 'Where is the strategic reserve?' and, breaking into French, which I used indifferently (in every sense): 'Où est la masse de manœuvre?' General Gamelin turned to me and, with a shake of the head and a shrug, said: 'Aucune.'

WINSTON CHURCHILL

THE THREE cardinal blunders of the first phase of the campaign of 1940 lie basically in the sphere of strategy. The French had failed to continue their defence line to the sea. As the German attack developed, they failed to provide an adequate substitute for that defence line. Now, overshadowing all that had gone before, it was apparent that they had established no reserve, no *'masse de manœuvre'*, which could be moved to redress disaster.

It is true that in 1949 Gamelin claimed that he had not answered: 'There are none' but: 'There are no longer any.' The basic fact remains the same: such reserves as there were were so exiguous that they had no effect on the situation. There was, in fact, no *masse*.

The relative strength of the two sides is of importance here. The Germans disposed of 136 divisions, the Allies, including Belgium and Holland, theoretically of 135, though in actual fact the Allied total of manpower was substantially higher than that of the Germans. It is widely believed that the German power lay in a vast superiority in tanks – a figure of 10,000 was accepted in French official circles. In fact, the Germans attacked with some 2,800 tanks and 700 armoured cars. The four Allies between them had a total of 3,000 tanks and a rough parity in armoured cars. These were dispersed over a frontier that stretched from the River Ems to the Mediterranean.

Winston Churchill, flying to France on May 16th on the first of his urgent journeys, found in the great rooms of the Quai d'Orsay an atmosphere of defeat. In the gardens they were already burning the archives. Everywhere the word was that the Germans would be in Paris within a few days. The position was beyond hope. General Héring, the Military Governor of Paris, had advised the French Government to evacuate the capital.

That night Gort carried out his successful withdrawal to the Senne. The Belgian Army, to his left, and the French First Army, hotly engaged on his right, carried out their withdrawals in conjunction. There was never any possibility of holding the Senne line, though General Georges had envisaged a twenty-four-hour delay on it. On the night of the 17th the Allied armies fell back again, this time to the line of the Dendre. On the night of the 18th they began a fresh withdrawal to the line of the Scheldt and on the 19th they were in position. But the Scheldt was no longer a real barrier; the French First Army had lowered the sluices to establish inundations in the Valenciennes area, and the depth on the British section of the river was reduced to three feet.

Though enemy pressure had been heavy on the French First Army sector of the front and only slightly less heavy on the front of the BEF and the Belgians, these successive withdrawals were dictated not by that pressure but by the impossible situation that had developed in rear of the Allied line. As the three armies fell back in the north the 'bulge' in the south had developed into a salient, the salient into a break-through, the break-through into an axe stroke that severed France and with it severed the life of the Armies of the North. By the 17th the spearheads of the German armour in the south were at the outskirts of St Quentin. By the 18th they had captured Péronne. On the 19th they were across the Canal du Nord and in full career towards the sea.

May 19th is an extremely important date in the campaign of northern France. With the establishment of the Escaut position the situation of the Armies of the North became for the first time static. To the south, on the other hand, the German lunge to the sea continued with unabated speed. In Paris Reynaud had decided finally on the dismissal of Gamelin, and Weygand was in process of making up his mind to accept the post of Supreme Commander. In London a degree of optimism, based on delayed and unrealistic information from French sources, still prevailed.

Lord Gort at his Command Post considered the immediate position of the British Expeditionary Force. Despite last-minute efforts to establish a defence of Abbeville, it was now obvious that nothing would stop the Germans from reaching the sea. Already his lines of communication were severed. He was cut off from his main supply dumps and from this day onward he knew that he would have to fight on the forward echelons of ammunitions, fuel and food, with such supplies as could be brought in by sea. He knew, further, that his one hope of armoured reinforcement – the First Armoured Division – could not now get to him, that the headquarters of the Air Component, driven out of its airfields, was already moving to England and that his future air support was problematical. Finally, he knew that from the moment the Germans reached the sea 85 miles of his rear from the right flank of the French First Army to the Channel coast was open to the enemy. His estimate of the situation is outlined with admirable clarity in his dispatch. He gives three possible courses of action: the first, the maintenance of the Escaut line in the event of a successful simultaneous counter-attack from the north and from the south which would reopen communications with France; the second, the possibility of a general withdrawal to the line of the Somme, which 'would obviously be unwelcome to the Belgians who would be faced with the alternatives of withdrawing with us and abandoning Belgian soil, fighting on a perimeter of their own, or seeking an armistice'; and, finally, the possibility of a withdrawal towards the Channel ports.

'I realised that this course was in theory a last alternative ... It involved the virtual certainty that even if the excellent port facilities at Dunkirk continued to be available, it would be necessary to abandon all the heavier guns and much of the vehicles and equipment. Nevertheless, I felt that in the circumstances there might be no other course open to me. It was therefore only prudent to consider what the adoption of such a plan might entail.'

At 1.30 pm the Chief of the General Staff of the British Expeditionary Force, Lieutenant-General H. R. Pownall, telephoned the Director of Military Operations and Plans at the War Office and presented these alternatives to him.

It is on the basis of this presentation that criticism of Gort became vocal. This criticism had two streams. The first was French: it began with accusations that Gort was 'independent' and it ended with denunciations of 'desertion'. The second stream was British: it is crystallised in a comment written by

38

General Alan Brooke, then Commander of II Corps:[1]

'He had the most wonderful charm, and was gifted with great powers of leadership . . . I could not help admiring him . . . But I had no confidence in his leadership when it came to handling a large force. He seemed incapable of seeing the wood for the trees.'

The acid and insinuating character of these remarks may be accepted as common to those who disapproved of Gort. To them was added subsequently by other critics the suggestion that Gort was always looking over his shoulder towards the sea. The validity of these criticisms will be considered in a later chapter. What is important here is the character and capacity of Gort himself, for upon his decisions rested the fate of the British Expeditionary Force and, in addition, that of 140,000 Frenchmen of the First and Seventh Armies.

John Vereker, 6th Viscount Gort of Limerick, was gazetted to a commission in the Grenadier Guards in 1905. In the First World War he held a succession of Staff appointments until in April 1917 he returned to regimental duty in command of the 4th Grenadier Guards. In a series of actions he established a reputation for courage and audacity not often equalled even in the bitter fighting of that war. In the course of these he won the DSO with two Bars, and the MC. In September 1918 he commanded the 1st Grenadier Guards at the crossing of the Canal du Nord. Wounded early in the action, he refused to surrender the command and at a critical moment went into the open to lead a tank into position on foot. Wounded a second time, he continued to exercise command from a stretcher, and for his superb courage and leadership he was awarded the Victoria Cross.

Between the wars his career was varied. In 1936, as a young major-general, he was appointed Commandant of the Staff College. The following year he went to the War Office as Military Secretary. There is a story that he first met Hore-Belisha, then the new broom at the War Office, by colliding with him on a snow slope in Switzerland. The story is probably apocryphal, but it is quite certain that Belisha early decided to use Gort's reputation as a fighting soldier in his campaign for arousing interest in and enthusiasm for the Army. In due course out of that association came Gort's appointment as Chief of the Imperial General Staff. This appointment was made over the heads of a number of generals older than Gort

[1] *The Turn of the Tide* by Arthur Bryant.

and senior to him in the Army List.

The decision to send a major expeditionary force to fight in France was, as has been recorded, taken late. At the beginning of September 1939 a staff for that force was only in process of being assembled, and no decision had yet been announced as to the appointment of a Commander-in-Chief. On September 2nd the officers organising staff duties at Aldershot were informed unofficially that General Sir Edmund Ironside would command the force. On the morning of Sunday, September 3rd, Ironside's Military Assistant arrived with full powers, but on Sunday afternoon, immediately following the declaration of war, it was officially announced that Lord Gort was to be Commander-in-Chief and that Ironside was to take over the office of CIGS in his place – he had been one of the senior officers passed over at Gort's appointment. Two other officers who had also been senior to Gort on appointment were given the command of I and II Corps – Lieutenant-General Sir John Dill and Lieutenant-General A. F. Brooke. Gort's position, therefore, was one of considerable delicacy both with regard to the command at home and with regard to his immediate subordinate commanders in the field.

Three major factors emerge from this all too brief biographical sketch: that Gort was a man of immense courage, that he had been appointed 'out of turn' to high command with the inevitable consequences, and that he was believed to be a man of detail 'unable to see the wood for the trees'.

It is essential here to understand precisely his position in the general military hierarchy. As Commander-in-Chief of the British forces in France he was responsible to the Chief of the Imperial General Staff and through him to the Government under Mr Neville Chamberlain. But as commander of an army in the line he was responsible through the French chain of command to General Gamelin, Supreme Commander of the Allied Forces. Gamelin's authority devolved through General Georges, who commanded the French North-East Theatre of Operations.

This was the situation when the frontier was crossed on May 10th. Two days later at a meeting at the Château Casteau it was decided that the situation demanded a closer integration of the Allied armies, and the King of the Belgians and Lord Gort respectively were asked if they would accept co-ordination by General Billotte as General Georges' representative. Broadly speaking, then, Lord Gort's position lay at the fourth level of this complicated chain of command. He was personally responsible, therefore, only for his own army. The responsibility for operational control was that of the French generals.

From the moment the Meuse was crossed the French strategy broke down. With it the chain of command broke also. General Billotte was wholly unsatisfactory from the first. The British official historian says of him:[1]

'. . . the "co-ordinator" must be able to appreciate the position of the commanders who look to him, and to translate directives from the High Command into practical orders which they can carry out. On the other hand the commanders whose actions he is to co-ordinate must have confidence in his judgement and be willing to act on his orders. In this instance the arrangement worked but haltingly, for neither of these conditions was ever wholly fulfilled.'

The seven days that followed the crossing of the Meuse offer material for a profound study in the degeneration of a military machine. Before the end of the seven days was reached Paris was endeavouring to command by exhortation, and commanders in the field were interpreting exhortations in the sober light of practical possibilities.

There were therefore trees enough in the wood that Gort faced on May 19th. On this day he acknowledged formally the fact that from now on he would have to fight two battles and that he would have to fight them, in the main, on his own. At midnight of the previous night he had had a conference with General Billotte. Billotte's attitude was one of gloom: he had no confidence in any restoration of the Ninth Army front; news from the First Army was depressing. The French had no constructive suggestions to offer. Late on the 19th Gort, therefore, divided his staff into two sections: one, under Brigadier Sir Oliver Leese and Lieutenant-Colonel P. G. S. Gregson-Ellis, to deal with the original front that was hereafter to be called the Eastern battle, and the other, under Major-General T. R. Eastwood and Lieutenant-Colonel the Viscount Bridgeman, to deal with what now was to become the Western battle. The two sections were under the unifying direction of General Pownall as Chief of General Staff.

It is necessary to go back here for two days in order to understand the beginnings of the Western battle. On the 17th, while the second phase of the retreat from the Dyle was in preparation, it became evident that the German advance was

[1] *The War in France and Flanders* by Major L. F. Ellis.

threatening the area of Péronne far to the south and, in consequence, of Arras, the area of rear Headquarters. On this day General Georges made one of his ineffectual efforts to dam the tide that was flooding across France. The British 23rd Division, a territorial formation which was engaged on lines of communication and rear area duties, was ordered to take up a position on the line of the Canal du Nord between Ruyaulcourt and Arleux. It had neither artillery nor signals, its transport was exiguous, and it lacked almost all administrative units. Shortly after it reached its allotted position it was ordered to take up another location to the south. This it was unable to do. No French troops arrived to relieve it or to take up position on its flank, and it waited 'in the air' for the enemy attack.

At the same moment Gort, who was losing faith in the character of French resistance, decided that it was necessary to make some provision to guard his right flank. He therefore organised a mixed force of armour and infantry, and appointed Major-General F. N. Mason-MacFarlane, his Director of Intelligence, to command it and to cover the area from his right flank at Maulde down to Carvin on the La Bassée Canal. This was the first move in the establishment of the long series of Special Forces which were eventually to hold the German swing to the north. It was probably the least effective since the French First Army maintained its positions in the end with great courage.

Simultaneously with the establishment of Macforce a general defence of the Arras area was initiated by rear Headquarters and subsequently consolidated on May 18th under Major-General R. L. Petre. This was known as Petreforce. On the 19th, following the gloom of Billotte's midnight conference, the 50th Division, then in army reserve, was rushed in improvised transport to continue the flank from Carvin to La Bassée.

By the evening of May 19th Gort had taken the necessary action to guard his right flank from any sudden thrust up from the south-west. It must not be assumed from this, however, that a line had been established. The forces – all that could be gathered in the short time available – covered areas rather than lines, but by the afternoon of the 19th news from the French First Army front was more satisfactory and it appeared certain that it would now hold its position in the half-circle that stretched from Maulde through Valenciennes and came back to Douai. On the enemy side too the position had become more definite. The break-through on a broad front had divided now into two separate thrusts: one down the valley of the Somme towards the sea at Abbeville, the other through Hesdin and Montreuil towards the Channel ports. Gort was allowed a momentary leisure to consider the next moves.

In London the effects of General Pownall's telephoned outline of the situation were serious. Ironside and Dill (who had left the BEF to become Vice-Chief of the Imperial General Staff in April) were not prepared to accept Gort's assessment of the crisis with its possible third course. Information from Paris was still unreliable, late and unrealistic, and the War Cabinet decided that Ironside should proceed to France to view the position on the spot.

Gort himself was not yet examining his third course in detail. He had stated it in plain terms, but on what information he could glean from the French he believed that there was still a possibility of a double counter-attack from north and south. He now sent the 5th Division to join the 50th in the area of Vimy and began an outline plan for an attack to the south to take place on the 21st through Arras towards Cambrai.

Ironside arrived early in the morning armed with instructions from the Cabinet that:

'. . . the BEF was to move southwards upon Amiens, attacking all enemy forces encountered and to take station on the left of the French Army.'

This was the new French Army that was reputed to be forming along the line of the Somme. There was no basis of realism in this order. It ignored all the hard facts of the situation. In the Eastern battle the main forces of the British Expeditionary Force were engaged along the whole line of the Escaut, ammunition was reduced to that which was carried in the mobile echelons, food was already short, transport was diminishing, petrol was in reasonable supply but only in the Lille area, and a general withdrawal to the south would involve the abandonment of the Lille dumps. The hope that the Belgians either could or would take part in a movement which meant the final abandonment of Belgium and a problematical adventure to the south was illusionary, and the belief that the French First Army could operate in strength was equally far from the truth.

If anything were needed to convince General Ironside once he had seen the position as it existed, it was the news as he reached Headquarters that enemy tanks were already attacking to the south of Arras. It was rapidly made clear that Gort's

43

plan to attack south with the 5th and the 50th Divisions and what armour he could raise was the only practicable measure in the circumstances, and the meeting ended with Ironside's departure for French Headquarters to carry that plan to Billotte.

The one alternative to this plan was offered by General Brooke, who appears at that time to have been in favour of a retirement on Ostend and Zeebrugge with Belgian co-operation. This extraordinary idea seems to have been dismissed early.

Billotte agreed at once to co-operate with Gort's plan to the extent of two divisions and the French Cavalry Corps, which had been reduced to about 25 per cent of its armour. By 6 pm that evening the 12th Lancers, under Colonel Herbert Lumsden, whose scouting operations throughout this campaign represent the very highest achievement of their kind, were forced back to a line from Arras to St Pol. The weight and the direction of the German thrust from the south was now apparent. At this hour Major-General H. E. Franklyn had called a conference as Commander of Frankforce – the name which had now been given to the 5th and 50th Divisions – to settle final details for the attack of the 21st. The French, who had promised to send representatives on the basis of Billotte's agreement to attack simultaneously with two divisions, failed to arrive.

Meanwhile, at Headquarters, Gort continued to work on the construction of stop-gap forces. The information that came in as to the speed and spread of the German advance was swiftly establishing the fact that no point of the 85-mile line of canals from the French flank at Millonfosse to Gravelines was safe against attack. Polforce was set up in the St Pol–Carvin area of the Canal Line under Major-General H. O. Curtis, and Colonel C. M. Usher, who had been in command of a section of the communications area and who had already set in motion on his own responsibility elaborate measures to safeguard the approaches to Dunkirk in his vicinity, was ordered to set up a special force to be called Usherforce for the northern end of the line at Bergues, just outside Dunkirk.

Later in the day Gort was informed from England that the new Supreme Commander, Weygand, would be in the area on the 21st. The news of Weygand's assumption of the Command had been received with enthusiasm at Headquarters, as it was felt that any change from Gamelin's nerveless handling

44 ·

of the situation must be for the good. While he waited for Weygand Gort received at 12.30 pm a letter from Blanchard, which stated that it was impossible for the French First Army to move in conjunction with Franklyn's attack until the 22nd or even possibly the following night.

To the south Rommel, flushed with his magnificent feat at the crossing of the Meuse, fresh from his race across the heart of northern France, had already turned towards Arras with the 7th Panzer Division. Franklyn himself had received the news that the French could not move until the 22nd earlier than GHQ. Through General Prioux, however, he had received a promise of light armoured formations to cover his right flank. Reconnaissance reports made it clear that he could not delay the preliminary clearance operation which he had set for this day, and in the early afternoon of the 21st Frankforce moved forward to clear the area south-east of Arras and to deny the approach roads to the enemy. It charged headlong against the weight of Rommel's armour.

From the moment the leading German elements had streamed out through the broken Ninth Army the German Command had awaited counter-attacks from the north and from the south. Now at last counter-attack had materialised. Rommel himself, as was his custom, was up with the leading elements of his troops. The vigour and the élan of the British attack appears to have upset his judgement.

'Every gun, both anti-tank and anti-aircraft, was ordered to open rapid fire immediately and I personally gave each gun its target. With the enemy tanks so perilously close, only rapid fire from every gun could save the situation. We ran from gun to gun . . .' [1]

This was the first real opposition that his force had met with. Its effect was entirely disproportionate to the real weight and the intention of the attack. The SS Division *Totenkopf*, which had not yet been blooded, began to display signs of panic. Rommel himself described it as 'a very heavy battle against hundreds of enemy tanks and following infantry'. On his situation map for that day he showed the attack as being delivered by five British divisions in the immediate vicinity of Arras. In fact, it was launched by the 1st Army Tank Brigade, which mustered a total of 74 tanks, many of them desperately in need of overhaul and with their tracks worn out. In support of the tanks were two battalions of infantry, and operating on the

[1] *The Rommel Papers*. Edited by B. H. Liddell Hart.

right flank was the French armoured force, small in numbers and consisting almost entirely of light tanks.

Rommel's report went back to Rundstedt. Rundstedt hesitated. Though Rommel had halted the 'counter-attack', it seemed that the danger the German Command had always feared was about to materialise. In 1945 Rundstedt said:[1]

'A critical moment in the drive came just as my forces had reached the Channel. It was caused by a British counter-stroke southward from Arras on May 21. For a short time it was feared that our armoured divisions would be cut off before the infantry divisions could come up to support them. None of the French counter-attacks carried any serious threat as this one did.'

The attack was already in progress when Weygand arrived at Ypres for his meeting with the King of the Belgians. No information had reached Lord Gort with regard to the time and place of this conference. In his absence Weygand outlined future strategy to King Leopold and endeavoured to persuade him to withdraw to the Yser to cover a combined attack by the BEF and the French First Army to the south. The Belgians were left with the impression that 'the Supreme Commander was not aware of the situation'. None the less, the plan as outlined heavily involved the BEF and it was obviously necessary that it should be discussed with Gort, who was accordingly sent for. Before he could reach Ypres Weygand had left, and there was at no time any direct contact between Gort and the new Supreme Commander.

In the interim Gort had already held a conference with his corps commanders on the development of the Eastern battle. Brooke and Lieutenant-General M. G. H. Barker, who succeeded to the command of I Corps, are recorded as being pessimistic. Lieutenant-General Sir Ronald Adam, who commanded the new III Corps, was, according to a contemporary account of the conference, sound in his appreciation of the circumstances. All three generals, however, agreed that it was impossible to sustain the front on the Escaut for more than twenty-four hours, and the question of a withdrawal to the old frontier positions to take advantage of the pill-boxes, trenches, and anti-tank works, which had been built during the winter, was examined. The meeting decided that no alternative existed.

Gort's subsequent conference with the King of the Belgians

[1] Ibid.

and General Billotte was unsatisfactory. Billotte said frankly that the French First Army was 'too tired' to take part in offensive operations in the immediate future. The retirement to the old frontier positions was, however, decided upon, and in conformity with it the Belgians agreed to pull back to the River Lys. At the end of the conference Billotte asked the King of the Belgians in set terms if in the event that he was forced to withdraw from the Lys, he would fall back upon the line of the Yser.

'His Majesty,' said Gort, 'agreed, though evidently with some regret, that no alternative line existed.'

On the way back from the conference Billotte was fatally injured in a road accident.

On balance the effects of the Ypres conference were depressing. Weygand had engendered no confidence: he had made it obvious, in fact, that he had no confidence himself. The news that was beginning to reach Headquarters as to the progress of the Arras battle was good but it was not yet sufficient to counter-balance the general effect of doubt that had sprung from Weygand's lack of realism.

That night General Pownall ordered Colonel Bridgeman to begin work on a plan for the evacuation of the British Expeditionary Force in conjunction with representatives from each of the three corps. This order is important. Gort had listed the possibility of evacuation as the third of his three courses on May 19th. This was the first moment at which that possibility entered into the practical planning of GHQ. Planning had actually started in England thirty-six hours before at the Dover meeting and, as will be seen later, Gamelin had given Admiral Darlan orders to investigate the possibilities of evacuation as early as the morning of May 19th.

On the morning of May 22nd there was room for a small degree of optimism in the position of the BEF. In the Western battle Arras was holding, the special forces were getting into position on the Canal Line, and the French First Army appeared to have established itself firmly. In the Eastern battle preparations for the withdrawal from the Escaut were well under way and, though a strong German attack had developed on the left flank, it was being held. At 9 am, when the draft plan for evacuation was complete, Colonel Bridgeman was informed that it was not yet wanted.

Churchill had flown to Paris. Late in the morning Churchill and Dill met Reynaud and Weygand. In the afternoon Gort

47

received a message from the Prime Minister which gave the decisions of the conference: that the Belgian Army should withdraw to the Yser; that the British Expeditionary Force and the French First Army should attack southward 'certainly tomorrow with eight divisions' and with the Belgian Cavalry Corps on the right of the British; that the British Air Force would give the utmost help; and that the new French Army Group, 'advancing upon Amiens', would strike northwards and join hands.

Later in the day General Weygand issued his Operation Order No. 1. Indefinite almost to the point of incomprehensibility, it was an expression of policy and not a plan. There was no possibility of attack with eight divisions. Weygand, despite the information that Billotte had given him at Ypres, had wholly misrepresented the potential strength of the French First Army and wholly disregarded the fact that on the main front the First Army, the BEF, and the Belgians were under heavy pressure from Bock's Army Group. This in turn was followed by Operation Order No. 17 from General Georges, which stated that 'the task of the Armies remains unaltered'. It gave no direct orders for attack, it outlined no definite plan, and on it General Blanchard (who had succeeded to General Billotte's command following the road accident on the 21st) took no positive action. The plans at the end of the day remained unchanged.

The general situation of the Armies of the North had by that time worsened considerably. Arras was invested on three sides, and both to the east and to the west of the town heavy German forces were making important advances. Boulogne was besieged. Enemy armour was within nine miles of Calais. In the Eastern battle considerable loss was being sustained in the effort to disengage on the northern end of the line of the BEF. Any question of attack 'with eight divisions' on the 23rd was patently absurd.

The morning of the 23rd brought little news that was good. The French Army, it is true, had recovered itself sufficiently to initiate an attack to the south. In a strength of slightly less than two divisions it advanced with very little opposition almost to the outskirts of Cambrai. At this point, heavily attacked by dive bombers, the advance was abandoned, the force withdrawing to its original line.

There was some comfort in the fact that the British Expeditionary Force had carried out its withdrawal through roads

48

desperately congested with refugee traffic to the old frontiers and that the relief of three British divisions was in progress. There was less comfort in the supply position. Ammunition, equipment, and ordnance stores were already at a low ebb, and the food situation had reached a climax. On this day the British Expeditionary Force was put on half rations. This was a precautionary measure. In fact, the Army was retreating through its existing dumps, and though the effects of the order varied from unit to unit, it is probable that with local improvisations (Montgomery, for example, drove a herd of cattle on the hoof) there was no serious shortage.

In the Western battle Boulogne was doomed, Calais would be besieged before the day was out; the panzer divisions had reached the Canal Line at St Omer and forced a crossing against stubborn resistance, and Arras was now hopelessly outflanked; the Germans had crossed the Scarpe, and the French Light Armoured Division had been forced off the high ground to the north of it. The position was one of swiftly increasing danger.

Then at six o'clock the whole situation changed decisively. At this hour Rundstedt made his decision to halt the German panzer divisions on the line of the Aa Canal. His records show that he had lost 50 per cent of his armoured vehicles to enemy action and to wear and tear. The terrain beyond the Canal Line was seamed and broken by dykes and flooded areas. He was convinced by Franklyn's counter-attack, by the stubborn heroism of the garrison of Arras, and by the grim defence of the Special Forces along the canal area that he would have to pay heavily for any further advance. Moreover, he had to prepare and ready his forces for *Fall Rot*—Operation Red—the attack across the Somme against the heart of France. At 6.10 pm the order to halt and re-group was entered in the Fourth Army War Diary. It was obeyed reluctantly by some of the armoured commanders, in fury by others. The German attack lost impetus and, like a stone that rolls down a hill and finds lodgement for a moment, it never recovered its original momentum.

At Gort's Headquarters there was as yet no indication of this vital decision. At Arras the garrison still held out, but already, flooding past it, the Germans had advanced as far as Béthune and now on the east they had forced a second crossing of the Scarpe and were thrusting towards Bailleul. Gort's first orders had been for the garrison to hold on to the end. Now, with three panzer divisions and a motorised division poised along the Béthune–Arras road, it was desperately obvious that the Arras area could never be used as a springboard for the attack to the south. Late in the evening Gort issued orders to Franklyn to withdraw to the Canal Line.

The morning of the 24th brought a tirade of fury from Weygand: the English were retreating towards the ports, they had abandoned Arras without being compelled by the Germans to do so, the retreat had forced him to abandon the Weygand Plan. The very heat of Weygand's accusations, the speed with which he changed his charges to include the British Government, appear to indicate a desperate search for a scapegoat. The loss of Arras was unquestionably important, but by the evening of the 23rd there was no longer any possibility whatever of holding it. Franklyn's brilliantly conducted retreat through a gap barely five miles wide between the jaws of the German pincers had at least saved Frankforce for a second attempt at the attack to the south if it could still be mounted.

It is at this point that Hitler comes into the immediate picture. At about eleven o'clock this morning he reached Rundstedt's Headquarters. After discussion he confirmed the standstill order – confirmed it on the military grounds which Rundstedt had presented to him. At 11.32 am a signal was put out *en clair* ordering the 'attack on the Dunkirk–Hazebrouck–Merville line to be discontinued for the present'. That signal was intercepted and was carefully weighed at GHQ. Neither Gort nor Pownall accepted it as proof that the German impetus had spent itself. Reports that had been received of the beginning of Weygand's thrust from the south, however, led to a temporary belief that Rundstedt's action might be due to fears for his southern flank – it was not until much later that Gort learned that there was no French thrust from the south and that the German panzer divisions remained a major threat to the safety of the BEF. It is salutary, therefore, to examine the position of Rundstedt's armies at this moment.

The German situation map for the 24th is painfully revealing. To the west of a line drawn from La Bassée on the canal to Amiens – the line roughly of any attempt to strike through to the south – were all ten German panzer divisions and two motorised divisions. Of these, four panzers and the two motorised divisions were uncommitted. To the east of the line, and sufficiently close to it to have come into operation long before any attack from the north could hope to reach the area of Amiens, were ten infantry divisions and one motorised division. Weygand had persuaded himself that it was possible to mount an attack of eight divisions from the north. The fight around Arras had destroyed, for practical purposes, the last of the British armour; the French had little left that was of significance. An advance of eight divisions of infantry with limited ammunition and failing transport into the heart of that enormous concentration of men and armour would have been military suicide.

The full strength of the German force was not known at Gort's Headquarters – it should have been known at Wey-

The position on May 23rd. The diagram illustrates the success with which the German armour under Manstein's plan reached the Channel coast, and shows the last attempt to hold on to Arras in the hope of effecting a junction with the south.

gand's – but both Paris and London continued to call for the attack to the south. Churchill this day was again in Paris, and Gort received from Anthony Eden, the Secretary of State for War, a telegram which said that Reynaud and Weygand were

'Both convinced that Weygand's plan is still capable of execution and only in its execution has hope of restoring the situation. Weygand reports French VII Army is advancing successfully and has captured Péronne, Albert and Amiens.'

Gort's dispatch says quietly: 'It later transpired that this information was inaccurate.' It later transpired, in cold fact, that it was of an unparalleled mendacity – no advance of any consequence whatever had been made, no towns had been recaptured. But on the basis of these exhortations Gort continued his planning for an eventual attack to the south, which it was now hoped would be possible on May 26th with five divisions and what was left of the French Cavalry Corps. At the same time he continued to strengthen the defence of the Canal Line, ordering down to it the 2nd and 44th Divisions, which had now been relieved with the general retirement to the old frontier defences. General Eastwood was appointed to the command of the Canal Line. His appointment marks the virtual end of the Special Forces.

It is one of the extraordinary facets of the campaign that Gort incurred considerable criticisms in his establishment of these forces. Admitted they were never at any time militarily 'tidy' – they were, in truth, in every instance desperate groups desperately got together. They were composed of every branch of the British Army: dismounted gunners, tunnelling companies, chemical warfare units, signal corps, railway companies, even a mobile bath unit. To them were given what was available in their particular areas in the way of anti-tank guns and artillery. The artillery itself was so exiguous that the 392nd Battery of the 98th Field Regiment, RA, for example, posted single guns at seven critical points, and those guns held up the German advance with magnificent self-sacrifice until they were relieved, destroyed or overrun. It is a fantastic page in the history of the British Army. Often these formations lacked signals, supplies, transport – everything except courage. Yet there was behind the whole, behind even the desperation of their establishment, always a coherent plan. Gort, feeling blindly for the enemy's intention, blocked it at every major point. The achievement of the Special Forces was Rundstedt's decision on the evening of May 23rd to halt and regroup. They were not militarily 'tidy', but they stopped the northern thrust of the German Army and that is their Battle Honour. Now, as the evening of May 24th drew on, they were placed under the direction of III Corps.

At that same moment a new threat developed in the Eastern battle. On either side of Courtrai Bock opened a heavy attack on the Belgian line, and General Brooke on the left of the BEF began to grow increasingly anxious as to the danger to his flank. He had never held a good opinion of the fighting capacity of the Belgian Army. Now he was certain that it was about to collapse immediately and he began to demand reinforcements from GHQ.

It is desirable to attempt to visualise the shape of the area held by the Armies of the North at dawn of May 25th. It may most easily perhaps be compared with a boot. The sole was the Belgian shore with the toe at the estuary of the Scheldt and the heel at Gravelines. The back of the boot was the Canal Line running up to Valenciennes. The instep was the line of the old frontier defences manned again by the BEF, and from there to the toe the Belgian Army still stood against the main weight of Bock's attack. Ten German infantry divisions were concentrated between Halluin at the left flank of the BEF and Ghent; it was evident that Bock was launching his full weight against the Belgians and the British, and at 7 am it was reported that he had pushed back the Belgian front to a depth of a mile and a half for 13 miles between Menin and Desselghem. The French were being attacked in the area of Denain.

Because of these developments Colonel Bridgeman, who had been examining the situation to the south, was brought back to Headquarters to complete the draft plan for evacuation. He had begun it on the night of the 21st when the Channel ports from Boulogne to Zeebrugge were at the disposal of the Allies. He completed it with the available coastline shrunk to the sector from Gravelines to Nieuport.

The Western battle front was comparatively quiet, though the enemy was still nibbling out from the bridgeheads across the Canal Line. The 2nd Division had taken up its position to the right of the French, the 44th was in line between the Forest of Claimarais and Aire, and the 48th was being moved to form garrisons at Cassel, Hazebrouck and Wormhoudt.

Brooke was early at GHQ again demanding reinforcements. His fears for his left flank had grown with the news of the night. It seems probable that he had overestimated the rate of advance possible to Bock's army. It is necessary to remember that there was an essential difference between the time-space calculations with regard to the movements of Rundstedt's army of motorised divisions and those for the foot soldiers of Bock. It is equally certain that Brooke never visualised accurately the state of the Western battle or the threat of the armour. Though Rundstedt had issued the standstill order on the 23rd and Hitler had confirmed it on the following morning, it was at least as obvious to the German High Command, as to Gort, that from the bridgehead at St Omer there was a route of approach to the rear of the Armies of the North which ran through high ground and which would not expose the German armour to the dangers of the canals and flooded areas. On the morning of the 25th the High Command, in fact, issued an order for the armour to resume the advance along this axis. Rundstedt, secure in the personal authority that he had been given by Hitler, rejected it. But this, of course, was not known at British GHQ, and Gort had to concentrate on the most probable danger at the same time as he maintained his preparations for the attack to the south. Brooke was given the sole reserve that remained in GHQ's hands – a brigade of infantry and two battalions of machine guns.

Shortly after seven o'clock that morning Sir John Dill arrived. Gort had asked him to come over to ascertain for himself the position in the area. It was obvious early in the discussion that no accurate knowledge of the situation existed in London even now, and Dill hinted at dissatisfaction with Gort's generalship. He appears rapidly to have become himself convinced of the desperate nature of the crisis. At the end of the discussion he reported to the Prime Minister:

'There is NO blinking the seriousness of situation in northern area. BEF is now holding front of eighty-seven miles with seven divs. . . . two BEF divs. in reserve preparing attack in conjunction French for evening 26. Germans in contact along whole front and are reported to have penetrated Belgian line north-east Courtrai yesterday evening. In above circumstances attack referred to above cannot be important affair.'

A meeting with Blanchard followed, and at its conclusion Dill returned to London. Gort was left to face the possibility of a collapse of the Belgians on the left flank of the Eastern battle and the probability of an early resumption of the German armoured thrust on the Western side.

The long day wore on. In the château at Premesques, that

small undistinguished country house that was GHQ, Gort fought a battle by himself. He was a Guardsman; by training and tradition he was imbued with the spirit of obedience. Weygand, Georges, Blanchard, each in his different way had ordered the attack to the south. He had a loyalty, however, outside this obedience, a loyalty to the British Government. But London also had ordered the attack to the south. Now, as the Saturday afternoon drew on, Gort came reluctantly to the conclusion that it was no longer possible. The inexorable

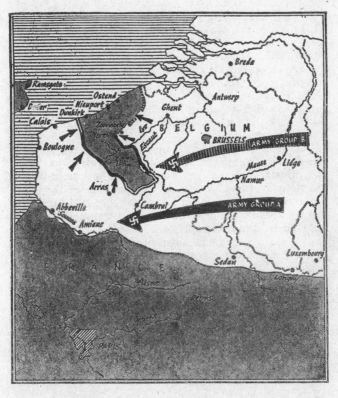

The extent of the Allied pocket as the breach between the British left flank and the Belgian Army developed on May 25th. This was the day on which Gort finally abandoned all hope of attacking to the south.

movement of time had brought him to the point where the use of the whole of his resources was necessary to ensure the very survival of his army.

For a long time he sat alone and silent at a desk in the drawing room of the château with a map spread in front of him. Just before six o'clock he walked out of the room and into Pownall's little office next door. Without preamble he said: 'Henry, I've had a hunch. We've got to call off the 5th and 50th Divisions from the attack to the south and send them over to Brookie on the left.'

Pownall said: 'Well, you do realise, sir, that that's against all the orders that we've had and that if we take those two divisions away, the French First Army is very unlikely to attack without British support?'

Gort considered his Chief of Staff's words for a moment and answered: 'Yes, I know that quite well. All the same it's got to be done.'

So, very simply and without heroics, one of the cardinal decisions of the war was taken. The official historian describes it in these terms:[1]

'But at six o'clock Lord Gort had already taken his most fateful action during the whole campaign. Without waiting to ask authority from the French commander he ordered the 5th and 50th Divisions to abandon preparations for the attack southwards on the 26th and to move at once to the threatening gap between the British and Belgian armies. By doing so he saved the British Expeditionary Force.'

That decision is the highlight of Gort's military career; it is one of the climactic moments of the war. Half an hour after it had been taken a signal came from the Needham Mission at Belgian Headquarters to say that at five o'clock a gap had broken between Gheluwe and the River Lys. The Belgians had expended their last reserves – they could offer no hope of closing it.

[1] *The War in France and Flanders* by Major L. F. Ellis.

56

CHAPTER V

The Week Before 'Dunkirk'

The harbour of Dunkirk is approached by a fine natural
roadstead entered on the east and west ... From the road-
stead, entrance is by a channel into the outer harbour,
which communicates with seven floating basins about 115
acres in area and is accessible to the largest vessels.
Encyclopaedia Britannica (*14th Edition*)

THE BLOCKING of Antwerp and Flushing brought an end to the first phase of the naval operations made necessary by the attack on the Low Countries, and the three days which followed were relatively quiet. A French plan for the evacuation of 350,000 civilian refugees from Ostend and Zeebrugge put forward during this period hardly emerged from the planning stage.

The situation began to crystallise on May 19th. On this day General Pownall, as has been described, informed the Director of Military Operations and Plans in London of Lord Gort's views on the possible necessity for evacuation. A meeting was called at once by the War Office at which Admiral Ramsay was represented. It was presided over by General Riddell-Webster, and its primary object was to consider the problem of organising alternative supply routes. The situation was examined in detail and it was determined that, while the decision as to the actual ports to which the ships should go would rest with Admiral Ramsay, Calais and Boulogne should be used as much as possible as it was more difficult to give air protection to Dunkirk. Various alternative methods, such as barge traffic to Gravelines, Étaples and other small ports, were discussed. In addition the meeting considered the question of evacuation of personnel. This was dealt with under three headings: the first, the orderly evacuation of personnel not required in the changed circumstances of the BEF, amounting to 2,000 a day from May 20th onwards; the second, the possible emergency evacuation of base units, hospital staffs and odd personnel, which might amount to some 15,000 in all from the night of May 22nd onwards; and the third, 'the hazardous evacuation of very large forces' – this was considered unlikely!

It was decided to utilise merchant vessels for these purposes, and the Ministry of Shipping was requested to make the necessary arrangements. It was agreed that control would be delegated completely to Admiral Ramsay and that he was to investigate the question of the number of ships that might be able to work from the existing French ports and whether additional loading places could be used by small craft in the event of emergency. The War Office and the Ministry of Shipping were to attach liaison officers to the staff at Dover.

Simultaneously on May 19th General Gamelin sent a telegram to Admiral Darlan which read:

'. . . Although the situation does not justify the immediate taking of this step, it would be prudent to provide for it from this moment by assembling transports to evacuate certain units, without it being possible to establish in advance the number of ships necessary and the ports of embarkation.'

The first directives to both the British and the French navies were thus issued simultaneously and in remarkably similar terms. Darlan, in execution of the first part of that directive, set on foot planning for a supply operation for the northern French armies, utilising stocks accumulated at Brest, Cherbourg, and Rouen for the Norwegian campaign.

* * *

The Ministry of Shipping took over the management of all British merchant vessels at the outbreak of war. As the débâcle of April and May developed, Norwegian, Danish, Dutch, and Belgian shipping also came under its direction. It was therefore the appropriate authority for large-scale transport demands. The Minister of Shipping at that date was Mr Ronald Cross. The work fell principally upon the Sea Transport Department, which was under the direction of Mr W. G. Hynard (who had as his Deputy Director Mr D. H. Edwards), and on Captain J. Fisher, the Director of Coastwise and Short Sea Shipping. The military side of the Sea Transport Department, under Mr C. E. W. Justice, assisted by Mr B. E. Bellamy, dealt with larger vessels and, as need arose subsequently, the smaller vessels were dealt with by Mr A. L. Moore and Mr H. C. Riggs.

In peacetime the British Merchant Navy totalled some 10,000 ships. Superficially it would appear that the Ministry of Shipping had an inexhaustible supply of vessels upon which to draw. In actual fact supply was small and most drastically limited by the circumstances of war. Of ships based on home ports a reliable estimate before the war placed 1,850 ocean-going vessels at sea on any given day, with a further total of 1,650 smaller and coasting vessels. The number actually in British ports at any one moment was, comparatively speaking, small. Of this residue a proportion at any given time was under repair, and a very much larger proportion was in process of loading or discharging and therefore not available for immediate service. Owing to the necessities of war and of a quick turn-round that proportion in May of 1940 was even greater than normal. The residue of *available* shipping was, therefore, extremely small, and of that available shipping a considerable proportion was not suited to the needs of the operation. The shallows off northern France, the ever-increasing possibility of air attack, made it quite impossible, for example, to use large ships. Only the extraordinary efforts of the Ministry and its responsible departments made it possible for the final sifting of suitable ships to be brought together at the right place and at the right time.

*　　*　　*

There remained the 'purely' naval side of the operation. It had a deceptive simplicity. In its essentials it consisted of the protection of the flanks of a transportation movement which covered a rough quadrilateral whose southern side was the narrows of the Straits of Dover and whose northern side was a line leading from Nieuport to the estuary of the Thames.

The southern side can be dismissed in a few words. It was in the highest degree improbable that attack on a serious scale could come from here. Though the Germans held the coast from Calais through Boulogne to the mouth of the Somme, it was impossible that they should yet have been able to bring even mosquito craft to the Channel ports, and the speed of the débâcle as a whole had been so great that it was improbable that U-boats in any strength could have been brought up through the Channel in an attempt to attack from the west. But the eastern flank of the movement was intensely vulnerable. The Dover Command was no longer a small enclave separated by 300 miles of neutral coast from the sea bases of the enemy. German E-boats were known to be using the port of Flushing at the entrance to the Scheldt. There was only the narrow fringe of the Belgian coast between it and the enemy's springing place.

To achieve a just balance of the possibilities it is necessary to examine the naval position in the last week of May as a whole. Britain had a big navy, Germany a small one. It is easy to argue from this that no problem should have existed, but the tendency to over-simplification is a dangerous one. For a variety of obvious reasons Dunkirk could not be – on either side – in any way a heavy-ship affair. The shoals off the French and Belgian coasts precluded the possibility of the use of heavy ships, but infinitely more important was the threat of the new air weapon, still in its most doubtful stage. It was not in 1940 thought possible in many places that battleships would ever again be brought within gun range of an enemy's territory. But the tortuousness of the channels, the alignment of the shoals, the confusion caused by the use of air power made the quadrangle of the evacuation a paradise for the *Schnelboote*. With destroyers, torpedo-boats, motor torpedo-boats, and, in a lesser degree, submarines, the Germans could have made the evacuation not merely precarious but impossible.

Since it was a small-ship operation, therefore, it is in the sphere of light craft that any balancing of the problem must be attempted. At the outbreak of war the Royal Navy possessed 202 destroyers. This number was already considerably reduced. The ordinary loss of war was responsible for six destroyers during the period up to the Norwegian campaign. The accelerated hazard of the following month saw another five ships lost, together with one Polish destroyer. The fighting in Holland saw a further two ships bombed and lost, and Calais a third. But this total of fifteen does not represent the whole casualty of the sea war. There were as many ships virtually lost to the Navy through serious damage. There were numerous others in dockyard hands for major repairs. Amongst these were many of the destroyers which had taken part in the Boulogne and Calais operations. *Keith*, *Venetia*, *Vimy*, *Vimiera*, and *Whitshed* were all hit at different times, and in point of fact only one of the eight destroyers which evacuated Boulogne on May 23rd–25th was completely unscathed, while *Venetia* and *Vimiera* were so badly damaged as to be unable to take any part in the subsequent operations.

Of the remainder that were fit for service a large proportion was 1,500 miles to the north, engaged in the complexities of the last phase of the Norwegian campaign. This was a phase of constant movement, of landing and evacuation, supplied by convoys over a route of 1,000 miles from the north of Scotland – a route subjected to constant U-boat attack along most of its length. Every destroyer of the Home Fleet that could be spared from the actual work of screening the heavy ships was engaged without rest or respite in this task.

But Norway was not the only commitment. Already the Mediterranean situation was beginning to cause anxiety; the few destroyers in southern waters could not be detached from their bases. And in addition to the preoccupations in the far north and the far south there was the deadly preoccupation of the Battle of the Atlantic, then in its first phase. Destroyers in May of 1940 were still the mainstay of convoy escort. The 'Hunt' class escort vessels were not yet in commission. Only five ships of the huge corvette programme had yet materialised.

Yet with these three great responsibilities the Admiralty somehow found forty destroyers to take part in the defence and in the carrying work of Dunkirk. It was one of the major naval achievements of the war. That it was done in the face of loss that became terrifying in the swiftness of its upward curve demanded a degree of courage on the part of the Admiralty that has not yet perhaps had its due meed of recognition.

The proper measure of this aspect of the operation is to be found in a speech made by the First Lord of the Admiralty nearly two years later, when it was stated that in the week after Dunkirk for all the enormous commitments of the Royal Navy through a world growing swiftly colder, swiftly more hostile, there were only seventy-four destroyers out of dockyard hands.

*   *   *

Naval headquarters at Dover were set in the deep galleries of the east cliff below Dover Castle, galleries hewn in the chalk by French prisoners of war in the first years of the nineteenth century. The nerve centre of the headquarters was a single gallery which ended in an embrasure at the cliff face. This was used as an office by Admiral Ramsay. A succession of small rooms leading deep into the chalk housed the Secretary, the Flag Lieutenant, the Chief of Staff (Captain L. V. Morgan) and the Staff office itself. Beyond these was a large room used normally for conferences in connection with the operation of the base. In the First World War it had held an auxiliary electrical plant and it was known as the 'Dynamo Room'.

On Monday, May 20th, a conference was called at Dover under Admiral Ramsay to decide upon the detailed measures made necessary by the rapidly changing situation. On the agenda for that conference – so much had the position altered in the twenty-four hours since the preceding meeting – was 'Emergency evacuation across the Channel of very large forces'. At this meeting (which was continued at the War Office the following day) it was decided that if emergency evacuation became necessary, it was to be carried out from the three French ports Calais, Boulogne and Dunkirk. The estimated capacity of the arrangements, 'allowing for moderate interference', was 10,000 from each port in each twenty-four hours.

The first list of ships available had been prepared. At the disposal of Admiral Ramsay at Dover were *Biarritz, Mona's Queen, Canterbury, Maid of Orleans, King George V, Queen of the Channel, King Orry, Mona's Isle, St Helier* and *St Seiriol*, and at Southampton were *Normannia, Manxmaid, Royal Daffodil, Royal Scot, Archangel* and *Lorina*. From this it will be seen that the authorities had selected the obvious and natural form of shipping for use in these waters – passenger ferry steamers. Most of them had been built for the purpose of using the French and English Channel ports. They were conditioned by years of experience and handled by men who had grown old in the trade. No better selection could have been made. It was proposed that they should work the three French ports in pairs, not more than two ships to be in any harbour at any one time. In addition to this list, and to be ready when the Southampton ships had been called forward, were another fourteen of similar type. To supplement these were twelve drifters and six small coasters.

Captain Fisher, at the War Office meeting, stressed the value of British self-propelled barges, and of the flat-bottomed Dutch *schuits* which had come over to Britain in large numbers after the fall of Holland. Subsequently he selected forty of these Dutch coasters, and (known thereafter irrevocably as 'skoots') they were manned by naval crews from Portsmouth and Chatham.

The Sea Transport Officers at Harwich, London, Newhaven, Southampton, Poole and Weymouth were instructed to record all small ships up to 1,000 tons, including paddle-steamers and pleasure craft. Arrangements were made for passing this information to V.-A., Dover.

The meeting of the 20th made it obvious also that a re-organisation of the base staff at Dover was urgent in view of the press of work that appeared inevitable. It was decided to set up this new body in the Dynamo Room itself, and from that arose the code name for the evacuation – Operation 'Dynamo'. The Dynamo Room organisation, first composed principally of members of Admiral Ramsay's own office, was later supplemented by what was virtually a duplicate staff sent down from Admiralty, and, as the operation got under way, Vice-Admiral Sir James Somerville (subsequently to win fame in command of Force H in the Western Mediterranean) came down to assist Admiral Ramsay and to take – in effect – alternate shifts. In addition to the naval officers of the staff, Captain, L. E. L. Wright, RA, of the War Office Movements Branch, a Mr J. L. Keith of the Ministry of Shipping, and a representative of the RAF were included. Signals and the highly important navigational details remained under normal Dover organisation. Officers were appointed to deal with spare crews, provisions, repairs and maintenance and, as the condition of Dunkirk became known more fully, with water.

It is impossible to say precisely when this staff became complete as its members were added to and its functions altered in accordance with the desperate succession of events. But it was the 'Dynamo' staff, with the supplementary officers from the Admiralty, who were responsible both for the planning of the operation in every vital detail and for its subsequent control, and it is essential to remember that that planning, spread out over the six days from the meeting of Monday, the 20th, to the executive signal for Operation 'Dynamo', was carried out while the situation in the immediate area changed almost with every hour.

As the first day's work ended the preliminary benefit of the Arras counter-attack was felt, for the panzer divisions advancing on Boulogne and Calais were halted late in the day.

On May 22nd the War Office stated that it did not anticipate any decision to evacuate before Friday, May 24th, nor did it contemplate anything in the nature of 'panic' evacuation, believing that the movement would take place in an orderly manner. It considered that the flow of ships arranged would be sufficient to cover the necessities. On the afternoon of the

22nd, however, the armour surged forward again. By the morning of Thursday, May 23rd, it was possible to see from the windows of Ramsay's office in the cliff the shell-bursts of the attack of the 2nd Panzer Division on Boulogne. In the brilliant afternoon, while the coast of France stood clear in every detail from the English shore, the watchers at Dover saw the first elements of the plan go down in ruin.

*   *   *

The swift advance of the panzers made desperate measures necessary. Rear headquarters of the British Expeditionary Force had already moved all elements not needed in the actual fighting to Wimereux, near Boulogne, and Lieutenant-General Sir Douglas Brownrigg had been given instructions by Lord Gort to move all 'useless mouths' from Boulogne, Calais and Dunkirk as rapidly as possible. The phrase requires a certain explanation.

Behind the British Expeditionary Force as it lay during the first nine months of the war along the Franco-Belgian frontier had collected all the enormous 'tail', the non-fighting element that lies behind a modern army. It was very much larger than the size of the expeditionary force itself warranted, for the BEF was considered by the Government the nucleus of the enormous expansion made possible by its introduction of conscription. Behind it, therefore, were training units, administrative echelons, stores, development, experimental units, designed to handle the influx from Britain when the great training programmes initiated at the beginning of the war finally began to produce men. Of necessity a high proportion of these units was composed of non-combatant troops, and an even higher proportion of troops either untrained or unequipped for fighting. Those closest to the actual battle were drawn on in the formation of the Special Forces of the Canal line, but the rest were a drain on the diminishing food supplies of the Army and an unnecessary target for the Germans. They were 'useless mouths', and in the planning of the Dynamo Room cognisance had to be taken of that fact and ships provided to lift them.

*   *   *

It is as well to have a picture of this week in mind in considering the problem which faced the Dynamo Room in the final planning. It will be remembered that just before the week began HMS *Westminster*, a British destroyer of the old 'V' and 'W' class converted for escort purposes, was bombed. On May 19th the Dover rescue tug *Lady Brassey* was ordered to proceed to Dunkirk for the purpose of towing her back to an English port. Her master, G. W. Blackmore, reported on the evening of this day that the West Hinder lightship was anchored in Calais Roads. There is a significance in this. The sea marks were going already. That night, anchored off Gravelines, from the *Lady Brassey* they watched Dunkirk and Calais being raided from the air and saw large fires burning. On this same day farther up the coast between Nieuport and Ostend HMS *Whitley*, operating under French orders, was badly damaged by bombs and forced ashore.

At dawn on Monday, May 20th, *Lady Brassey* proceeded to Dunkirk and was bombed off the port. At 9 am she entered harbour – with instructions to keep 150 feet off the outer moles as a magnetic mine was reported near – to take HMS *Westminster* in tow. Five miles north-west of Calais her crew saw the London steamer *Mavis* bombed and abandoned. *Mavis* was one of the first of the small ships utilised in the plan for supplying the BEF through the Channel ports.

Meanwhile the French supply operation had been badly held up by the aerial mining of the estuary of the Seine. Though it had been hoped to sail the first ship on May 20th, it was not until May 24th that a convoy was got away. Thirty-seven cargo vessels had been requisitioned and, in all, eleven convoys were dispatched. They met with heavy loss. Only thirteen ships finally arrived at Dunkirk and, of these, five were destroyed in the harbour by enemy bombing. It was therefore decided to abandon the direct attempt with cargo vessels and instead to anchor the ships in the Downs close to Dover and tranship their supplies to small craft for transport to Dunkirk.

Meanwhile subsidiary operations were in progress at Dunkirk itself, and on May 20th, following serious loss from German bombing, Admiral Abrial decided to evacuate all large French vessels from the port. The first flight of vessels was got clear without trouble. On the next tide it was proposed to sail the 20,000-ton tanker *Salome*, the tanker *Niger*, the cargo vessel *Pavon* (which had on board 1,500 Dutch troops), and certain other craft. The movement began at midnight and was almost immediately subjected to heavy attack. The attempt to tow out the *Salome* had to be abandoned. The *Niger* was attacked as she cleared the piers and in a subsequent attack was set on fire. She was sunk finally off Gravelines. The *Pavon*, badly damaged, was beached between Gravelines and Calais. The destroyer *L'Adroit*, waiting to cover the operation, was hit and beached in a sinking condition off Malo-les-Bains, the Chasseur 9 was damaged and forced ashore a little farther up the beach.

Two days later the destroyer *Jaguar*, approaching Dunkirk Roads with demolition parties, was torpedoed, presumably by an enemy E-boat, and sank a short distance off the port.

Subsequently, damage to lock gates rendered a number of the basins tidal, and Admiral Abrial ordered a second evacuation – this time of small craft.

The work of supplying the BEF according to the new plan, therefore, proceeded in circumstances of great difficulty and very real danger. The loaded store-ship *Firth Fisher* was sunk by bombing, but the shelling of the motor-vessel *Sodality* by guns mounted in the vicinity of Calais introduced a new factor which was to have an important effect on the movement as a whole. The Germans had established batteries, first, of light field guns but later, as their equipment came up, of heavy guns on the rising ground near Calais from which they controlled to considerable extent the close route to Dunkirk Roads.

*   *   *

Supply had the first priority, but the problem of the wounded during this period was almost equally important and even more difficult. The prearranged system of evacuation had collapsed with the changing situation. The improvised base hospitals that had been set up in the northern area to replace those severed by May 20th from the Army were themselves in increasing danger, and together with the normal flow of wounded from the fighting areas the personnel of these improvised hospitals had now to be withdrawn.

An example of what that withdrawal entailed is contained in the work of the hospital carriers *Isle of Thanet* and *Worthing* on May 23rd. They sailed on the afternoon of that day from Newhaven and arrived off Dunkirk in the early evening with an air raid in progress. The Gare Maritime, the old cross-Channel berth, was bombed shortly before their arrival, but the quay still stood and they went alongside. While *Isle of Thanet* took on board 300 wounded and *Worthing* lifted a full load, there were enemy aircraft almost continually overhead and they worked under a curtain of anti-aircraft fire from ships' guns and shore batteries until they pulled out at eleven o'clock. With them worked cross-Channel steamers taking off civilian evacuees. *St Helier*, for example, picked up 1,500 British and French this day.

The scale of enemy air attack was increasing rapidly. The air raid which *Isle of Thanet* and *Worthing* endured was part of an attack that went on with brief intervals throughout the day either on the town or on the water. Off Calais, where the 30th Brigade was still holding out superbly, the Royal Navy lost the destroyer *Wessex*, in the course of a bombardment of enemy positions on the flank of the Calais perimeter, to a furious raid. In the same attack the Polish destroyer *Burza* was hit and lost most of her bows. Four destroyers had been lost and six put out of the battle in forty-eight hours. The cumulative effect of this was enormous, but the planning for 'Dynamo' went on, its ardour in no way diminished. And with it the ordinary business of the waters continued.

On top of these things, however, a new complication now presented itself. In its endeavours to find some means of checking the desperate situation that prevailed along the Flanders fronts the War Office had taken, at Lord Gort's request, the dramatic decision to throw the 1st Canadian Division into the fray. As the primary object of this move was to strengthen the already tired units of the British Expeditionary Force, the division could only be shipped through ports that were already intensely occupied with the work which has been described in this chapter – supply, preliminary evacuation, and wounded. On the 24th advance units of the division were embarked. *St Seiriol*, for instance, took on board units of the Canadian Provost Corps, and other ships at the different ports of the south coast were earmarked and held for this purpose. At the last moment, when a number of men were already aboard, the decision was countermanded. The view was taken that the situation was beyond such degree of restoration as could be effected by the throwing in of a new division and that evacuation was now inevitable, in which circumstances an extra 15,000 men would be merely an added embarrassment and a source of confusion to the lines of movement set up by the retreating army. The men who had already been loaded were disembarked.

*   *   *

It is not easy for those who did not see it to picture Dover harbour at this time and in the days that followed. Dover harbour, as has been said, is big but the actual quays were small and, save for the cross-Channel berth on the Admiralty Pier, unsuited for heavy working. The harbour was designed more as an anchorage for the old Channel Fleet than as a working port.

At the Admiralty Pier there were eight berths for cross-Channel steamers. During the height of the movement there were often sixteen, eighteen, or even twenty ships at these eight berths. They moored in tiers two and three deep, and because of the difficulties of turning space – there is a ridge of rock and shoal between the Prince of Wales Pier and the Admiralty Pier at low water – almost all these ships had to be handled by tugs, and with the utmost expedition. They came alongside, the weary and exhausted soldiers were sent ashore as swiftly as might be, and the ships pulled out again to refuel and return.

In the main harbour there were between forty and fifty mooring buoys. These were constantly occupied with ships taking stores, repairing minor damage, very occasionally resting. At one of the buoys the oil tanker *War Sepoy* was berthed, and incessantly alongside her the destroyers and the oil-burning cross-Channel steamers, the pleasure boats, and the rest made fast for fuel. Here too they had to be worked by tugs. The great part of the work was done by the four tugs *Simla, Gondia, Roman* and *Lady Brassey*. In his report of this period Mr G. D. Lowe, the master of *Simla,* said:

'The fortnight commencing the 20th of May 1940 at the time of the evacuation, the tug *Simla* assisted, inside and outside of Dover harbour, 140-odd ships. The crew and myself were practically on our feet night and day. I have great praise for my crew. . . .

'The tugs had orders to shift two destroyers from Admiralty Pier on May 24th, in the early hours of the morning, to buoys in the harbours to make room for other ships to berth. They were the HMS *Whitshed* and *Vimy,* but the crews of the destroyers were so tired and exhausted from their recent experience at Boulogne that we let them sleep on, and shifted the destroyers without them. I expect that when they turned out from their much-needed sleep they were surprised to find their ship in a different position, but were all fresh to go to sea again, and carry on the good work.'

Simla's account may serve to epitomize the work of the tugs which were based on the different ports. They had their share of danger both from direct attack and from the more insidious threat of the magnetic mine; but, for the most part, it was the incessant toil of the work that bore on them. Like *Simla*, other tugs went out to rescue work. *Doria* and *Kenia* were at sea almost throughout the period as inspection vessels at the approaches to the great anchorages. Still other tugs were occupied in the essential work of removing the constantly growing fleet of damaged ships clear of Dover and Ramsgate and taking them to the repair yards of the Thames, of Portsmouth and of Southampton.

Complementary to the work of the Dover tugs was that done by other tugs across the Channel. Various British ships took part in this, some of them staying for as much as five days at a time. But a little fleet of Belgian tugs – *Elbe*, *Thames*, *Max*, *Vulcan* and *Goliath* – from the Belgian North Sea ports began to work inside Dunkirk harbour on May 25th and continued throughout the whole of Operation 'Dynamo' until the first four were sunk on the last day and their crews brought to Dover in the surviving ship, *Goliath*.

On the 25th much of the recorded activity was again on the part of the hospital carriers, who were now desperately trying to get away the last of the casualties from the base hospitals, together with the rapidly accumulating casualties of the actual fighting and the additional wounded of the air bombardment. The *Isle of Thanet*, *St David* and other ships were all engaged this day in lifting wounded. *St David* arrived in Dunkirk in the morning and lay alongside receiving wounded into the evening. All day the town and the quays were subjected to severe aerial bombardment. On her way out, when passing the Gravelines beaches, she came under heavy shelling, one large-calibre shell falling less than a ship's length ahead of her.

The transport *Canterbury*, which had been shelled on her way to Dunkirk, carried out this evening one of the first really big liftings of men, embarking 1,246 troops from the Gare Maritime. These were mainly base personnel and line of communication troops who were no longer required.

Meanwhile yet another complication had presented itself. The incessant bombing had destroyed the waterworks and mains. There were only wells left within the area that was to become the perimeter, and few of these, and into them the brackish water was seeping from the flooding of the lowland levels. An urgent signal was made to England asking for water, and the water boat *Goldeve* was loaded and dispatched. She was followed by the water boat *Claude*.

* * *

This is at best a fragmentary picture of the week that preceded the main evacuation but its episodes have been chosen to show the main facets of a period of intense complexity and danger. The original basis of the plan, first for supply and then for evacuation, had already been broken under the speed of the German advance. The Channel ports themselves were falling inexorably into enemy hands. The last hopes on the day on which Operation 'Dynamo' was put into motion rested upon Dunkirk and the beaches that adjoined it. These stretched from Gravelines, midway between Calais and Dunkirk, to Nieuport across the Belgian frontier, a distance of 25 miles. Flat, level, featureless except for the little seaside resorts that were scattered along them, they had no piers, no harbour facilities; the sand shelved out for a long way to the deep water and they were completely exposed to all northerly winds.

The focus of all this area was, for obvious reasons, Dunkirk town. It is an ancient harbour. Thirteen hundred years ago in the dunes that fringe the beaches St Eloi built a chapel – the Dune Church. That chapel became a place of pilgrimage: a fishing village grew about it and enlarged itself. Three hundred years later Baldwin, Count of Flanders, made a fortress of it, ringing it with a moat and walls. By then a harbour was already established. It grew to be the third port of France, a fine modern harbour with seven dock basins, accessible to big ships and amounting in all to approximately 115 acres. It had four dry docks, it had 5 miles of quays, and three of the fine canals of the Low Countries fed into it. The docks were deep-set into the town and from them a dredged channel led through to the sea. Long piers protected it against the swirl of the tide along the coast: the West Mole that came out from the oil storage area, the East Mole that sprang out from the ancient fortifications and thrust 1,400 yards into the roadstead. A fine harbour – had it been possible to use it the British Expeditionary Force might have got away 'horse, foot and guns'. But the docks were useless. There were left only the two great moles and the guiding jetty to the new basin. Of these the East Mole was the vital factor.

It is essential to carry in one's mind a clear picture of this mole. It was not a stout stone breakwater with mooring places for ships along its length. It was a narrow plank-way barely wide enough for three men to walk abreast, with on either side a protective railing of moderately stout timbers above which longer piles projected at intervals to make samson posts by which a ship could be warped in emergency. At the far end was a nose with a substructure of concrete on which a short lighthouse stood. It was not designed for ships to berth against it; it was not calculated for the stresses and strains set up thereby. The free movement of the tide beneath the piles made it extremely difficult to bring craft alongside. All these things were to play intensely important parts in the evacuation.

In the week's working the authorities had learned harsh lessons as to the efficacy of German bombing. They had watched the facilities upon which they had relied in the early stages of the plan disappear one by one in smoke and fire. They had found a new responsibility in the necessity to supply Dunkirk with water, and they had learned that even the approach route, the main channel to Dunkirk, was now under the fire of enemy guns. In the course of the week's fighting the entire force of destroyers based on Dover had been sunk or damaged, and the French Navy had suffered proportionate loss.

On the afternoon of Sunday, May 26th, as the Secretary of State for War communicated to Lord Gort the Government's decision to begin the evacuation, the situation was as black as either soldier or sailor could conceive.

CHAPTER VI

Boulogne and Calais

*The answer is no, as it is the British Army's duty
to fight as well as it is the German's.*

BRIGADIER NICHOLSON's reply
to the German demand for the
surrender of Calais

THERE IS one other phase of the operations in this week
consideration of which is essential to a proper understanding of the main evacuation. The defence of the Channel ports
has achieved its place in history as one of the heroic exploits
of the British Army. It has another importance: it was the
pattern for Dunkirk, the pattern both for success and for
failure. It is necessary to go back a little in time to examine it
adequately.

About midnight of May 20th the Spitta Battalion of the
2nd Panzer Division passed through the village of Noyelles at
the edge of the marshy estuary of the Somme and reached the
sea. It is not the least extraordinary aspect of this remarkable
campaign that at this moment neither Guderian, who commanded the three panzer divisions of the spearhead, nor
Kleist, in overall control of the armour, had received any
directive as to future operations. Quite literally Guderian did
not know whether he was to turn north or south with his
armour. The decision to turn north was made on the 21st, but
it was instantly affected by the results of Franklyn's counterattack on Arras, and a standstill order was issued which lost
twenty-four hours to the leading elements of Guderian's force.

When, finally, Guderian was given the signal to move on the
Channel ports he was shorn of almost half his strength. His
own plan was simple in its ruthlessness: the 2nd Panzer Division was to advance on Boulogne by way of Samer, the 1st was
to press through Desvres to Calais, the 10th was to thrust by
way of Hesdin and St Omer to Dunkirk. But in the caution
that enveloped the Command after Arras the 10th Panzer

Division was detached to go into Panzer Group reserve and units of both the other divisions were held back to secure the Somme bridgeheads.

French morale at Boulogne was of uneven quality. The naval commander on whom the defence devolved allowed himself to be influenced by reports of senior officers who had come in from the fighting at Hesdin. Unable to make contact with Admiral Abrial, he ordered the evacuation of the port on May 21st. A subordinate officer of coast defence artillery, however, managed to establish contact with Dunkirk and was ordered to 'resist the enemy as long as it is necessary'. On May 22nd the defence was taken over by Commander Henry Nomy, and finally General Lanquetot, with the remnants of the 21st Infantry Division, arrived. The number of fighting troops, however, remained small.

British reaction to the threat was slow and, in the circumstances of the time, inadequate. On the morning of May 21st the 20th Guards Brigade, which was training at Camberley, was ordered to Dover. Within twenty-four hours it had entered Boulogne in the cross-Channel steamers *Biarritz* and *Queen of the Channel*, escorted by the destroyers *Whitshed* and *Vimiera*. It had with it the Brigade Anti-Tank Company and one battery of the 69th Anti-Tank Regiment.

The landing operation was not without its difficulties. The convoy arrived at dead low-water, and *Whitshed*, which had put in in advance of the transports, only made the Quai Chanzy with the aid of the tug *Gondia*. The harbour area was congested with refugees, base details, and unorganised parties of French and Belgian troops. Valiant efforts were made by units of the Royal Engineers to clear the Quai Chanzy, and after civilians had been moved from the area *Mona's Queen* disembarked the greater part of the two Guards battalions which were sent over and embarked lines of communication units and others in remarkably good order.

The 2nd Panzer Division was still hung on the Canche. At noon it moved forward. An entry in the German War Diary says:

'. . . the corps commander sent 2nd Armoured Division towards Boulogne at noon without waiting for orders from [Kleist] group. In consequence the division succeeded in penetrating to the town.'

At five o'clock it attacked. The respite had given time for the Welsh Guards to dig in on the shallow perimeter that it was possible for two battalions to man. They held the attack.

At first light of the 23rd the Germans attacked again. *Vimy*, *Wild Swan* and *Keith* of the Dover destroyers worked off the port under air attack, firing at targets of opportunity. German tanks, guns and motorised formations were clearly visible in the brilliant morning light.

Admiral Abrial had concentrated off the port two large and eight small French destroyers under Captain Urvoy de Portzamparc in the *Cyclone*. These answered fire calls from a fortified position known as the Tour d'Odre until it was taken by the Germans in mid-afternoon.

HMS *Whitshed*, with other destroyers, covered a second movement of troops – this time the Rifle Brigade to Calais. As she approached Dover on the return trip, her captain, Commander E. R. Conder, received orders to proceed to Boulogne 'with utmost dispatch'. On her arrival it was clear to him that the situation had deteriorated with alarming speed. Fort de la Crèche was already in enemy hands, the heights above the town were occupied and only the area about the harbour appeared still to be secure. *Keith* and *Whitshed* entered the harbour. As they entered, machine-gun fire broke out close at hand. *Vimy* had already landed in the course of the morning a party of 200 seamen and Royal Marines to restore order in the harbour area. The personnel ship *Mona's Queen* was still in the harbour, partially loaded. Seventy-two stretcher cases were lying on the quayside. *Whitshed* embarked these and withdrew, engaging machine-gun posts with her main armament at a range of barely a hundred yards. As she came out, *Vimy* was ordered in and berthed alongside *Keith*. *Whitshed*, securing sea room, engaged Fort de la Crèche and caused an explosion in what was apparently an ammunition chamber. Rescuing a French seaman a little later, she came under fire from field guns and engaged them successfully.

It was now late in the afternoon. *Venetia*, *Vimiera* and *Venomous* arrived from Dover, and *Keith*, still lying alongside, ordered *Whitshed* to return to England and discharge her wounded. As *Whitshed* set course she intercepted a signal ordering evacuation to be started immediately. The time was 5.30 pm.

It was decided that only two destroyers should berth simultaneously. *Keith* and *Vimy*, already alongside, began to take on troops. As they did so, a strong force of enemy aircraft came in from the north. While the destroyers at the berth waited for the bombs and troops took what cover they could on the battered quayside, a formation of Spitfires swept in and broke up the attack. From the ships they saw enemy bombers come down in flames. But, as they watched the battle develop, a second attack – estimated at 60 dive bombers – came in from a fresh direction and delivered a concerted raid on the harbour and the ships immediately outside. At the same time a general assault developed on the town. Mortar fire began to fall on the two destroyers in the harbour and *Keith* was hit on her fo'c'sle. Both ships came under heavy machine-gun fire. Over the noise of the machine-guns and the mortars, the scream of falling bombs and the thunder of the explosions turned the harbour in the brief space of seconds into an inferno. By astonishing fortune neither ship was hit by bombs, but one fell on the quay within three yards of *Keith* and caused considerable damage. Her commanding officer, Captain D. J. R. Simson, was killed early by machine-gun bullets, the captain of *Vimy*, Lieutenant-Commander C. G. W. Donald, was fatally wounded, and other officers and men were killed or severely wounded.

Meanwhile, the ships outside were heavily attacked. *Whitshed* was near-missed and her gunner was killed. The French suffered still more heavily. The *Orage* was set on fire and sank after her survivors had been removed. A second destroyer, the *Frondeur*, was seriously damaged.

The attack ended almost as swiftly as it had begun. From seaward it was evident that heavy damage had been suffered in the harbour, and *Whitshed* at once closed to see if assistance was required. As she approached she saw that *Vimy* was coming out stern first, apparently on fire aft. *Keith* followed her, firing all the time at targets to the north of the town. With the death of *Keith*'s captain, who was Captain (D), the command devolved on *Whitshed*. Her commander signalled Dover asking for air support, as in his opinion it was impossible to continue the evacuation without fighter protection. Fifty minutes later Spitfires arrived overhead. Immediately *Whitshed* signalled Dover: 'Going in.'

Once again it was low water. With considerable difficulty *Whitshed* and *Vimiera* negotiated the entrance channels. As *Whitshed* entered, she engaged machine-gun nests and other targets. 'X' gun, damaged, had to be trained by the shoulders of its crew. Oddly enough, neither ship came under fire as she entered. *Whitshed* embarked the demolition party, found that not all the assigned tasks had been completed and sent details off to complete them. Commander Conder considered that the opportunity had now arisen to extricate the Welsh Guards from a wood on the other side of the harbour and called them by megaphone to withdraw. The detachment of the Guards concerned formed up and marched with parade-ground precision round the harbour to where *Whitshed* was lying. With over 500 troops she pulled out, followed by *Vimiera* with 550 men in addition to the demolition party and the wounded who had been picked up earlier. It was impossible to carry more owing to the state of the tide. As they cleared the harbour, *Wild Swan* and *Venomous* went in.

It was decided now to put in a third destroyer as time clearly was growing very short. The two leading ships entered without opposition but, as *Venetia* closed the breakwaters in the dusk, a sheet of flame flared on the hills to the north of the town and a hot bombardment of the entrance opened. It is probable that the Germans hoped to sink *Venetia* in the channel and thereby block it against further evacuation. She was hit on 'B' gun platform, the gun's crew was wiped out, and her captain, Lieutenant-Commander B. H. de C. Mellor, and the bridge crew dangerously wounded. The ship ran aground with her engines stopped, but Sub-Lieutenant D. H. Jones, RNR, took over command on the bridge and eventually brought her out of harbour stern first.

Wild Swan, already alongside, opened fire with her after guns and a moment later sighted enemy tanks in the town, one of them coming down a side street to the quay. This was destroyed with a direct hit.

Venomous, as she went alongside, came under heavy fire but one of her sub-lieutenants jumped ashore and secured her wires. At the same time a midshipman sighted an enemy motor-cycle detachment debouching from the main street on to the quay. Opening fire with the pom-poms, he broke up the column. All through the embarkation fire was maintained. At 9.0 pm the two ships had taken on approximately a thousand men between them. As the state of the water still prevented heavier loading, they cast off. On the way out the steering gear of *Venomous* jammed but she steered by her engines and got clear; *Wild Swan* grounded but managed to get off again, and with the damaged *Venetia* the three ships returned to Dover.

There were still troops ashore. Admiral Ramsay ordered HMS *Windsor*, which was working off Calais, to Boulogne and she reached the port at about 10.30 pm. In circumstances of tremendous confusion she was worked into the port and alongside the Quai Chanzy, and there picked up 600 men and some 30 wounded.

Only two undamaged destroyers were now left to the Dover Command – *Vimiera* and *Wessex*. These were in turn ordered to Boulogne, but *Wessex* was diverted to Calais and *Vimiera* entered alone. In an absolute silence she approached the harbour. To her captain, Lieutenant-Commander R. B. N. Hicks, any attempt to reach the inner harbour seemed suicidal and she secured to the outer jetty. For a long while she lay there in the same complete silence. To her hails there was no reply. It seemed to her people that the port had capitulated and she was at the point of slipping when a disorganised rush of civilians, refugees, and French and Belgian soldiers came from behind the quayside building. Almost simultaneously a Guards officer reached the ship. He was asked how many men were left and answered that there were a little over a thousand. By 2.45 am *Vimiera* had taken on board 1,400. Only the spaces round her guns were left clear. Outrageously overloaded, she slipped and headed for the English coast. As she cleared the breakwaters the jetty came under heavy shellfire and a bombing attack developed over the town.

French resistance in areas remote from the harbour continued the following day, and in giving supporting fire the French destroyers again suffered heavily. The *Fougueux* was badly damaged. The *Chacal* was hit and lay stopped in a sinking condition under fire from German batteries while her men took to the water. Some of the survivors, under the command of Lieutenant-Commander Ducoing, reached the shore at Gris Nez and joined in the defence of a small fortified position until it fell on May 25th.

Because of these losses Admiral Abrial withdrew the remainder of the destroyers, but General Lanquetot, with a handful of men, continued his resistance until the morning of the 25th, when he too surrendered.

The brief epic of Boulogne was over.

*　　*　　*

The story of Calais is a story of deliberate sacrifice – the sacrifice of a brigade to win time for an army.

The French stand at Desvres won the first brief breathing space, but by May 22nd the 1st Panzer Division was close to

Calais. On the afternoon of the 22nd the 10th Panzer Division was restored to Guderian's command, and he decided to move the 1st Panzer north at once, leaving Calais for the time being in order to effect a crossing of the Aa and an advance on Dunkirk – the mission that had originally been intended for the 10th Panzer. This formation Guderian now directed to take over from the 1st Panzer opposite Calais and to undertake the assault. The respite that this rearrangement gave is important.

On May 22nd, as the Germans closed in on Boulogne, reinforcements to the minute British force at Calais were sent forward. The Queen Victoria's Rifles, a territorial battalion, reached the port first and moved out at once to block the principal roads into the town; they had no transport. Behind them came the 3rd Royal Tank Regiment – part of the 1st Armoured Division – and a little later their vehicles. Harbour facilities had been badly damaged by air raids and the absence of quay personnel completed the trouble. Unloading began with ship's derricks and was not completed until the following day. The Tank Regiment was, however, ordered by General Brownrigg, who was moving back now to Dover, to thrust south-west to join in the defence of Boulogne. Long before it could get under way an officer from GHQ arrived with orders for it to proceed towards St Omer and to make contact with GHQ. As there was no prospect of its moving for some time, light tanks were sent forward to reconnoitre the St Omer road. They found St Omer in flames and narrowly escaped destruction by the 6th Panzer Division.

On the 23rd, escorted by the Dover destroyers, the 30th Brigade, under Brigadier Nicholson, reached Calais. This too was directed by General Brownrigg to move south-west to hold at Boulogne. It sailed with that intention.

Meanwhile the Royal Tank Regiment sent back the liaison officer to GHQ with an escort of light tanks. The party ran into the 1st Panzer Division and was destroyed. Behind it the regiment moved forward and fought a brisk action. After an initial success it lost twelve more tanks, and it became obvious that a break-through to St Omer was impossible. The surviving tanks accordingly fell back on Calais.

When Brigadier Nicholson arrived at Calais it was to find that his armour had already suffered heavy loss, that the enemy was closing in almost on the outskirts of the town and that any question of a sortie either to Boulogne or to St Omer was impossible. Doggedly he set to work to consolidate a perimeter of defence in conjunction with the French. While he was doing this he received a third order: to take through to the British Expeditionary Force 350,000 rations. The order was underlined as 'over-riding all other considerations'. The Royal Tank Regiment sent out one of its dwindling squadrons to reconnoitre the road to Dunkirk. Once again it ran into the 1st Panzer Division. Three tanks broke through, the remainder were lost. At first light on the 24th, when infantry and another squadron went forward to clear the road, a bitter battle developed. At its end the Tank Regiment was reduced to nine cruiser and twelve light tanks. Calais town itself was under heavy artillery fire from the guns of the 10th Panzer Division and an attack was developing against the western sectors.

Throughout the 23rd destroyers had maintained patrol up and down Calais Roads and had fired when opportunity arose at enemy targets. On the 24th Admiral Ramsay, who had now received reinforcements, sent *Grafton, Greyhound,* and the Polish destroyer *Burza* to the area. All through the day they carried out supporting bombardments under heavy air attack. It was in the course of these that *Wessex* was sunk and *Burza* and *Vimiera* damaged.

At two o'clock that morning the War Office informed Brigadier Nicholson that evacuation had been decided on 'in principle'. In view of that decision wounded were loaded aboard ships which had not yet completed their discharge of vehicles and *matériel,* supply personnel, stevedores, and noncombatant troops were embarked, and the ships were dispatched to Dover. As the day wore on an ammunition shortage developed, and the destroyers *Wolfhound* and *Verity* were sent over from Dover with replenishments and with a Royal Marine guard for the port itself.

Late in the afternoon the 10th Panzer Division launched heavy attacks on all three sides. Fort Nieulay was surrendered by the French commander, Fort Lapin was abandoned after the coastal defence guns had been disabled, the British perimeter was pierced in the south, and the enemy obtained a foothold in the town.

The Germans suffered heavy loss in the process but the attacks continued. To Brigadier Nicholson it was evident that he could not hold the original perimeter much longer. A new message from the War Office now reached him confirming that evacuation would take place – but not until seven o'clock the following morning. At dark Nicholson brought his men in to the old ramparts that had been built by Vauban. As the withdrawal was in progress he received a signal from the CIGS which said that General Blanchard 'forbids evacuation' and that this 'means that you must comply for the sake of allied solidarity'. The tone and tenor of the message were heavily castigated by the Prime Minister.

That night Admiral Somerville crossed to discuss the situation with Nicholson and reported that 'Given more guns which were urgently needed, he was confident he could hold on for a time', but it was agreed that there was no purpose to be served by keeping ships in the harbour.

On the morning of May 25th the Mayor of Calais, who had been captured by the Germans, was brought forward under enemy escort with a proposal for surrender. He was detained under guard and his escort returned to the enemy.

All through the morning the bombardment continued remorselessly. The water mains had broken and the troops were critically short of water. Almost all Nicholson's guns were out of action now and, though the destroyers made every effort to help him, lack of fire control and shore spotting parties restricted their value. Fires burned through the old town, streets were blocked by fallen masonry, dust and acrid smoke shrouded the defence. On the east side a sortie was made to relieve pressure but it broke down in the sandhills. At last the enemy crossed the canals and the defenders fell back to the area of the docks. Brigadier Nicholson had established at the old Citadel a joint headquarters with the French Commander. Here in the course of the afternoon a German officer was brought under a flag of truce with a demand for surrender.

The German War Diary records Nicholson's reply with admiration:

'The answer is no, as it is the British Army's duty to fight as well as it is the German's.'

At once the attack was resumed but by nightfall resistance was not yet crushed and the Germans, disappointed of immediate victory, broke off the assault. At midnight the War Office sent a final exhortation:

'Every hour you continue to exist is of greatest help to the BEF. Government have decided you must continue to fight. Have greatest admiration for your splendid stand.'

These signals and cross-signals in the confusion of the hour were not clear at Dover. Admiral Ramsay would not abandon the hope of rescuing at least some of the garrison. On the night of the 25th a force of yachts, trawlers, and drifters, with some small craft, was sent over to wait in case there was a last-minute change of plan. Some of these small vessels entered the port and brought off a number of men, most of them wounded. The Belgian launch *Semois* went in four times and each time brought away wounded. HM Trawler *Conidaw* went in in the early hours of the 26th, grounded and remained there until the afternoon. When she left she had 165 men on board, including the survivors of the Royal Marine guard, whose officers had been killed or captured.

In the defence positions all through the night they rested as they could – short of water, short of food, short of ammunition. On the morning of May 26th the bombardment began again, heavier than before, for fresh artillery had come up from Boulogne. The German War Diary says:

'The combined bombing attack and artillery bombardment on Calais Citadel and on the suburb of Les Baraques are carried out between 0900 and 1000 hours. No visible result is achieved; the fighting continues and the English defend themselves tenaciously.'

Dive bombers, high-level bombers, fighters joined in. Each phase of the bombardment was followed up by tanks and infantry. Gradually the defenders were forced back into the northern half of the old city. The Citadel was surrounded and isolated. Coherent defence broke under the overwhelming strength of the enemy and the defenders were split up into separate parties which yet maintained themselves in battered bastions and heaps of rubble. Late in the afternoon the Germans fought their way into the Citadel and captured Brigadier Nicholson with his headquarters. As dusk came one point of resistance after another failed. Slowly the sound of battle died and silence fell on Calais.

In that silence HM Yacht *Gulzar* entered the harbour, as *Vimiera* had entered Boulogne. She berthed at midnight, and her crew searched the ruins of the captured town for wounded. At 1.0 am – hours after the enemy had secured the town – they picked up fifty men from the end of the breakwater. The story of Calais was ended:

Yet it was not wholly ended. General Guderian said:[1]

'As the commander on the spot I am able definitely to state that the heroic defence of Calais, although worthy of the

[1] *Panzer Leader* by General Heinz Guderian.

highest praise, yet had no influence on the development of events outside Dunkirk.'

Is Guderian correct in his assumption? It seems at the very least improbable. Had Calais fallen early, had neither Calais nor Boulogne been defended, the situation must have been very different. When the armour was halted on the 23rd the 1st Panzer Division had actually crossed the canal at Watten. If there had been no defence of Boulogne and Calais, there would have been instead of the somewhat attenuated 1st Panzer Division, three armoured divisions on the Canal Line, flushed with victory. It seems inconceivable that in the circumstances Guderian would not have gone straight through to Dunkirk, his avowed objective.

He makes his statement in the midst of a complex attempt to shift the blame for the German Army's failure at Dunkirk to Goering and the Luftwaffe. The one clear fact that transcends all explanations is that the defence of Calais won time – and time was the essential factor in Gort's conduct of the Western battle.

So in the fury of Boulogne and the last silence of Calais the pattern of Dunkirk was shaped and set.

CHAPTER VII

Sunday, May 26th

*A regular and orderly transport of large numbers
of troops with equipment cannot take place in the
hurried and difficult conditions prevailing. . . .
Evacuation of troops without equipment, however,
is conceivable by means of large numbers of smaller
vessels, coastal and ferry steamers, fishing trawlers,
drifters, and other small craft, in good weather, even
from the open coast. The Navy, however, is not in a
position to take part successfully in this with the
means at its disposal. There are no signs yet of such
transport being carried out or prepared. If it should
be started, the Navy considers the best counter-attack
to be the use of aircraft on moonless nights with
flares.*

ADMIRAL SCHNIEWIND to Field-Marshal Goering,
May 26th, 1940

AT 10.30 ON the morning of Sunday May 26th Gort was
handed a telegram from Anthony Eden, Secretary of State
for War, which read:

'. . . I have had information all of which goes to show that
French offensive from Somme cannot be made in sufficient
strength to hold any prospect of functioning with your Allies
in the North. Should this prove to be the case you will be
faced with a situation in which the safety of the BEF will
predominate. In such conditions only course open to you may
be to fight your way back to West where all beaches and ports
east of Gravelines will be used for embarkation. Navy will
provide fleet of ships and small boats and RAF would give full
support. As withdrawal may have to begin very early preliminary plans should be urgently prepared . . .'

The moment for decision was at hand. In his answer to this
telegram Gort said:

'. . . I must not conceal from you that a great part of the

BEF and its equipment will inevitably be lost even in best circumstances.'

What was the position on this morning?

Gort's decision the previous evening to abandon the attack to the south had set in motion a series of changes which were to have a crucial effect on the survival of the British Expeditionary Force. As he read Eden's message three factors dominated the situation.

The first was that the uneasy pause in the Western battle continued. Gort had already utilised it to the fullest extent to straighten and to strengthen the tenuous line of the western front.

The second was that he had reached agreement with General Blanchard as to the timing of a withdrawal to the River Lys. This would drastically shorten the front held by the BEF and the French First Army. Blanchard had himself abandoned all hope of attack to the south – he had issued orders to that effect just before midnight – but both at the meeting and in the orders it was apparent that he still believed that it would be possible to hold indefinitely an extended bridgehead covering Dunkirk, with its perimeter reaching the banks of the Lys. 'This bridgehead', he wrote, 'will be held with no thought of retreat.' The question of evacuation was not raised at the meeting. It was only on his return from Blanchard's Headquarters that Gort received Eden's telegram.

The third factor was that in the Eastern battle the 5th Division had established itself firmly in position on Brooke's left flank, thereby securing the vital opening advantage. Gort had won for the British Expeditionary Force another breathing space.

So much importance has been attributed to the Eastern battle – the Battle of the Left Flank – that it is desirable to consider it in its wider implications. In *The Turn of the Tide* Sir Arthur Bryant speaks of the BEF on the eastern front as 'defending the French frontier from the main German armies advancing from the north-east'. Were these in fact the main German armies?

Bock's Army Group B, part of which faced Brooke's II Corps, consisted of the 6th Army and the 18th Army, with a total of six corps. The armour with which it had begun the attack on Belgium had been taken from it after the Dyle and sent to Rundstedt. Army Group B on the 26th was made up of infantry divisions; it was not mechanised or motorised and its transport was mainly horse-drawn. It was in principle, if not in detail, a 1918-style army and its rate of movement was dictated by that fact. Rundstedt's Army Group A, part of which faced III Corps, in the Western battle, comprised the 2nd, 4th, 12th, and 16th Armies, with a total of seventeen infantry corps and four armoured corps. It was in manpower more than three times the strength of Army Group B but, incomparably more important, it included the entire weight of the armour. The whole potential of the German Army for the *blitzkrieg* was, therefore, concentrated in the south and west. Not all of either of these forces was involved with the Armies of the North. The German situation map for the evening of May 24th, which marks the beginning of the battle of the eastern front, shows nine and a half divisions in contact with the Belgians, one and a half disposed along the British positions on the old frontier lines, six against the French First Army, two infantry and three panzer divisions in contact with the British on the western front.

By this morning of May 26th Bock had made certain important changes. Three German divisions were approaching the position which Franklyn's 5th Division had taken up, two were in contact with the old frontier position; a total of five in all, with one more in close support. Rundstedt, however, had also made important changes. Five panzer divisions, one motorised, and three infantry divisions were in contact on the western front along the Canal Line, with two panzer and one motorised division in close support.

It is not possible to extract from these figures justification for the statement that the eastern front of the BEF faced 'the main German armies'. None the less the position on this flank was difficult and highly dangerous.

Brooke, however, had two inestimable advantages. The first was that he was entrenched in the old frontier positions and therefore had a solid anchor from which to begin the extension of his front to the left, coupled with a complete knowledge of the area and of its defensive possibilities. It should be made clear, however, that in general the defences had been planned for much larger numbers of troops than were now available to man them, and there was little time to disseminate necessary information about them to strange units coming into the area. The second was even more valuable; he knew his enemy's plans. On the 25th a patrol on General Montgomery's front had shot up a German Staff car. Its occupant, Lieutenant-

Colonel Kinzel, escaped but he left behind him a brief-case full of papers. Brooke, visiting Montgomery's Headquarters in the afternoon, found the staff busy over these papers and took them to GHQ, where they were translated. They contained an almost complete German Order of Battle, which was to prove invaluable both then and after in all assessments of German strength. More immediately important, however, they contained the German 6th Army's plan for its attack against the hinge of the BEF and the Belgian forces. Briefly, the plan provided for a holding attack on the frontier positions to pin down the BEF, and a main thrust towards the general area of Ypres in a strength of two corps. Brooke's final positioning of the 5th Division was made in the light of this knowledge and his immediate subsequent moves were conditioned by it.

A third advantage now demonstrated itself. The swift movement of the 5th Division (carried out largely by the GHQ transport companies, which had already given invaluable service during the retreat) indicated that Brooke had superiority in speed over Bock's infantry and horse-drawn transport. This superiority was to be of decisive importance throughout the battle of the left flank. It was because of these things that GHQ was able to view the position by the middle of the morning with a qualified optimism as to the immediate future.

Unknown to Gort, however, important decisions were at that moment being taken at Hitler's Headquarters. Brauchitsch on the previous day had attempted to re-start the Western battle. Rundstedt, secure in the personal discretion given to him by Hitler, had ignored the order. Now Brauchitsch was summoned to Hitler's Headquarters. The slow progress of Bock's armies was discussed, and it was decided to issue an order in the name of the Führer for 'a forward thrust from the west by armoured groups and infantry divisions in the direction Tournai-Cassel-Dunkirk'.

The fighting had never wholly ceased along the western front – despite the standstill order the Germans made constant efforts to enlarge their bridgeheads – nor did the order apply equally over the whole area. From St Venant to the south the terrain was favourable to tanks, and on this day preliminary moves were begun which were to develop into a pincer movement aimed at Kemmel with the object of making contact with Bock's 6th Army and cutting off the BEF and the French from the coast. As the day advanced fighting flared heavily in the vicinity of St Venant and along the 2nd Division's area.

The 50th Division, already allotted to Brooke and waiting for transportation, was drawn into the battle and the 151st Brigade became deeply involved at Carvin. When Brooke after a reconnaissance of the gap between his flank and the Belgians reached GHQ, he could only be given the 150th Brigade. In view of the situation to the west it was necessary to delay the movement of the others.

It is appropriate here to examine the claim made by Sir Arthur Bryant that 'At this time Brooke was co-ordinating the movements both of his own Corps and of the 1st Corps on his right and in retreat behind him, without orders from above and on his own sole responsibility.'[1] I Corps was composed originally of the 1st, 2nd, and 48th Divisions. Of these the 2nd Division had already been detached and was 'at this time' hotly engaged against German armoured forces on the Canal Line 20 miles from Brooke's position. 48th Division had also been detached and was 'at this time' 25 miles in the opposite direction setting up the blocks at Cassel, at Arneke, at Ledringhem, Wormhoudt and Bergues which were to save the western flank. 1st Division alone remained in position on the frontier line. 42nd Division, next to it, had been placed temporarily under I Corps command. Neither of these divisions was 'at this time . . . in retreat behind' Brooke. Neither of them, in fact, began to retreat until the night of Monday, when they moved in accordance with the general plan laid down by Gort and adapted to the necessities of the fluid situation.

As Gort at his headquarters strove to evaluate the new developments, he received a second telegram from the Secretary of State for War. It ended:

'. . . no course open to you but to fall back upon coast . . . M. Reynaud communicating General Weygand and latter will no doubt issue orders in this sense forthwith. You are now authorised to operate towards coast forthwith in conjunction with French and Belgian Armies.'

The British Government had reached decision.

*   *   *

At French General Headquarters Weygand received the signal outlining General Blanchard's order for the withdrawal to the Lys and 'sent for Admiral Darlan to study re-embarkation'.

*   *   *

[1] *The Turn of the Tide.*

87

At 1857 – three minutes to seven – on the evening of May 26th the Admiralty made the signal: 'Operation Dynamo is to commence.'

It had already begun: At three o'clock Admiral Ramsay, on his own responsibility and in the light of information from the French coast, had started the flow of personnel ships to Dunkirk. The leaders were already loading when the signal reached the far shore. His prevision was justified. At 10.30 that evening the first shipment of troops disembarked at Dover.

Ramsay's problem had two facets. The first of these was the purely naval task. From Dover he had to secure the area through which the evacuation was designed to take place. The Straits of Dover were no longer a sheltering enclave 300 miles distant from the nearest enemy base. Information showed that light enemy craft were already operating from the captured Dutch port of Flushing; U-boats had been reported in the southern area of the North Sea; the effectiveness of enemy air attack had been brutally demonstrated within view of the windows of Ramsay's office on the Dover cliff. His destroyer losses had been made good but he still had barely a flotilla available. With them and with the smaller vessels of the Dover Command, plus the reinforcements that were beginning to reach him, he had to establish a protective screen to the eastward of the evacuation area, to cover the actual routes of the evacuation vessels, to provide counter-bombardment against the German batteries near Calais, to ensure what anti-aircraft protection could be improvised out of the ships that he had at his disposal, and to sweep both the approach channels and the area off Dunkirk town itself for mines. He had, in addition, to arrange for the control of traffic and to maintain a rescue service.

The task was sufficient in itself. The all-out use of destroyers as lifting vessels was not contemplated at this period despite the experience of Boulogne. There were too few of them and the duties of conventional protection were too great. The second facet of the 'Dynamo' plan provided for the main lifting to be carried out by merchant ships – cross-Channel vessels, obviously the most suitable type for the work – together with coasters and the Dutch skoots, backed and supported where necessary by naval vessels. There were available on the 26th the following ships for this purpose:

The plan lasted little more than a few hours. Late on
Sunday evening Ramsay received a signal from the Admiralty
which informed him that:

  '. . . it was imperative for "Dynamo" to be implemented
with the greatest vigour, with a view to lifting up to 45,000
of the British Expeditionary Force within two days, at the
end of which it was probable that evacuation would be
terminated by enemy action.'

The reasoning on which this signal was based is obscure. It
did not originate from Gort's Headquarters. It was a decision
made in London. Gort's answer to Eden's first telegram
appears to have had an effect in Whitehall out of proportion
to its careful phrasing. London had other sources of information, however: local messages from Dunkirk itself were
agitated and inaccurate; credit was no longer placed on information from French Headquarters; news from the Belgian
side was increasingly despondent. The situation was examined
at the highest levels, London had as yet no news of the resumption of the armoured attack on the western front and it
was mainly on the basis of its estimate of the chances of the
Eastern battle that a decision was reached. In the light of after-
events it was clearly a mis-judgement. None the less Ramsay
was compelled to adjust his plans in accordance with it.

As the night wore on a second factor entered into calculation. Signals reported a steady increase in shellfire from the
Calais area and it was plain that the main channel of approach,
the short Route Z, would be too dangerous for use in daylight.
Ships began to turn back.

What were the conditions from their point of view this
Sunday evening? Captain R. Duggan, master of the Isle of
Man packet *Mona's Queen*, paints a graphic picture.

'Immediately hell was let loose on our ship. We were shelled
from the shore by single guns and also by salvoes from shore
batteries. Shells were flying all around us, the first salvo went

over us, the second, astern of us. I thought the next salvo would hit us, but fortunately it dropped short, right under our stern. The ship was riddled with shrapnel, mostly all on the boat and promenade decks. Then we were attacked from the air. A Junkers bomber made a power dive towards us and dropped five bombs, but he was off the mark too, I should say about 150 feet from us. All this while we were still being shelled, although we were getting out of range. The Junkers that bombed us was shot down and crashed into the water just ahead of us (no survivors). Then another Junkers attacked us, but before he reached us he was brought down in flames. Then the tension eased a little.

'Owing to the bombardment, I could see that the nerves of some of my men were badly shaken. I did not feel too well myself, but I mustered the crew and told them that Dunkirk was being bombed and was on fire. On being asked if they would volunteer to go in they did so to a man and I am glad to say we took off as many as *Mona's Queen* could carry. Coming back from Dunkirk, I made a route for myself and am glad to say we arrived safely at Dover in the early hours of Monday morning . . .'

It is not possible to draw a hard and fast line between the end of the preliminary evacuations and the beginning of the 'Dynamo' liftings. Ships of one kind and another had been moving all through the Sunday between Dunkirk and Dover. At 1.15 on the Sunday morning, for example, the hospital carrier *Isle of Thanet* sailed with a load of casualties. In the middle of the morning *Worthing* and *Isle of Guernsey*, also hospital carriers, left the Downs.

At about 4.0 pm, as the convoy approached Calais, which lay under a heavy pall of smoke, it was forced to deviate from the route laid down to avoid two destroyers which were engaging shore batteries. On arrival off Dunkirk, shrouded under an even heavier smoke pall than Calais, the ships were compelled to pick their way between the numerous wrecks, which were already making navigation hazardous. Loading began at once, and by 9.55 pm both ships had embarked wounded far in excess of their normal accommodation. Happily the return voyage was made without incident.

At the same time *Maid of Orleans* sailed with 600 two-gallon cans of water, and 250 men drawn from the RASC and the Signal Corps who were to help in the organisation of the port facilities. Using the short route, she came under the inevitable shelling from Calais. She arrived off Dunkirk moles to find the harbour under heavy air attack and, after lying some time off the entrance, was ordered back to Dover. In the late afternoon she made a second attempt and this time berthed safely.

Canterbury left about six o'clock and ran the gauntlet of the Calais guns. At Dunkirk she berthed alongside the *Maid of Orleans*, and the two ships loaded troops under continuous bombing. *Canterbury* sailed with 1,340 men and *Maid of Orleans* followed her with 988. The French cross-Channel steamer *Rouen* in the same period lifted 420 wounded and sailed for Cherbourg.

The reports of these ships demonstrate very clearly the appalling difficulties that faced Ramsay from the start: the heavy shelling of the Calais guns, the rapidly growing weight of the enemy air attack, the disappearance of the facilities at Dunkirk, and the danger of entering the harbour under bombing.

The port of Dunkirk as darkness fell this Sunday was a place of horror. To the west of the great basin enclosed by the outer moles the oil-tank farm was blazing. Flames silhouetted the moles and lit the underside of the bascule bridge that was jammed open at the entrance to the main basin, and the high, white column of the lighthouse. Warehouses up and down the 115 acres of the basins were burning. The wrecked cranes were outlined against their brilliance. Smoke lifted intermittently to show the fires of the town itself. And endlessly through the night the thunder of the bombs and the lightning flash of their explosions marked the progress of destruction.

It was possible to hear the bombs in the silence of the cliff tops at Dover, and in the Dynamo Room the staff began to plan for the use of the open beaches. The principal weakness of Ramsay's force at this moment lay in small craft. On this night he had available the motorboats of the Ramsgate Contraband Control base, the drifters and the small craft of the Dover base, and four Belgian passenger launches. That was all, except for the boats of the ships themselves. An urgent appeal was made to the Admiralty for reinforcement.

It was already on the way. On the Sunday morning Rear-Admiral T. S. V. Phillips, Vice-Chief of Naval Staff, called a conference on small craft. It was attended by Admiral Preston of the Small Vessels Pool and his deputy, Captain E. F. Wharton. Captain Wharton, certain from his reading of events that small craft would be desperately necessary in the very near future, had been collecting boats unofficially for several days. Forty were made fast in the neighbourhood of Westminster Pier, barely a quarter of a mile from the Admiralty building. No sanction had been sought for this requisitioning and there was some apprehension as to the official attitude. Now at this meeting the move was approved with acclamation. All officers who could be spared from the staff of the Small Vessels Pool (there were barely a dozen in all) were sent out to the principal yachting centres. HMS *King Alfred*, the south coast training establishment for the RNVR, was asked for help. Signals were sent to the Flag Officer Commanding the Port of London, the Commander-in-Chief, Plymouth, and other naval authorities; and individual yachtsmen on the list which was already in being as a result of the BBC broadcast of May 14th were telephoned and given instructions.

The movement of the little ships had begun.

*   *   *

'There are no signs yet of such transport being carried out or prepared,' said Admiral Schniewind, Chief of Staff to Admiral Raeder, in his memorandum to Goering on this day. In the minutes of the Führer Conferences the memorandum is annotated in pencil: 'Transport has certainly been going on for some time.'

By midnight on this Sunday a total of 27,936 men had been brought back to England. They were the men of the 'useless mouths' scheme, the men of the lines of communication, the base organisations, the training areas. All through the week there had been a constant movement of ships. Dover harbour was full, the Downs – the historic anchorage between the Goodwin Sands and the Kentish coast – was crowded with cross-Channel steamers and coasters and barges, Ramsgate was filling with small craft, and from every port between Plymouth and Hull the stream had already begun. The failure of German intelligence to inform the German Admiralty of these movements is extraordinary. The failure of Admiral Schniewind to evaluate the messages that must have reached him from Guderian's panzers at Calais, from the Luftwaffe, from his own E-boat patrols is almost beyond understanding.

CHAPTER VIII

Monday, May 27th

We were stopped within sight of Dunkirk! We watched the Luftwaffe attack. We also saw the armada of great and little ships by means of which the British were evacuating their forces.

GENERAL GUDERIAN

GUDERIAN'S HEART cry is the measure of the chagrin and the disappointment of the German panzer divisions. Rundstedt had halted them within sight of Dunkirk. From the hill of Watten they could see the houses of the port. For three days they had been held there in a furious impatience. Now they surged forward.

Hitler's orders for the resumption of the armoured attack were too late to be translated into action on the 26th, but at dawn on May 27th Kleist Group drove east on a 35-mile front between Gravelines and Robecq – the 1st Panzer Division on the coast, the 2nd between it and Arneke, the 20th Motorised Division between Arneke and Cassel, the 6th and the 8th Panzers between Cassel and Hazebrouck. Farther south Hoth Group, developing the pincer movement that had begun the previous day, flung four panzer divisions towards Armentières and Kemmel to cut off the BEF in the frontier positions, to encircle the French First Army, to strike at the rear of Brooke's new-established front, and to link up with the ponderous forward movement of Bock's 6th Army.

From the 7th Panzer Division at the tip of the southern jaws of the pincers Rommel wrote exultantly to his wife:

Dearest Lu,

I'm very well. We're busy encircling the British and French in Lille at the moment. I'm taking part from the south-west. I'm all right for washing, etc. . . .

Rommel wrote twenty-four hours too early. The pincers closed twenty-four hours too late. Through the gap – barely

10 miles wide – that was left between Comines and the leading elements of Rommel's tanks at dark on May 27th the 1st, the 3rd, the 4th and the 42nd Divisions of the British Expeditionary Force slipped clear, and with them a third of the French First Army. The pincers failed to close because the British 2nd Division, fighting alone, cut off from support, held throughout this thunderous day the heaviest attack of artillery, dive-bombers and tanks that was launched against the BEF in the course of the entire campaign. Slowly, defending its positions desperately, fighting for every foothold, it fell back over the ancient battle-grounds of Marlborough's wars – bypassed, surrounded, overrun. At nightfall the 4th Brigade in the centre had ceased to exist, the 5th and the 6th Brigades on either hand were cut to pieces. At full dark the division was reduced to the strength of one brigade. But it had held the weight of Hoth Group's armour, and with darkness the main withdrawal began behind it.

Down the Canal Line the garrisons of the stop points clung grimly to their blocks – Lestrem, Hazebrouck, Cassel, Arneke, Ledringhem, Wormhoudt – while the armoured flood swirled by them on either side; swirled, hesitated and halted.

On the eastern front three infantry divisions of Bock's 6th Army formed the other claw of the pincer movement. Their weight fell on Franklyn's reinforced 5th Division holding the railway line and the canal from Comines to Ypres. The attack began with heavy artillery and mortar fire, assisted by dive-bombers. By sheer superiority of numbers the 143rd Brigade, holding the Comines area, was forced back. Gallant counter-attacks by an improvised unit largely composed of Royal Engineers fighting as infantry, checked the German onslaught. The attack was held on the reserve position, and throughout the day Franklyn stubbornly countered the German moves.

Gort had extricated the second brigade of the 50th Division at nightfall on the Sunday night. Brooke used it with its companion brigade to extend his left flank once more, this time beyond Ypres. As with the first deployment of the 5th Division, the 50th was in position at dawn, long before Bock's infantry could cover the ground.

The handling of the German divisions in the eastern area on this day is of extreme interest. Far to the east nine divisions still pounded against the last flicker of Belgian resistance. Two of them – the 30th and the 255th – had broken through between Iseghem and Thielt, and were heading for Ostend.

Three divisions – the 18th, the 311th and the 61st – hammered against Franklyn's 5th Division. Two divisions were spread against the old frontier positions, but in the 6-mile gap which yawned between the British front at Ypres and the retiring Belgian flank at Zonnebeke nothing moved at all. No attempt was in progress, no attempt apparently was envisaged, to exploit the wide breach that opened to the sea. Over and over again 6th Army bewailed its lack of tanks.

Gort had committed the last of his reserves. There was little in this hour that he could do; the battles were in the hands of God, and of the commanders of his corps and his divisions, and of the men who fought and died to hold on to meaningless fragments of French villages and nameless stretches of Belgian waterways.

One thing, however, remained to be done: it was vital now to set up a defensive perimeter about Dunkirk. It was no longer humanly possible to hold Blanchard's perimeter on the Lys. The Belgian Army was breaking fast, the eastern front was desperately outweighted. The time had come to fall back on the last perimeter of all: the canals from Dunkirk to Nieuport, from Nieuport to Furnes, from Furnes to Bergues, from Bergues to Gravelines – the canals that ringed Dunkirk.

Late on the Sunday Gort had appointed Sir Ronald Adam to organise the defence of Dunkirk. There was inevitably an overlap here. Nominally Admiral Abrial, as *Amiral Nord*, was responsible for the defence of the great French base. Under him was a formation known as the SFF – the *Secteur fortifié de Flandres*. Its resources were small and its equipment limited. It was designed principally for coast defence. Weygand, returning from the Ypres conference, specifically charged Admiral Abrial to defend the whole area. 'I have complete confidence in you.' Abrial properly pointed out that he had very feeble means for such a task. Weygand answered that two divisions of the Seventh Army, still then fighting with the Belgians, were to be recalled and assigned to him under General Fagalde, commanding XVI Corps.

'. . . I am counting on you to save everything that can be saved – and particularly our honour.'

How Abrial was expected to cover an effective perimeter on the canals with two divisions was not made clear.

At seven o'clock on the morning of May 27th a meeting was called at the Hôtel du Sauvage at Cassel. Before the conference sat, Sir Ronald Adam and General Fagalde discussed the possibilities of the Dunkirk perimeter and reached a formal agreement. The sectors were marked on a map that Colonel Bridgeman had brought to the meeting. The British were to hold from Nieuport along the canals through Furnes to the town of Bergues, the French were to hold from beyond the limits of Bergues to Gravelines; the perimeter was divided in two by the canal between Bergues and Dunkirk town. This outline map was signed by both generals.

The sub-division of the eastern sector was a British matter. Briefly, it was devided into three areas, one for each corps: II Corps in the east, I Corps in the centre, III Corps next to Dunkirk town itself. A collecting area was appointed outside the perimeter for each corps, a sector was laid down for each to occupy, and a section of the beach was allotted to each for evacuation. Dumps of what ammunition and food remained were set up in the three areas, and medical arrangements were made to deal with the wounded. The problem of traffic was dealt with by the drastic step of ordering all transport, except for a very few headquarters vehicles and artillery, to be abandoned outside the line of the canals. Brigadier the Hon. E. F. Lawson was lent by 48th Division to assemble and post what troops were already in the area and to fill out the defence of the long line of the canals as men came in. The beach-head of Dunkirk began to take shape.

The meeting proper followed. It was attended by Adam, representing Lord Gort, with a group of senior officers, and General Blanchard, Admiral Abrial, General Prioux (now commanding the French First Army), General de la Laurencie (commanding the III Corps), and finally, General Koeltz, Chief of Staff to the Supreme Commander General Weygand. The formal Cassel meeting achieved perhaps the summit of unreality. After twenty minutes in which nothing germane to the situation was settled, General Koeltz rose. He said that he was 'in Weygand's mind', that the situation called for an all-out attack, that an advance towards the south-west should be initiated, and that the French XVI Corps should set out instantly on the recapture of Calais. Great enthusiasm was stirred amongst the French. It is not perhaps necessary to comment further on this.

At noon General Pownall reached Cassel to ascertain if it would be possible to move GHQ back to the town, which was on the line of the buried cable. He received his answer in enemy shellfire. The siege of Cassel had begun.

Through Sir Roger Keyes at Belgian Headquarters came a message from the Belgian King:

'. . . He fears a moment is rapidly approaching when he can no longer rely upon his troops to fight or to be any further use to the BEF. He wishes you to realise that he will be obliged to surrender before a débâcle.'

It was almost immediately after he read this signal that Gort was given one of his last messages from Weygand:

'General Weygand makes a personal appeal to General Gort. The British Army must participate strongly in the necessary joint counter-attacks. Situation demands hard hitting.'

What counter-attacks Weygand had in mind were not mentioned. What hard hitting he believed possible with the pincers closing on the French First Army, the ammunition resources almost gone, the food and fuel vanishing, has never been made clear.

The new GHQ was set up at Houtkerque, 9 miles north of Cassel, wireless communication with the three corps headquarters was established and, as the movement was in progress, Gort received from the Secretary of State for War a telegram which said:

'. . . want to make it quite clear that sole task now is to evacuate to England maximum of your forces possible.'

The unrealities of the Cassel conference were such that Gort set out himself to find Blanchard. He went first to La Panne, drew blank and went to Dunkirk. At Bastion 32 Admiral Abrial and General Fagalde had their headquarters. Blanchard was not there either. It was late now. A little before eleven o'clock General Koeltz asked Gort casually whether he had heard that the King of the Belgians had asked for an armistice from midnight.

Gort set out at once for Houtkerque and his headquarters. Almost immediately he was forced off the road by traffic retreating into the area of Dunkirk town. In a nightmare journey he struggled through roads crazy with refugees, cumbered with horse-drawn traffic, blocked with broken vehicles. For four and a half hours of that time he knew that his ally to the north had ceased fire, that for 20 miles his left flank was open to the sea.

But even as Gort fought his way through the fantastic press of the traffic Montgomery with the 3rd Division had disengaged from the old frontier positions and was coming down close behind the battle-front of the 5th Division, his vehicles moving at times under an arch of fire from the batteries that were covering the battle, to extend the left flank from the 50th Division towards the new Dunkirk perimeter. Behind them the 4th and the 42nd Divisions fell back to the line of the River Lys and formed a defensive flank from Comines to Armentières. The 1st Division passed through them. The French III Corps manned the river from Armentières to Estaires. The remnants of the 2nd Division fell back to the bank between Estaires and Merville, and the 44th filled from there to Hazebrouck. It was nowhere as neat as it appears subsequently on the situation maps. There were gaps, there were long unmanned sectors of line. In the darkness and the horror of the roads units lost touch with each other, commanders lost contact. The night was full of terrors. But incredibly, on the lines laid down by Gort, the divisions came out of the turmoil and the new front was established.

*　　*　　*

Why did Leopold surrender?

The blunt fact is that the Belgian Army was defeated in the field. That fact was obscured at once by a dense smoke screen composed in varying parts of the political quarrel between Leopold and his ministers, the French search for a scapegoat, Reynaud's impassioned accusations, and Churchill's second reference to the capitulation in the House of Commons. Gort lent himself to the subsequent clamour.

It is an unhappy story. Leopold made mistakes – they will be examined in a later chapter – but the facts on this Monday are militarily plain. The Belgian Army was severed irrevocably from the BEF – neither side had the resources with which even to attempt to close the gap. In addition, and perhaps even more important, the Belgian Army was broken in two; Bock had forced a fatal penetration between Iseghem and Thielt. Short of ammunition, short of transport, without armour and virtually without air support, the position of the Belgians was hopeless.

Leopold from the Ypres meeting on the 21st had left no doubt whatever in Gort's mind as to the fighting efficiency of his forces. As the days passed he had issued further warnings. On the 25th and the 26th GHQ was kept informed of the failing strength of the Belgian Army. Leopold's first message of the 27th has already been quoted. The last message failed to reach Gort, but it is difficult to see what more the King

98

of the Belgians could have done. It has been suggested that he should have conferred directly with Gort, or at least with Blanchard and the French, before he made his decision. The stark truth is that no attempt was made to confer with Leopold when the British Government took its decision to evacuate. Leopold was not informed of the intentions of the British Government until this Monday morning. He must have known that partial evacuation had been going on for a week – 27,000 men, after all, had already been embarked. When he sent his plenipotentiaries to meet Bock, Operation 'Dynamo' – full-scale evacuation – had been in progress for twenty-four hours. Gort subsequently resented references to that fact. It remains, none the less, a fact.

* * *

At dawn on May 27th the position at sea was confused and obscure. Ships were turning back in the face of the shellfire from Calais and of the increasing attacks of the Luftwaffe. The tally of loss and destruction had begun. The armed boarding vessel *Mona's Isle*, for example, had berthed at Dunkirk the previous evening. She embarked 1,420 troops, cleared the harbour early on the Monday morning, and was straddled by the German batteries between Gravelines and Les Hemmes. Shortly after she was attacked from the air. Twenty-three men were killed and sixty wounded. This was the first heavy loss of the evacuation.

The reinforcements under way for Dunkirk began to suffer. The SS *Yewdale* and the motor vessel *Sequacity* sailed from the Downs. The report of Captain J. MacDonald, the master of *Sequacity*, is an admirable essay in objectiveness.

'All went well until we arrived off Calais, then I noticed some shells falling in the water ahead of us. I then thought it was land batteries ashore firing at some mines, but soon after the shells started dropping all round my ship, and one came through the port side, at the water line in the main hold and went out the starboard side.

'I sent my mate down into the hold with some of the crew to try and patch the hold up. The next shot came through the port side of the engine-room and smashed up the auxiliary engines that drove our dynamo, etc., put our switchboard out of action, and went out the starboard side.

'This put our pumps entirely out of action for pumping water out of the hold.

99

'Another shot came through the wheelhouse and went through the hatches, down the forehold, and right through the ship's bottom.

'We then shaped our course away from the shore and the *Yewdale* which was outside of us did likewise.

'In the meantime eleven German planes appeared overhead and bombed both the *Yewdale* and ourselves. Another shell burst over our fiddley and put the Bren-gun out of action, and wounded the chief engineer.

'Meanwhile the wind increased and caused a nasty chop on the sea, which allowed a lot of water to come through the hole in our side, and as we were unable to pump our hold out the ship began to take a nasty list.

'I blew for the *Yewdale* to stand by us, but he did not appear to notice our signal. A British plane then appeared and saw the trouble we were in, and flew ahead to the *Yewdale* and dropped some red flares.

'The *Yewdale* then returned to us, and we launched our lifeboat, and then after we got aboard the *Yewdale* she went down by the head and sunk.

'I should add that in addition to the two soldiers that worked our Bren gun, before we left the Downs we took on a young naval rating named Evans with Lewis guns. We had to fix these on the open bridge, and all the time we were being attacked by the planes he kept up incessant fire with the Lewis guns and stuck his job manfully.

'The *Yewdale* landed us at Ramsgate. . . .'

One after the other the signals came in to Dover, signals that made it brutally certain that the short route to Dunkirk would have to be abandoned during daylight hours.

There were two other possible routes. Route Y, of 87 miles against the short route distance of 39, ran to a point well out at sea off Ostend, turned acutely off the Kwinte Buoy and came in from the east through the Zuydecoote Pass. Route X, of 55 miles, cut across the Ruytingen Bank and came into the inshore channel midway between Gravelines and Dunkirk moles. Route X was known to cross minefields; Route Y might or might not be mined. Grimly Admiral Ramsay accepted the risk. At eleven o'clock, though it had not yet been possible to sweep the full length of Route Y, the transports *St Helier* and *Royal Daffodil* and the hospital carriers *St Julien* and *St Andrew* were ordered to proceed by it, escorted by two destroyers.

The long route more than doubled the time necessary for

the run, which logically increased the number of ships required. The loss of time had to be accepted, and with it – and perhaps more important – the increase of opportunity for the German Air Force. This last point was to some extent offset by a heavy increase in fighter patrols. On this day Fighter Command had ordered sixteen squadrons to operate as nearly as possible continuously from five o'clock in the morning until dusk. Patrols varied from nine to twenty aircraft, and some squadrons carried out as many as three patrols. Though the major weight of the Luftwaffe was still directed against the weakening Belgian Army and in spite of the increase in the number of patrols, Dunkirk itself was bombed heavily in twelve separate raids.

The situation ashore was, from the naval point of view, equally obscure. The previous day Captain W. G. Tennant, Chief Staff Officer to the First Sea Lord (who had just been appointed captain of HMS *Repulse*), had volunteered to help with the evacuation. He was ordered to Dunkirk as Senior Naval Officer ashore. Early on the afternoon of this Monday he sailed from Dover with twelve officers and 160 ratings, together with a communications staff, in HMS *Wolfhound*. At half-hourly intervals the ship was attacked by dive bombers on the passage across. When at six o'clock Tennant landed at Dunkirk the town was burning, most of the harbour facilities were in ruins, the bombing appeared to be continuous, and the local information he received was alarming. At eight o'clock he sent a signal which said:

'Please send every available craft to beaches East of Dunkirk immediately. Evacuation tomorrow night is problematical.'

He followed this with a more detailed analysis of the situation and immediately afterwards ordered *Wolfhound*, which had originally been intended to remain in Dunkirk as communications ship, to clear the harbour and to proceed to the beaches to pick up men. These two signals were followed shortly afterwards by a report from two unidentified officers from GHQ to the effect that the situation of the BEF was precarious. On the basis of these signals Admiral Ramsay ordered all available ships to the beaches. The patrolling destroyers were called in, and very rapidly a force consisting of the anti-aircraft cruiser *Calcutta*, nine destroyers, two transports, four minesweepers, seventeen drifters, and a number of skoots was spread between Dunkirk and La Panne, working the beaches with their own boats. They joined HMS *Sabre*, one of the oldest destroyers in the Navy, which was already operating in the area.

The first of the cross-Channel steamers to work off the beaches were *St Seiriol* and *Queen of the Channel*. They had crossed in the early afternoon by the long route and had entered the harbour. *Queen of the Channel* had already picked up fifty men when, with *St Seiriol*, she was ordered out to lie off the beaches. Again the words of one of her people best describe the difficulties and the dangers. Her chief officer, Mr J. McNamee, wrote in his report:

'There was an air raid in progress as we arrived alongside. Our guns with others were in action. We landed a man on the pier to hang on to our ropes. About 8 pm Lieutenant-Commander Williams, RN, came on board and told the captain to proceed out of the harbour, lower his boats, and get the men on board from the beach. We got to the anchorage. I lowered the first boat in charge of the second officer and the second boat in charge of R. Thomas, AB. The third boat was taken by the crew of a trawler.

'When I was about to lower the fourth boat we received information that there were a number of troops arriving at the pier. With the remainder of the crew we still had on board we proceeded alongside the pier. We got about 600 men on board, they were arriving in batches, about 11 pm we were told there were no more men in the vicinity, so we cut our mooring ropes. On hearing more men running along the pier we got the ship alongside the pier again and got about 80 more men on board. During our stay alongside the pier we had four air raids. While we were leaving the pier the enemy dropped illuminated parachutes which lit up the whole sea front. Our captain backed the vessel up the harbour under the smoke screen made available to us from the burning town of Dunkirk.

'We then proceeded to try and pick up our boats and crew, but were ordered by a destroyer to proceed to Dover via Calais. When off Calais we were attacked by bombs and machine-gun fire, the plane coming down to the level of the navigation bridge, but fortunately for us a destroyer was passing at the time and came into action and the plane was destroyed . . .'

The work off the beaches was desperately slow. Ships used their own boats, the heavy, clumsy lifeboats approved by the Board of Trade and designed for deep-sea work – nothing more inappropriate could have been thought of for the shallows of Dunkirk. The naval vessels used cutters and whalers. Lord

Gort said in his dispatch that on the 27th only 200 men were embarked from the beaches. The number actually was considerably higher, approximately 2,500 in all (*Queen of the Channel*, for instance, herself picked up 200 men), but the lifting was, none the less, painfully slow.

There were two solutions: one lay in the provision of suitable small craft, which was already in hand; the other was more radical. Captain Tennant, weighing up the possibilities of the harbour itself in the light of the flames of the burning warehouses, decided to experiment with the practicability of berthing vessels alongside the East Mole. As has been said before, it had not been built for this purpose – but there was a chance. With a magnificent disregard for the consequences he signalled a ship to come alongside. She berthed without trouble, and the pattern was set.

*   *   *

The withdrawal to the Lys had, as outlined in the previous chapter, driven Weygand at last to consider the possibility of 're-embarkation'. On the morning of this day Captain Auphan, Assistant Chief of Staff to Admiral Darlan, arrived at Dover to discuss the situation with the Deputy Naval Commandant of Dunkirk and the Chief of the French Naval Liaison Mission from London. After a brief discussion the three men met Admiral Ramsay. Auphan, in a later account of his mission, said that despite 'the confidential liaison' which had existed between the two navies, no information had been given to the French of the decision to evacuate. The implications of this are discussed in a subsequent chapter. For the moment it is only necessary to remember that Reynaud had been fully informed of the position at the London meeting the previous day.

Despite whatever bitterness he may have felt, Auphan was a man of great energy and he began at once the very difficult task of improvising a complementary French effort to work with the enormous machine that Ramsay had already thrown into action. The collection of small boats in the nearer French ports began, all immediately available naval craft were ordered up, and Rear-Admiral Landriau was appointed to command in the area and was ordered to proceed to Dover at once in the sloop *Savorgnan de Brazza*, which was to act as headquarters vessel. It was impossible, however, to make a practical contribution to the work on this day. Two minesweepers brought back a total of 175 wounded to England and that was all; the hospital ships which attempted to enter the port were turned back in the face of heavy bombing.

*   *   *

At Dover the provision of small craft became a matter of first priority. Essentially it was a matter of time, and time, in the view of every man at Dunkirk, was running desperately short. In England every effort was being made to expedite the movement. The first results were, in fact, already showing with the arrival of the Dutch skoots. The Small Vessels Pool was hurrying everything that it could down the river and from the ports. Rear-Admiral A. H. Taylor had been appointed to Sheerness as 'Dynamo' Maintenance Officer to receive and to pass on the boats from the Thames and from the East Coast. With a limited staff, he set up headquarters in the gloomy and ancient Admiralty House under the shadow of the ramparts.

Working with the Small Vessels Pool was the small craft section of the Ministry of Shipping under Mr A. L. Moore. Mr H. C. Riggs of this department had been warned by telephone during the night of the urgency of the situation and with the early morning he began to get in touch with Ministry officials in various ports. Up the Thames Messrs Tough Brothers, boat-builders of Teddington, were approached to act as agents for the collection of craft in their area, while all through the Port of London officials of the Authority were warned to expedite the passage of small craft in every possible way. The Ministry of Shipping undertook the whole responsibility towards crews and towards the small craft themselves in regard to financial problems. Payments for runner crews, for travelling expenses and for necessary stores were undertaken by Mr Moore's department, and by that department eventually all responsibility for craft damaged and lost was assumed. With the Ministry, as with the Admiralty, the story was the same – everywhere it was met by an almost importunate desire to help. And here, as in the Admiralty, the narrative of these days is marked by a complete and utter absence of red tape, a deliberate abandonment of any rules or restrictions which might tend to hamper the mighty effort that had sprung into being.

The spirit of those first hours is perhaps most abundantly manifested in the movement of the boats. Dr B. A. Smith, owner of the motor yacht *Constant Nymph*, for example, was rung up in the early hours of the 27th from the Admiralty and asked to confirm the fact that his boat was ready for sea. At 8.30 that evening, and without waiting for the convoy of boats with which he was to have sailed, Dr Smith took *Constant Nymph* down to Sheerness.

The small boats had started. It was painfully apparent that until sufficient of them could reach the beaches loading would be slow. This was a day of failure: 7,669 men only were landed in England. One thing redeemed it. It was impossible yet to estimate its worth, impossible to balance hopes upon it, yet Tennant's signal that ships could be berthed at the East Mole remains one of the turning points of Dunkirk.

CHAPTER IX

Tuesday, May 28th

The man that once did sell the lion's skin
While the beast liv'd was kill'd with hunting him.
SHAKESPEARE, *Henry V*

ONE FACTOR dominated the situation on the land on the morning of May 28th – the consequences of the capitulation of the Belgian Army.

At midnight on the 27th twenty miles from the left flank of the 50th Division at Boesinghe to the sea at Nieuport lay open to the power and the weight of Bock's inevitable assault. As Gort fought his way through the crazed roads from Dunkirk town to Houtkerque that single fact occupied his mind to the exclusion of all lesser dangers. There was, as has been said, little, if anything, left that he could do. He had used his last reserves.

The left flank now was Brooke's responsibility. It was his urgent task to fill that gap, to cover the eastern front, to establish some sort of defence to the sea at Nieuport. Bock's problem was, from the opposite side of the field, in equal measure urgent. Somehow, without armour, without motorised divisions, without proper transport, he had to fling his infantry in a great enveloping movement from the sudden silence of the Belgian front in the few hours that were left before Brooke could bar his way.

Both men failed.

Bock's manoeuvre has an almost text-book solidity and a lack of inspiration that is wholly text-book. The nearest of the divisions that had been fighting on the Belgian front were swung stolidly round against the Canal Line from Ypres to Noordschote – the 254th, the 14th, and the 19th. The two divisions that had broken through the Belgians, the 30th and the 255th, he sent farther north to the line of the Yser between Noordschote and Dixmude. The next two divisions he dispatched to the stretch of the Yser between Dixmude and

Schoore; and the last two divisions of all, the 208th and the 256th, which had been battering against the Belgian left at Bruges, he swept in a long, swift right hook across the Belgian coastal plain to Nieuport town.

There is a parade-ground precision about the movement. It was a gigantic left wheel pivoted on Ypres, and it almost worked. Bock had had six hours from the moment when Leopold's plenipotentiaries reached his headquarters to plan and prepare his move. It began at midnight. At 11 am, eleven hours after the Belgian cease-fire, the leading elements of the 256th Division raced into the coastal area before Nieuport. With improvised transport the 256th had executed the fastest move of the campaign on the eastern front.

It was not fast enough. They were met by the armoured cars of the 12th Lancers – which had remained, despite Brooke's complaints, under the command of GHQ. In a brisk and bloody skirmish the Lancers crowned the splendid record of their campaign. For the moment the attack was held.

That afternoon Brooke drove to La Panne. Sir Ronald Adam told him there that the Germans were at Nieuport. Writing after the war, Brooke said that he had believed that he had checked the German westward advance in the Ypres-Comines area.

'I sent off instructions at once to divert Hawkesworth and his 12th Infantry Brigade from Dixmude to Nieuport, and remainder of 4th Division to follow, so as to cover perimeter defence from Furnes to Nieuport.'[1]

The implication is that this order restored the situation. It did nothing of the sort. The Lancers' skirmish was followed that afternoon by a full-dress German attack. By then, however, Adam's measures for the defence of the perimeter had taken effect. Brigadier Lawson had moved into Nieuport a mixed force of men drawn from medium artillery, heavy anti-aircraft regiments, and Royal Engineers, fighting as infantry. With elements of the French 60th Division, they met the German onslaught. Difficulties and misunderstandings between the French and Belgians had led to a failure to blow up the principal bridge across the Yser. With great *élan*, the leading Germans rushed it. The last barrier between Bock and Dunkirk was carried, the last ditch crossed. Then in the narrow streets and the houses, from the cellars and the barricades began the heroic defence of Nieuport. The Germans

[1] *The Turn of the Tide* by Arthur Bryant.

were held to a narrow bridgehead. By nightfall the German 256th Division was joined by the 208th, but all through the night the defence clung grimly to its lines. On the morning of the 29th Brooke's 12th Brigade at last reached the Nieuport area but, when it arrived, it was impossible to move it into position – the flat terrain was swept at short range by enemy fire. Throughout the day the gunners and the engineers endured. Not until the second night fell was II Corps able to take over the last-ditch stand from Adam's improvised force. Once again Gort's prevision had averted disaster.

Far up the line from Nieuport the Eastern battle thundered. From the Loo Canal to 'Plugstreet' five British divisions stood firm against eight German divisions. Bock mourned again his lack of armour – the race for Dunkirk was lost.

On the opposite side of the pocket the pattern of the Western battle at dawn was bitter and confused. Deep enemy penetrations had been forced between the stop points and one by one they were overwhelmed or abandoned. The 44th Division, farthest down the line, moved slowly back towards the position on the Mont des Cats, suffering heavy loss as it withdrew. The battered survivors of the 2nd Division were sent back past Poperinghe towards the sea. Everywhere along the desperately extended line the Germans advanced. At dusk only Cassel of the forward stops, with Ledringhem completely surrounded, held out. To the Germans it was a day of victory. It is in keeping with the strange irony of the time that for the Germans it was a day of failure also.

As the British stop points fell, new stop points formed behind them. For Arneke and Wormhoudt, for Hazebrouck and Lestrem, were substituted Quaedypre and Wylder, Bambecque, Vyfweg and Bergues itself. This was a battle of divisions now. Major-General S. R. Wason had succeeded to the command of III Corps, but the command never became effective until III Corps entered the perimeter. Its component parts were cut off from each other, communications were impossible (the armoured car, for example, that was sent to carry to the exhausted garrison of Cassel the order to withdraw was forced off the terrible road and the message reached the hill too late). It was a battle of divisional generals and of brigadiers, a battle of small bodies of surrounded men – but it held the German armour.

Late in the morning, Guderian made a tour of the front of XIX Corps, the front of the stop points and of the western perimeter of Dunkirk. In the night the French, under Fagalde, who had talked boldly at Cassel of an attack towards Calais, had fallen back six miles to the line of the old Mardyck Canal. The leading tanks of the 1st Panzer Division were a bare eight miles now from the harbour of Dunkirk, the moles were already under fire, but Guderian, when he had inspected the area, wrote: 'Further tank attacks would involve useless sacrifice of our best troops.'

The hard facts of the terrain and the defence of the stop points had convinced him at last. The rebel had reached the same opinion as Rundstedt.

Victory and failure were greatest of all along the new central front – the front from La Motte through 'Plugstreet' to Comines, which linked the Western and the Eastern battles. The 44th Division, as it moved back towards the Mont des Cats, formed the right flank of it; III Corps of the French First Army, with the remains of the Cavalry Corps, held the centre from Estaires to 'Plugstreet'; the 42nd and the 4th Divisions of the BEF manned the left of the line to the junction with the Eastern battle. It was to the south of this central front that the jaws of the pincers slowly closed and Rommel's 7th Panzers linked with Bock's 7th Infantry Division. They closed too late; the British Expeditionary Force was gone. There was no triumph on that score – but six divisions of the French First Army were cut off, penned in the quadrilateral of the canals south-west of Lille.

Should they have been?

The story of the loss of the main body of the French First Army is one of the most dramatic of those strange days. At eleven o'clock on the morning of May 28th, before the pincers closed, Blanchard came to Gort's headquarters at Houtkerque. The fire and the enthusiasm of the Cassel meeting were gone. When Gort read to him the last unequivocal orders of the British Government to evacuate, he was horrified. Weygand had been informed of that decision on the Sunday afternoon. Now, two days after the decision had been taken, Blanchard still had no information – no directive. It was apparent that he could no longer appreciate the full meaning of the German moves, the full implications of the Belgian surrender. He could say only that his troops were tired, that he had no orders. At the height of the argument a liaison officer arrived from General Prioux. The First Army, Prioux said, was too exhausted to withdraw farther. Gort wrote in his dispatch:

'I then begged General Blanchard, for the sake of France, the French Army and the Allied Cause to order General Prioux back. Surely, I said, his troops were not all so tired as to be incapable of moving. The French Government would be able to provide ships at least for some of his troops, and the chance of saving a part of his trained soldiers was preferable to the certainty of losing them all. I could not move him.'

Wearily, Blanchard said that the British Admiralty no doubt had already made arrangements for the BEF, but that the French Marine could never do so for his men – evacuation from the open beaches was impossible, it was useless to try.

Prioux himself vacillated. Late in the morning he decided that the position of his V Corps at Lille was hopeless and that it would have to be abandoned, but that he would destroy his *matériel* and fall back with III and IV Corps across the open country. At half-past three in the afternoon he changed his mind again. He would stand instead with IV Corps on the Lys in accordance with Weygand's last wishes, his III Corps and the Cavalry Corps alone would retire at noon on May 29th.

At 11 pm on the night of May 28th General de la Laurencie, with great personal courage and decision, brought III Corps and the Cavalry out.

That night Blanchard sent a telegram to Weygand to say that Gort was directing on his own initiative the withdrawal of his army towards Dunkirk, with the result that the flank of the French First Army was uncovered. On the following morning Weygand asked the President of the Council to lodge a protest against 'Gort's too selfish attitude'.

For more than twelve hours already the IV and V Corps of the French First Army had been surrounded. For three days, under General Molinié, they fought on, gallantly, hopelessly, uselessly. On June 1st they surrendered with the honours of war. It has been claimed that the fight held off six German divisions which might otherwise have been thrown against Dunkirk. Even that claim will hardly bear examination. By the night of May 29th the maps show thirteen divisions in contact with the sides of the narrowing pocket, nine moving against it or in reserve. It would have been scarcely possible to deploy six more divisions against that shrinking front.

*　　*　　*

It is strange that simultaneously with this last uncertainty of the French Command a similar uncertainty entered into the German. Its reasons were different – opposite – but from the War Diaries of the Army Groups, from the records of the lower formations, it is patent that a fumbling and an indecision entered at this moment into the handling of the last stages of the campaign.

Guderian's change of heart has already been cited. He may have been correct, but from what is now known of the strength of the 48th Division at Bergues and the armour and artillery available to Guderian, it seems hardly questionable that he

The last withdrawal. The state of the pocket on May 28th after the capitulation of the Belgian Army and the junction between Army Groups A and B to the west of Lille. This pincer movement cut off the major part of the French First Army. It was from this line that the final withdrawal into the perimeter began.

could have carried Bergues and the key to Dunkirk port. Farther back behind the central front the indecision is more strongly marked. There seems to have been almost no co-ordination between Army Group A and Army Group B. Their forces in the Lille area became hopelessly entangled, with consequent loss of effort. Co-ordination at lower levels broke down also. There was a drastic failure to push home their advantage, and in the middle of it formations began to be withdrawn – two whole corps were pulled out before the day was over. The attitude on the part of Army Group A was: we have done enough. The attitude of Army Group B was one of pedestrian conventionalism.

And at La Panne, to which British Headquarters had finally withdrawn, Gort put the last touches to his plan for the night. The BEF was drawn back to the line of Poperinghe.

*   *   *

While the pocket narrowed, while the divisions fell back, while the stop-gaps held, the tide turned on the sea. Early in the morning of this Tuesday Tennant signalled for ships to come into the East Mole. In the night he had organised the flow of men, set up a control system, arranged berthing parties, appointed as pier master Commander J. C. Clouston.

At once the destroyers went in: *Mackay* and *Montrose*, *Verity*, *Sabre*, *Worcester* and *Anthony*. They loaded, pulled out of the harbour stern first, headed for Dover. And in the Dynamo Room Ramsay adjusted his plans again; the emphasis was shifted from the beaches back to the battered port, personnel ships were ordered to the moles to join the destroyers.

Then, as the afternoon wore on, the position on the beaches eased in turn. The first of the small ships reached the area. Tows of whalers and ships' lifeboats arrived off La Panne, Bray Dunes, and Malo-les-Bains. Reinforcements of minesweepers began to come in from as far north as Rosyth. The old paddle-minesweepers that had been working from the Dover area were diverted from the task of sweeping the new channels and sent into the harbour and the beaches. Destroyers from the North Sea and from the East Coast ports were ordered to Dunkirk to join the battered Dover flotilla. Tugs and yard craft, coasters and short-sea traders were started on their way.

Ship reinforcements, signals, orders are impersonal things.

Underneath all this was a fundamental humanity. Here is a 'master's report':

'I am writing the letter on behalf of myself, Harry Brown, and Fred Hook who were the crew of the *Gipsy King*, a small motor-boat. We went to Dunkirk on May 28th. We stayed there about forty-eight hours. We were under shell-fire and machine-gun fire. We stayed there till every British soldier was off the beach. I should like to mention Harry Brown who did a brave action. We just loaded boat with troops. We saw a pontoon with soldiers in, being swamped with waves. Brown, being the swimmer, decided to go over the side with a rope, he tied it to the pontoon and saved the soldiers from being drowned. I am writing this letter as Fred Hook and Harry Brown are in the minesweepers.

'If this letter is satisfactory please would you give me a reply.

A. BETTS.'

Gipsy King was a Deal beach boat. Her crew were lineal descendants of the famous Deal hovellers; they were professional seamen. Here is another 'master's report':

'*Advance* was a 40-footer, with a beam of 11 ft 6 in, an open bridge, and a 140 hp Thornycroft engine. We found that all the boats taken over by the Admiralty were to be away by 7.30 on the following morning, May 28th, and we also learned that there was an acute shortage of crews and volunteered to take her ourselves to Sheerness, this being her first call.'

The three men who took her – her owner, C. P. Dick, with Hamilton-Piercey and McGuffie – were amateurs. They sailed *Advance* to Sheerness and by persistence took her on from there to Dunkirk.

There is an apparent contrast in these reports – professional and amateur, longshoremen and yachtsmen. It is apparent only. Beneath each of them shows clearly the sense of duty, of determination, and of courage that were the essentials of the spirit of Dunkirk.

The armada of the little ships was under way.

*   *   *

The big ships worked on, their task harsher, their danger greater almost with every hour.

Dover harbour was crowded to capacity. To work a ship in and out of it, with its difficult tidal streams, was, particularly at night, an intricate feat of seamanship. Beyond Dover the ships using the new routes had to pass through the Downs. No one who went to Dunkirk will forget the tragic grandeur of the Downs. Ships threaded their way through a forest of masts and the upperworks of vessels that had been sunk in the magnetic mine campaign. Between them, off Deal and farther up, scores of ships were anchored, waiting without lights. Beyond the Downs the lightships were unlit. The personnel ship *Lochgarry*, for example, almost rammed the North Goodwin light-vessel. Beyond the lightships buoys were unlit or had been sunk, the channels were barely marked, and despite the efforts of the naval staff some ships sailed without charts.

Prague, one of the cross-Channel steamers, left Dover in the late afternoon in company with the Isle of Man ship *Manxman* and the hospital carrier *Paris*. She was drawing over 16 feet and had only a small-scale chart, which gave inadequate information about the Zuydecoote Pass.

On entering the pass all three ships grounded, *Prague* and *Paris* got off immediately, but *Manxman* remained fast for some hours. One of HM sloops supplied the master of the *Prague* with a large-scale chart and some local advice, as a result of which he realised that passage was impracticable until the tide had risen, so he anchored off the Nieuport Bank buoy, where he was joined some hours later by *Manxman*. *Prague* got under way again at 3.55 am and proceeded via the pass to Dunkirk.

Off Dunkirk itself and off the beaches the difficulties were wilder still. The offshore channel is narrow. Under air attack ships increased to full speed but it was almost impossible to take violent avoiding action in most areas. They were studded already with the wrecks of ships from the magnetic mine period and those sunk in the early days of the lifting, and as the evacuation proceeded the number of wrecks grew with a desperate swiftness. With them there was floating wreckage: water-logged boats, timber, lengths of heavy hawser, bodies.

At the end of that nightmare passage ships went either to the East Mole or to the beaches. Off the beaches they lay for hours while enemy attacks came over in waves, waiting for the men to come slowly off. In the harbour they loaded swiftly, but they loaded under the scream of the bombs, the whistle and crash of the shells of the German guns that all that day had crept closer and closer from the west.

*   *   *

Two of the personnel ships were lost this day. *Abukir*, coming from Ostend where she had picked up 220 soldiers and refugees, including the British Mission at Bruges, was not strictly a part of the evacuation, but she was sunk by an E-boat in the vicinity of the North Hinder buoy.

To Admiral Ramsay this loss indicated a new threat. For the first time the German Navy was interfering directly with the evacuation.

Just before sunrise the *Queen of the Channel*, which had left Dunkirk at dawn after picking up 920 men from the Mole and beaches, was bombed and sunk after an attack by a single aircraft. Her crew and passengers were rescued by the store-ship *Dorrian Rose*.

There was another loss. Despite the efforts of Captain Auphan at Dover on the 27th there was as yet no direct French participation in the evacuation, but on the 28th the French decided to bring out 'certain categories of specialists'. 2,500 men were embarked in a convoy assembled by Admiral Abrial. The first ships cleared the entrance to the harbour and set course for Route Y. Almost at once the cargo vessel *Douaisien*, with 1,000 men on board, exploded a magnetic mine and sank slowly at the side of the channel. Trawlers heading into Dunkirk picked up the majority of the survivors.

*   *   *

The loss was disregarded, the work went on and, as the day drew out, the reinforcements of destroyers came swiftly in. The ships that began the lifting from the East Mole have already been named. *Codrington*, *Grenade*, *Gallant*, *Jaguar* and *Javelin* (picking up the survivors of the *Abukir* on the way) reached the harbour in the later part of the morning under heavy air attack. *Harvester*, *Esk*, *Malcolm*, *Express*, *Shikari* and *Scimitar* came in. With extraordinary speed the rate of loading rose. *Codrington* berthed at the East Mole and lifted 700 men. *Grenade* lifted another 700. At 22 knots, because the shallow water prevented higher speeds, they returned to Dover, landed their men and came back for more. This time *Codrington* picked up 900 men. *Gallant* lifted 681, *Harvester* lifted 700.

115

These figures are vital, for this was the turning point of the evacuation. A destroyer is not built to carry men. These ships were, by modern standards, small. More than half their space was occupied by engine rooms and boiler rooms and magazines. Their decks were crowded with guns, torpedo tubes, depth-charge racks. It was almost inconceivable that they could load 900 men and stow them in safety, but they were to carry even greater loads as the evacuation went on. So crowded were their upper decks at times that they could not fight their guns; so top-heavy were they that, as they took avoiding action against falling bombs, they heeled over to wild and impossible angles.

With them worked the minesweepers: the 'Halcyon' class, ships of 800 tons, not unlike miniature destroyers; the 'Albury' class, old Fleet sweepers, coal-burning, that were known universally as the 'Smoky Joes'; paddle-sweepers like the *Sandown*, the *Gracie Fields*, the *Medway Queen* and the *Brighton Belle*.

The naval ships suffered loss, but the loss was never commensurate with the risks that were faced. The destroyer *Windsor*, which had done magnificent work at Boulogne, was bombed and seriously damaged. The destroyer *Wolsey* had her degaussing gear put out of action, ignored that fact and carried on. *Pangbourne* of the 'Smoky Joes' picked up 200 troops and a very heavy load of wounded. On the passage home, searching for a green light buoy, she headed for the starboard navigation light of another ship and ran aground. With the rising tide she clawed off by herself and reached Ramsgate safely. *Brighton Belle*, the oldest paddle-minesweeper in the Service (built more than forty years before), picked up 800 men. Threshing her way home, she hit the wreck of a ship that had sunk a few hours earlier and now lay hidden in the fairway. The bottom was ripped out of the old ship and she began to sink. Out of the procession of ships that now moved endlessly across the Channel the *Medway Queen* closed her and, as she sank, picked off her troops, her crew, her captain and her captain's dog.

* * *

The Army was reacting now to this surge of help. For the first time it was possible for the troops to see the tremendous numbers of ships that were being used, the calculated risks that they were taking in the harbour and off the beaches, the growing work of the small boats.

One of the best accounts of the chaos ashore was written at the time by Sir Basil Bartlett.[1] He had come in the previous day. Raids were taking place at intervals of ten minutes. He was told at the Town Major's office to destroy his *matériel* and make for the harbour. By the time he had brought his men in it was impossible to get back to the Town Major's office. He took his troops down to Malo-les-Bains, and from there helped to load parties as the boats came in throughout the night. On the following day he found it was impossible to move in Dunkirk except on foot. The streets were blocked by the ruins of bombed houses. Despite all this he wrote:

'. . . everyone was much more optimistic than I'd expected. The whole BEF has a blind faith in the Navy.'

The Army officer who used the *nom de guerre* of 'Gun Buster' said of his final moments on the beach:[2]

'We tacked ourselves on to the rear of the smallest of the three queues, the head of it was already standing in water up to the waist. Half an hour passed. Suddenly a small rowing boat appeared. The head of the queue clambered in and were rowed away into the blackness. We moved forward, and the water rose to our waists.

'Our only thoughts now were to get on a boat. Along the entire queue not a word was spoken. The men just stood there silently staring into the darkness, praying that a boat would soon appear, and fearing that it would not. Heads and shoulders only showing above the water. Fixed, immovable, as though chained there. . . .'

Eventually the boats came in. Weighed down by the weight of water in his clothing and equipment, 'Gun Buster' had found difficulty in climbing over the side. In the end he was hoisted in by the crew of the boat, falling on his head on the bottom boards.

'From the instant I landed on my head in the lifeboat a great burden of responsibility seemed to fall from my shoulders. A curious sense of freedom took possession of me. All the accumulated strain of the last few hours, of the last day or so, vanished. I felt that my job was over. Anything else that remained to be done was the Navy's business. I was in their hands, and had nothing more to worry about. There and then,

[1] *My First War.*   [2] *Return via Dunkirk.*

on that dàrk and sinister sea, an indescribable sense of luxurious contentment enveloped me.'

He wrote from an angle that was deeply personal, yet something of this contentment made itself felt over a wider field. This was the day hope began: for the first time the word 'failure' disappears from the record of Dunkirk. In the twenty-four hours of May 28th 17,804 men were brought back to England in safety. It was not enough but it was a beginning. The Navy had found a way to solve its problems.

CHAPTER X

Wednesday, May 29th

It will be impossible to carry out the evacuation.
ADMIRAL DARLAN to M. Reynaud

THIS DAY the Eastern and the Western battles merged. In the last hours of darkness a rearguard line was established which curved from Noordschote through Proven to Poperinghe. It was held by elements of Brooke's II Corps in accordance with Gort's plan of withdrawal, with certain amendments. To the south of the Poperinghe line the 44th Division was still clinging to the Mont des Cats position and the garrison of Cassel, deep now in enemy-held territory, was fighting on. Between them and the sea the 48th Division, reinforced by the 42nd, faced and held strong attacks by tanks and mechanised infantry of the 20th Motorised Division, the SS *Grossdeutschland* and the SS Adolf Hitler Regiments.

At the exposed ends of the Dunkirk perimeter itself the French, to the west, held to the line of the Mardyck Canal, while to the east Lawson's scratch defenders clung grimly to Nieuport.

In the middle of the morning the 42nd Division, attacked by dive bombers and under heavy mortar fire, began to move back. At noon the Germans made contact with the Poperinghe line, and thereafter it was under heavy shellfire. At dusk the general withdrawal began.

From Cassel the depleted garrison set out at 9.30 pm to cut its way back to safety. It was a march of desperate valour. Three regiments shared its tragic glory: the 4th Oxfordshire and Buckinghamshire, the 2nd Gloucestershire, the 1st East Riding Yeomanry. Throughout the night they fought their way dourly back. By dawn they were split into small detachments, fighting until they were overwhelmed. Very few passed through the enemy lines to Dunkirk. The defence of Cassel is one of the fine feats of British arms. For the five critical days of the retreat its battered garrison held to the hill of Cassel and denied to enormously stronger forces of the enemy the vital junction of the twelve roads that led to Cassel town.

At dark from the Poperinghe line the rearguards of the 50th Division and the 3rd fell back. From the secondary position along the upper waters of the Yser the 42nd and the battered 5th withdrew. One by one the garrisons of the stop points, many of them now in deep salients in the enemy advance, fought on to their appointed hours and slipped away. Through the congestion of the roads, the lack of co-ordination with the French, the chaos of rumour and uncertainty, the divisions, the brigades, the battalions – in many cases the individual companies and platoons – fell back; and through and behind all the apparent tumult of that movement ran the strong thread of Gort's plans. They were adapted by individual commanders, circumstances forced their alteration at numerous points, alternatives had to be discovered and utilised; but throughout the main lines persisted. By midnight the major part of the British Expeditionary Force had withdrawn into the perimeter, and the defences were manned from the sea at Mardyck to the sea at Nieuport.

The battle of the right flank and the battle of the left flank were all but over. Once again a German pincer movement had closed fruitlessly. Three divisions sent by Bock to link with Kleist's armour and 'cut off the enemy from Poperinghe' linked for a second time too late.

From this moment the two battles coalesced, and it is appropriate here to attempt some assessment of their separate merit and achievement. It ought not to be necessary – they were parts of a whole that is in the fullest sense indivisible – but dramatic claims have been made for the Battle of the Left Flank, and it is desirable to examine them with care.

In the 'Prelude' to his book *The Turn of the Tide* Sir Arthur Bryant makes a number of statements at to the conduct of the last phase of the campaign. These statements are based presumably upon Lord Alanbrooke's diaries; they are made certainly with the approval of Lord Alanbrooke. It is simplest to list them in order. In the first, Sir Arthur, speaking of May 25th, says:

'At that moment, however, it looked as though all of them would spend the rest of the War in German prisons. The Expeditionary Force's communications had almost completely broken down, its Commander-in-Chief, at his headquarters near the coast, had no means of knowing whether his orders were reaching the battle-line on the Belgian frontier . . .'

Again, discussing Churchill's statement 'It seemed impossible that any large number of Allied troops could reach the coast', Sir Arthur says.

'That they did so was due mainly to one man. During the four crucial days between the Belgian collapse and the beginning of the evacuation Alan Brooke, with the four divisions of his Corps, covered the long exposed flank opened by King Leopold's surrender, and took command of all the desperately pressed men fighting their way back down a narrowing corridor to the improvised evacuation lines which Lord Gort was throwing up in the marshes around Dunkirk.'

He follows this with:

'Though seventeen German divisions had been released by the Belgian capitulation, by his speed and foresight Brooke anticipated the attacker's every move . . .'

Finally he says:

'Thus the miracle of the Navy's evacuation was preceded by an equal miracle – that of the Army's reaching the coast at all. Alan Brooke's achievement in bringing it through the closing defile of its enemies was one of the great feats of British military history.'

At the most dispassionate reading the sum of these statements is that Lord Gort, by setting up his headquarters 'near the coast', lost command of the retreat – that General Brooke took over, that he personally commanded 'all the desperately pressed men fighting their way back', and that he was alone responsible for bringing it through 'the closing defile' to Dunkirk.

Let us examine each claim in turn. First: was Gort's headquarters 'near the coast'? On Saturday, May 25th, it was at Premesques. This was substantially farther from 'the coast' than II Corps headquarters which Brooke had established at Armentières on May 22nd. It was excellently situated in a central position between the Eastern and the Western battles. It had good road communications through Lille and Armentières, and it was on the line of the buried cable from England.

On May 26th it was still at Premesques.

On May 27th it was still at Premesques until the early afternoon, when GHQ withdrew to Houtkerque. It was unable to site itself at Cassel, on the buried cable, owing to the speed and strength of the German armoured advance. Probably it would have been more satisfactory if it had now pulled right

back to La Panne. The new position was still, however, a considerable distance from the coast and it was, again, well situated in the centre of the main area of the withdrawal. Immediately on arrival at the new position wireless communication was established with the three corps headquarters.

Gort knew perfectly well throughout this time that his orders were reaching corps headquarters. Brooke knew that he knew. His own diary shows that he visited GHQ on the 25th (twice), on the 26th (once), and on the 27th (twice). He reached Premesques a third time that day, just after GHQ had left for Houtkerque and just before closing down his own headquarters. On the 28th his Brigadier General Staff attended a conference at Houtkerque.

So much for the suggestion that Gort isolated – 'near the coast' – had lost touch with the situation.

Ignoring for the moment the opinion in the second extract that the Army's arrival in the perimeter was 'due mainly to one man', let us examine the statements of alleged fact. Did the Eastern battle cover 'the long exposed flank opened by King Leopold's surrender . . . during the four crucial days between the Belgian collapse and the *beginning* of the evacuation'? If we ignore the 28,000 men carried back to England before Operation 'Dynamo', the evacuation began officially with the transmission of the 'Dynamo' signal at 6.57 pm on May 26th. The first shipload of men was disembarking at Dover at 10.30 pm on that day. King Leopold did not surrender until midnight on May 27th – twenty-nine hours *after* the evacuation had begun. The first two days of the Battle of the Left Flank were fought out before the Belgian collapse, only two days remained after the Belgian cease-fire. On the third day after 'King Leopold's surrender' Brooke himself was on board a destroyer, bound for England. By midnight on the fourth day most of his II Corps was either in England or safely embarked.

Next: did Brooke in reality take command of all the desperately pressed men 'fighting their way back down a narrowing corridor'? The general withdrawal was made, as has been outlined already, in accordance with the broad principles of the GHQ plan which was drawn up by Colonel Bridgeman. The first phase of this plan was the withdrawal to the Lys agreed between Gort and Blanchard on Sunday, May 26th. The second phase was that communicated by Gort to Blanchard at the painful meeting of May 26th. The orders to withdraw to the Poperinghe line, which it entailed, were issued at two o'clock on the afternoon of May 28th. Broad control of the fighting in connection with the withdrawal was exercised by a succession of orders issued from GHQ by Colonel Gregson-Ellis and Brigadier Leese.

Corps commanders were given permission 'within the outline of these orders' to use the fullest discretion to move as many men as possible back to the Dunkirk bridgehead. By that permission Gort provided against the difficulties of communication and the unstable nature of the situation. Simultaneously orders were issued for phasing the withdrawal from the stop points of the Western battle.

Control necessarily was exercised on the broadest possible basis, but it was maintained with only minor breakdowns throughout the last and final phase of the retreat on the night of the 29th/30th, and corps and divisions alike moved with a remarkable precision, considering the circumstances, into the areas prescribed for them by the GHQ plan and prepared for them by General Adam.

Sir Arthur Bryant's claim that Brooke co-ordinated the movements of I Corps has already been examined. This claim to have taken command of 'all' the men appears to have a similar lack of justification.

With regard to the next point: did Brooke, in fact, anticipate 'the attacker's every move'? After the war Brooke wrote of the information given him by Adam at La Panne:

'I thought that I had checked the German advance westward in the battle that had been raging in the Ypres-Comines area . . .'

It is obvious from this that Brooke had completely underestimated Bock's capacity to effect a rapid out-flanking movement along the coastal area and had made no disposition whatever against that possibility. He was, in fact, saved by Gort's forethought, and the energy of Adam and Lawson.

Upon the final claim it seems, in the circumstances, hardly necessary to comment.

None of this, of course, detracts from the fighting of the battle itself. The analysis is directed at the inflated claims made on Brooke's behalf in matters to some extent outside the actual fighting.

What, then, was the stature of the Battle of the Left Flank? It was not, of course, fought against 'the main weight of the German armies'. This has already been dissected. What *was* the weight of the enemy?

On May 26th, according to the official situation maps, three divisions under II Corps (one of them already considerably reinforced) faced four German divisions.

On May 27th four divisions under II Corps faced four German divisions. On each of these days the main weight of Bock's Army Group (itself, it will be remembered, the German second eleven) was, of course, directed against the Belgians.

On May 28th four divisions under II Corps (one of them reinforced to about double strength) faced eight German divisions.

On May 29th two divisions under II Corps are marked as in contact with four German divisions.

The maximum strength brought against Brooke's corps at any one time, therefore, appears to have been eight infantry divisions. The enemy had a considerable weight of artillery, a moderate air support and no armoured formations.

None the less, it was a hot and bloody battle in which the heaviest attack was held throughout by the gallant 5th Division, under General Franklyn. Strengthened by a brigade group of the 48th Division, two brigades and the RE of the 4th Division, three battalions of the 1st Division, two battalions of machine guns, and the artillery of I Corps, it defied every effort to break across the dry canal between Ypres and Comines. By its courage and its ardour it blunted the eastern claw of the German pincers.

That Brooke had certain specific advantages from the outset does not detract from the great quality of the 5th Division's stand, but it is as well to list those advantages again. The extension of the flank began from the anchor of the old frontier positions, which continued to be held until long after the first extensions had been completed. The overall tactics of the battle were, in principle, simple. It was like the child's game of extending a wall by picking up the bricks from one end to add them on at the other. In doing so Brooke had the advantage of the defensible position – weak though it unquestionably was – of the incomplete Ypres-Comines Canal and the railway embankment which ran along it. Beyond them he had the line of the canal from Ypres to the Yser. From Comines to Ypres, where the main fighting took place, the front was only 8 miles, from Ypres to Noordschote was another 9. It was long enough in all conscience for a single corps to cover, but in relation to the uncomplicated nature of the terrain and the fact that defensive positions (even though they were weak) existed, it was a task that was never impossible.

The contrast between the Eastern battle and the Western is absolute. It has already been stressed that the types of fighting involved were different by a whole generation of war, but the physical complexity of the Western battle was at the very start appalling. Again it is necessary to outline the basic facts. Gort had to prepare a defence from May 17th onwards to cover a front that stretched from Douai (the last point at which the French appeared able to exercise effective control) through Arras and on eventually to the coast at Gravelines. The distance involved was substantially over 80 miles. It was a complex area in which, though there were certain positive advantages to be obtained from the canal lines and the line of the River Scarpe, there were also positive disadvantages in areas of high ground, which could only be controlled with difficulty or not at all. To begin the defence Gort had no firm anchor – he had, in fact, no anchor at all. He had no large organised mass of troops with all the organisational details of supply lines, dumps and supply trains, such as existed in the old frontier area; no communications were in being except in and out of Arras; and no fortunate capture of documents gave him a clear description of the enemy's intentions and the direction of his attack.

The fundamental basis of the battle was precisely the same as that for which such melodramatic claims have been made in the case of the Battle of the Left Flank – the collapse of an ally – but the collapse of the Belgians came two days after the Left Flank battle had begun and many days after it had become obvious that it would happen. The famous gap that developed was 6 miles wide at the outset of the battle and was only a potential 20 miles at the middle of it. On the Western battle the ally collapsed four days before the battle started. The collapse let through the strongest and swiftest armoured force that war had ever known until that date to range unhindered over the hinterland of France, and the 'gap' when Gort took up the challenge was 80 miles across.

Because of these basic facts the picture of the Western battle never has a simple whole. It was a battle of desperate expedients, a battle of sieges and strong points, of stands as tremendous as the defence of Arras and the holding of Cassel, and as small as the stand of the gun at St Momelin. It was fought in its early stages by scratch bodies of troops often drawn from branches theoretically non-combatant; it was fought with limited weapons and deficient ammunition and non-existent supplies. And it achieved, before Gort was able by retiring to the old frontier positions to release major formations to relieve it, two signal victories.

The first was the victory of the 'counter-attack' at Arras, which held Rommel and caused Rundstedt to call the first halt. Gort used the brief hours of that halt to add to his stop points, and the determined resistance that Rundstedt's panzers met when the attack went forward again, added to his knowledge of the terrain that he was entering, brought the other victory. It caused Rundstedt to halt for a second time on the 23rd.

Because of that decision, and its subsequent confirmation by Hitler, it has been loosely assumed that fighting ceased. Nothing could be farther from the truth. The major advance ceased along the northern sector of the front – the Canal Line proper – but even there the bridgeheads that had already been won were steadily and methodically enlarged. At the southern end of the line it never ceased. Rundstedt's rejection of the High Command's orders did not include the area of St Venant, and, as has been seen, the tragic and glorious stand of the 2nd Division beyond all doubt held the armoured claw of the great pincer movement on the 26th and 27th. By the afternoon of that day Hitler's own orders for the general advance had been promulgated. By the morning of the 27th the advance was in progress. By the evening of the 28th, when the situation map shows eight infantry divisions in contact with Brooke's eastern front (the heaviest onslaught which the Eastern battle sustained), the same map shows the 1st, 2nd, 6th, 8th and the 3rd Panzer Divisions attacking between Gravelines and Lestrem, and with them four motorised divisions. The strength, the fire power and the mobility of this armoured attack was incomparably greater than that of Bock's old-style infantry divisions to the east.

The western front held. It was not easy even now always to say why, nor is it easy to present the battle as a coherent picture. It was disconnected – a battle of divisional generals – but always the lines of its control ran directly back to GHQ. In every sense of the word it was Gort's battle, and, like the Eastern battle, it also 'saved the British Army at Dunkirk'. Had the Western battle failed at any point along the 80-mile front, had it failed at any time in the twelve days of bitter holding, the campaign must have gone down in tragedy.

*   *   *

On the sea the day began with disaster. At midnight the destroyers *Wakeful* and *Grafton*, loaded with troops from the Bray Dunes area, left almost simultaneously for home by the Zuydecoote Pass – Route Y. At 12.45 am off the Kwinte Whistle Buoy, while she was zigzagging at 20 knots, *Wakeful* sighted two torpedo tracks. One missed, the other hit amid-ships. The destroyer broke in two and sank in fifteen seconds, the separate halves of the ship standing upright with the stern and bow sections above the water. Most of the troops were below and went down with the ship. Only a handful of the crew drifted clear.

After thirty minutes the motor-drifter *Nautilus* and the dan-layer *Comfort*, themselves loaded with troops, reached the scene of the tragedy and began picking up survivors. *Comfort* took on board the captain of *Wakeful*, Commander R. L. Fisher. *Grafton* and the minesweeper *Lydd* closed the area and lowered boats. Commander Fisher shouted to *Grafton* that she was in danger of being torpedoed and, as he did so, a torpedo hit her. *Comfort* herself was lifted in the air by the explosion and Commander Fisher was washed overboard again. She was going full speed at the time, and as she came round, *Lydd* and the sinking *Grafton* opened fire on her in the belief that she was the enemy E-boat which had launched the torpedoes. Most of *Comfort*'s crew and all except four of *Wakeful*'s survivors were killed. Then *Lydd* bore down on her, rammed and sank her.

The *Grafton* had stopped two torpedoes, one of which had exploded under the wardroom, killing the thirty-five Army officers sleeping there. Her captain was machine-gunned and killed on the bridge. She remained afloat long enough for most of the survivors to be rescued, but the casualties were heavy.

Whilst this double tragedy unfolded, the hospital ship *Dinard*, with 271 stretcher cases on board, was attacked be-tween the Kwinte Bank and West Hinder Whistle buoys, but escaped unharmed.

Still closer to England, at the far end of the Dunkirk area, another destroyer was in process of rescue. HMS *Montrose*, coming back with a full load of troops, had been in trouble earlier. At midnight she was lying within range of the Gris

Nez searchlights, helpless, with her bows blown away. At 12.30 pm the tugs *Lady Brassey* and *Simla* were ordered out of Dover to her assistance. They picked her up at three o'clock and she was towed stern first into Dover.

Three destroyers were lost or out of action in the first hours of the morning. The loss was accepted. The work went on.

At dawn a division of four destroyers was attacked by a submarine. A torpedo passed through the line, and the Polish ship *Blyskawica* carried out an immediate depth-charge attack which was followed up by one of the British ships. As they made ready for a second attack they were dive-bombed out of low cloud. Subsequently British aircraft arrived. Though no observable result was obtained submarine attacks in this area ceased.

The air attacks, on the other hand, continued. *Intrepid*, a little later, was also bombed and damaged; *Saladin* suffered slight damage from a near miss; *Icarus*, coming through the crowded channel, was attacked by ten aircraft, one of which came in persistently at low level, but by using smoke and zig-zagging violently she got clear. *Sabre*, whose boats had been left on the beaches, steaming through a position where another ship had been sunk ahead of her, manoeuvred to pick up individual survivors. While she was doing this she was attacked from the air, but continued until all the men in the water had been picked up. Every ship that crossed seems to have had some experience with enemy aircraft. *Scimitar*, *Wolsey* and *Malcolm* all reported attempts at bombing.

To the air attacks another complication was added now. At dawn enemy guns were brought to bear on Route Y where it closed the coast off Nieuport. The transport *Scotia*, coming in through the narrows, found destroyers heavily engaged with shore batteries in the area. With the transport *Malines* she went on to Dunkirk. Owing to dense clouds of smoke the two ships missed the entrance to the harbour and steamed a little to the west. As they came clear of the smoke, guns opened fire on them from the area of Mardyck. They turned under fire, and *Scotia* was hit abaft the engine-room on the port side. Her master, Captain W. H. Hughes, said:

'We berthed at about 1.30 am close to the lighthouse, East Pier. Immediately the vessel was alongside the Embarkation Officer requested that I should take as many troops as possible. This I did. The count showed 2,700, but many more had been taken aboard of whom no account could be taken. The

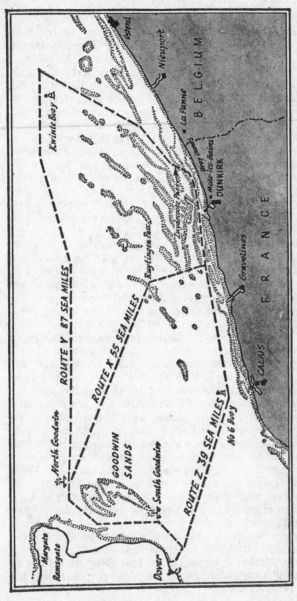

The three swept channels which were maintained for the Dunkirk evacuation. Of these the first, Route Z, came under enemy fire from the Calais area in the early stages of the evacuation. The second, Route Y — of more than twice the distance — eventually came under fire from the Nieuport guns. The last, Route X, was finally brought under fire at its point of junction with the original channel.

Scotia, I estimated, had fully 3,000 troops on board, as every available space had been taken up. The troops (British) were very exhausted and many of them could hardly walk along the pier . . .'

A little later HM Tug *St Clears* came in by the same channel. She had attempted late the previous day to use the old short route and had lost two of her tow of naval cutters to the Gravelines guns. Now she lost two more cutters to the Nieuport guns and a third broke adrift. French destroyers near by engaged the batteries and the tug herself got clear.

The sea approaches to Dunkirk were shrinking. As the news filtered back to Dover Admiral Ramsay was forced to another decision of courage. The sweeping of the new central route – X – was not yet complete, but shortly before noon he sent the destroyers *Jaguar*, *Gallant* and *Grenade* to test the opposition of the shore batteries and to evaluate the possibility of using this route as an alternative to Route Y. All three ships were bombed and *Gallant* was damaged, but they drew no fire from enemy guns. The sweeping of the route went ahead and by mid-afternoon ships were ordered by signal to operate it, 'exercising navigational caution'. The words have an almost ironical air in this holocaust of shells, bombs and torpedoes.

Yet despite all these things the troops were getting away. The cruiser *Calcutta* had returned. She picked up 1,200 men from the beaches, loading largely from drifters, themselves fed by small craft. *Calcutta* was a cruiser, shaped and manned for war. *Bullfinch* and *Yewdale* were small coasters, but their record is equally impressive. *Yewdale* on her first trip lifted over 1,000 men. *Bullfinch* arrived at the same time, and her master, Captain H. Buxton, was ordered to beach his ship. Troops waded off to her as the tide fell and embarked up ladders. When she finally floated off she had 1,500 men aboard. On her return voyage she was repeatedly attacked by German aircraft and her steering gear was put out of action. Emergency repairs were made, however, and she returned in safety. These were little ships – less than 1,000 tons, without the wide decks of the personnel ships, in no way suited for carrying large quantities of men. These facts must be remembered in judging their performance.

The personnel ships had another advantage. Built for the cross-Channel run, their speed was high. *Royal Sovereign*, for example, berthed at 4.45 am at the East Mole, cleared at 5.45 with a full load, reached Margate at 12.15 pm, discharged her men in an hour and a quarter, and at 5.30 was back off La Panne. At 6.20 pm the report of her master, Captain T. Aldis, says briefly: 'Commenced embarking troops from beaches.'

Royal Sovereign got back safely a second time. Not all ships were so fortunate. The Isle of Man Steam Packet *Mona's Queen* sailed during the morning. The report of Captain A. Holkam, who had taken over the command of the ship, reaches new levels of understatement.

'I joined the *Mona's Queen* on May 28th. On the evening of that date I received orders to leave Dover in the early morning of the 29th to carry fresh water to Dunkirk and return with troops. Everything was uneventful until we reached to within about half a mile off Dunkirk, when the ship was mined and sank within two minutes, the survivors being rescued by the destroyer *Vanquisher*.'

There is a succinct brevity in this that defies comment.

The personnel ship *Killarney*, lying to off the entrance to the harbour, saw *Mona's Queen* sink. About an hour later she went in to the Mole, picked up 800 men and the report of her master, Captain R. Hughes, says that she had extreme difficulty in preventing what appeared to be the whole canine population of France and Belgium from taking passage with her. These animals had attached themselves to the Tommies, and hundreds of them were shot on the quays to prevent their starving to death.

On her return journey, with her decks covered with men, she came under fire from the Gravelines guns. It was estimated that three batteries of 6-inch guns were firing. Heavy smoke was made from the funnel in an endeavour to set up some sort of smoke screen and, despite the narrowness of the sand-banked channel and the known minefields, she zigzagged violently. (The ship was not degaussed.) During forty minutes about ninety shells were fired and one hit on the after end of the boat deck, killing eight men and wounding thirty. A little later she was attacked by machine-gun fire from enemy aircraft.

'But,' her master's report continues, 'to our great delight a Spitfire came right out of the clouds on to the German's tail, and giving him a good burst of his guns sent the enemy crashing in flames into the sea, on our port side, about 600 yards away. We did not dally any further to look for survivors.'

A little later *Killarney* sighted a raft, made of wood and an old door, bearing one French officer and two Belgian soldiers.

'The commissariat of the raft was most complete – two tins of biscuits and six demijohns of wine. Also, carefully lashed on the raft was a bicycle of ancient vintage.'

The Southern Railway vessel *Lochgarry* watched *Killarney* come out. The tide was low and falling, and her master, Captain Ewen MacKinnon, had considerable anxiety as to whether there would be sufficient water for him to go alongside. *Killarney* drew roughly as much water as his ship and he hoped to take her berth, but it was taken by a shallow-draught vessel before he could reach it and he was forced to go farther up the harbour.

'There we met two very brave and cheerful men – the Commander and the Lieutenant-Commander, who were carrying on their work and directing operations as if no danger existed. There was no bustle or commotion, but everything was orderly and well regulated. The Jerry shells were dropping in the harbour about fifty yards from the bow of the *Lochgarry* at 11.25 am when we were fixed in our berth, but they did not appear to explode, and all of them could be heard coming, screaming through the air, through the smoke and haze, and dropping in the very centre of the harbour. They had the range perfectly. Well, it was all right so long as they did not alter it a degree the one way or the other. There was nothing but thick black smoke and fire everywhere round the harbour, and parts of several sunken vessels were projecting in the inner harbour at low water . . .'

Lochgarry loaded through air raids and shell-fire with a destroyer berthed alongside her and loading across her decks. Astern of her were three destroyers loading, and she had some difficulty in getting out. A drifter, trying to assist, cut her degaussing wires and started a small fire, but that was soon put out. When she cleared the harbour, she waited for a short while for her escort, the destroyer *Greyhound*. As *Greyhound* closed her and started to pass a signal, three successive salvoes landed. The *Lochgarry* was missed, but the third salvo hit *Greyhound* and holed her in the engine-room, and the *Lochgarry* was told to carry on without her escort. By supreme efforts the *Greyhound*'s engine-room staff managed to make good the damage, and after a long interval she limped away under her own power.

In the early evening *Blyskawica*, still working her patrol somewhere near the West Hinder buoy, sighted her and took her in tow to Dover. Even off Dover she was by no means safe, for German planes dropped magnetic mines about 3,000 yards ahead of the ships on their course. They avoided the dangers, however, and the cripple was taken safely in.

Magnificent as was the work of the personnel ships on this day, it was matched in every particular by the work of the destroyers. Over and over again the accounts of the masters of the personnel ships stress the difficulties of going alongside the East Mole. Though as 'ferries' they were built with their sides specially stiffened and with thick rubbing strakes to berth against quays and jetties of widely differing constructions, they still found the problems of the East Mole hazardous.

Destroyers are built for speed. They are light craft, fragile, difficult to handle at slow speeds. Their side plating is astonishingly thin. They have no rubbing strakes, no extra stiffening. And these destroyers were working themselves alongside Dunkirk Mole, slamming up against wood and concrete, jamming themselves into berths between other ships, sandwiching themselves against paddle-steamers and turbine-steamers alike. The sheer handling of the destroyers in Dunkirk harbour is one of the most astonishing facets of the whole operation.

The day wore on. About 3.45 pm the ss *Clan MacAlister* was bombed. The story of this 6,900-ton ship, the largest merchant vessel used at Dunkirk, is a record of tenacity. She was ordered to carry to Dunkirk a number of Army motor landing-craft and she represented the one major effort made by the Army itself to get troops away from the beaches.

With considerable difficulty Captain R. W. Mackie, her master, took the *Clan MacAlister* in to the edge of the shoal water. The landing-craft were lowered with some damage and, as the *Clan MacAlister* began to take the first loads of men on board, she was attacked from the air and set on fire. Desperate efforts were made to fight the fire, while HMS *Malcolm* came alongside to take off her wounded and the troops that she had already embarked. The ship, however, was still capable of movement, and Captain Mackie decided to put to sea. While the anchors were coming in she was attacked again and her steering gear was wrecked. She was abandoned fiercely on fire.

As the *Clan MacAlister* burned, the day drew towards the greatest disaster of all. At four o'clock a heavy air attack began on the Mole at Dunkirk. All through the day a pall of smoke from the burning town and the flaming oil tanks drifted over the harbour and over the roadstead just beyond it. Now the wind changed. As it changed the smoke drifted inshore and the Luftwaffe seized its chance. The Mole was crowded. On the eastward side at the end of it lay the two big paddle-steamers *Fenella* and HMS *Crested Eagle*. Against its inside face, level with them, were the destroyers *Grenade* and *Jaguar* berthed alongside each other, six trawlers inshore of them, and astern of these the personnel ship *Canterbury*. Farther in were the destroyers *Malcolm*, *Verity* and *Sabre*. The French destroyers *Mistral* and *Siroco* were at the guiding jetty, and at the Quai Félix Faure, farther up the harbour, was the *Cyclone*. It was on the target at the end of the Mole that the Luftwaffe concentrated.

There is a remarkable cinema film extant taken from the nose of a German dive-bomber. It shows the approach to the harbour and the smoke and flames of the town; then it concentrates on the great raft of ships at the end of the long, straight tongue of the Mole. It shows the aircraft going down and down and down while the ships seem to come up to meet it. Finally, as the bombs are released, it sweeps away, and ships and sea are lost and there is only sky.

At five o'clock *Fenella*, which had already taken between 600 and 700 troops on board, was hit. A bomb passed through her passenger deck, killing a number of men. Another hit on the concrete of the Mole below her. Lumps of concrete were blown through the ship's side beneath the water-line. The blast drove the oil cooler off its seating, and all pumps and pipes in the engine-room were wrecked. Her master, Captain W. Cubbon, wrote:

'I inspected the damage in company with the Chief and Second Officer – the ship was listing badly – fortunately inclining towards the jetty – and was rapidly making water. Our examination of the damage proved that the ship was doomed and the only course open was to disembark all troops and abandon ship. I instructed the OC troops to this effect.

'As the jetty abreast of gangways had been blown away, the only method of disembarkation was to climb over the rails on the forecastle head which fortunately was level with the jetty. The enemy was particularly active at this time and several times his bombing and machine-gunning held up the disembarking of the troops, but owing to the skilful handling of my Chief and Second Officers, all troops and stretcher cases were safely disembarked and taken on board the *Crested Eagle*.'

Meanwhile, HMS *Grenade* was hit and a raging fire developed, her mooring lines parted, and she swung into the fairway out of control. For desperate minutes it seemed certain that she would sink and block the fairway in the very entrance to the harbour. Heavy explosions followed each other, but by heroic efforts and the admirable seamanship of a trawler, she was got under way and, burning and sinking, was towed outside. It was a desperately close thing. *Grenade* was barely clear of the entrance before she went down, sufficiently near for some of the few men left alive on board to swim in to land. A drifter picked up others, to be sunk in turn herself. Only a handful of survivors finally reached England.

The trawlers *Polly Johnson* and *Calvi* were sunk. *Canterbury* and the destroyer *Jaguar* got clear, though both were hit and badly damaged. The French destroyers, the first ships to arrive in obedience to the others that followed on Weygand's decision to evacuate, suffered as well, though in a lesser degree. *Mistral*'s superstructure was wrecked by a bomb which exploded on the quay abreast of her. *Cyclone* and *Siroco*, however, each cleared the harbour with about 500 men on board.

HMS *Crested Eagle* completed the embarkation of the survivors of *Fenella* and slipped her lines. She had barely got clear of the Mole when she was hit in her turn and, blazing furiously, went slowly in to the beach between the Mole and Malo-les-Bains, where she grounded and burnt out with heavy loss of life.

The destroyer *Verity* got clear but grounded for a brief moment on a sunken drifter near the entrance. All movement along the Mole ceased. On the French side the harbour was empty. Dunkirk was out of action.

In spite of this one more attempt was made this evening. At six o'clock the armed boarding vessel *King Orry* arrived to find the harbour occupied solely by sunken and burning ships. She had been attacked on the way across and set on fire, but the fire was put out and she entered the shambles which was Dunkirk. Lieutenant J. Lee, RNR, her First Lieutenant, said in his account:

'We only received one direct hit, on the stern, which blew the rudder off, and we just drifted alongside the Mole. The *Fenella* was alongside the same Mole only on the outside, the *Grenade* was blazing away furiously, and whilst we were drifting both her magazines blew up. After drifting alongside we moored up, and the CO and myself carried out an examination of the ship, and found so many holes from shrapnel that it was considered impossible to do anything, and it was only a question as to whether or not we could get her away from the Mole. We eventually decided that we must make the attempt, because, if the ship sank, she would be certain to turn on her starboard side and thus block the entrance with her funnel and masts. This was all about 8 pm. The tide was low and the ship resting on the bottom, so we had to wait for about two hours. Then when we came to shift we found that the rubbing strake on the port bow was actually resting on the Mole and the Mole was virtually carrying the whole weight of the ship. It took a tremendous effort of the ship's engines to get the rubbing strake clear and about two hours for us to get the ship out of the harbour stern first, just using the two engines. Our intention was to beach her out of the way, but suddenly she took a heavy list to starboard and sank almost without warning. This was at about two o'clock on the morning of May 30th. We all took to the water, my watch stopping at 1.59 am.'

At seven o'clock Admiral Ramsay was informed through a telephone message from military headquarters at La Panne that 'Dunkirk harbour was blocked by damaged ships and that all evacuation must therefore be effected from the beaches'. Admiral Wake-Walker wrote subsequently that this was due to the breakdown of a junior member of the naval shore party, who, affected by the bombing, made his way to GHQ with an alarming account of the state of the harbour. Great difficulty was being experienced at the time in communicating directly with the Senior Naval Officer at Dunkirk. In the circumstances all ships were diverted to the beaches.

But the swift increase in the weight of the enemy air attack had caused havoc off the beaches also. The Southern Railway ship *Normannia* was bombed and settled in shallow water near No. 9 buoy off Mardyck on an even keel with all her flags flying. The *Lorina*, also a Southern Railway ship, was hit amidships and broke her back. A gallant attempt was made to beach her but she sank in shallow water – eight men were lost.

The paddle-minesweeper *Gracie Fields*, with 750 troops on board, was hit soon after taking departure from La Panne beach. Her engine-room and her upper deck were swept with steam from burst pipes, and it was impossible to stop her engines. With her rudder jammed, she circled at 6 knots. Very gallantly two skoots came alongside, made fast and filled themselves with troops. They were followed by the mine-sweeper *Pangbourne*. *Pangbourne* was already damaged (she had been holed on both sides by near misses and had lost thirteen men killed and eleven wounded), but she went along-side the *Gracie Fields* and took off another eighty men. Then she managed to pass a towline to the damaged ship and headed for England. Night came, and in the darkness the *Gracie Fields* sank lower and lower in the water until finally *Pangbourne* was forced to slip the tow and take off her crew. Very shortly after the *Gracie Fields* sank.

Reinforcements of minesweepers had come in from Harwich at midnight – the 12th Flotilla, which consisted of the paddle-minesweepers *Waverley*, *Marmion*, *Duchess of Fife* and *Oriole*.

Waverley worked through the day off the beaches. At 3.30 in the afternoon, with 600 troops on board, she left in a heavy air raid. At about four o'clock she was attacked by twelve Heinkels. She was near missed early, but, twisting and turning, she dodged the rain of bombs for half an hour until a second near miss ripped off her rudder, and finally a direct hit wrecked the ward-room flat and passed through the bottom of the ship leaving a hole six feet in diameter. Out of control and sinking by the stern, *Waverley* continued the battle. With her one 12-pounder, Lewis guns, and the massed rifle fire of the troops on board, she fought off low-flying machine-gun and bomb attacks until it became apparent that the end had come. Within a minute of the order being given to abandon ship she had disappeared. Her captain, Lieutenant S. F. Harmer-Elliott, RNVR, went down with her but managed to kick himself clear of obstructions under water. When he sur-faced again, the sea was thick with troops, but gradually the concentration thinned. The first ship to reach the survivors was a French destroyer. Shortly after, HMS *Golden Eagle*, with drifters and a tug, was guided to the scene by aircraft. Lieutenant Harmer-Elliott was rescued after three-quarters of an hour, but many of his ship's company and between 300 and 400 of the troops on board perished.

Yet even off the beaches the story is not altogether of disaster. *Oriole*, of the same flotilla as *Waverley*, having no motor-boat and realising the tremendous difficulties of taking men off with the inadequate boats she possessed, solved the problem by empirical means. Boldly and deliberately her captain, Lieutenant E. L. Davies, RNVR, ran his ship on to the beach, trusting that when the tide ebbed far enough men would be able to wade out and climb aboard and, using his ship as a pier, pass out to other ships in the deeper water astern of him. The account of her sub-lieutenant, Sub-Lieutenant John Crosby, RNVR, gives a striking picture of the method used.

'We still had about two hours flood so when we got off a busy looking part of the beach, her head was brought slowly round until we were facing dead on to the beach, everybody went aft to raise the bows as much as possible, and we went lickity-split for the shore and kept her full ahead until we jarred and came to a full stop. As we went in we dropped two seven-hundredweight anchors from the stern, to kedge off with. The men waded and swam out and many of them had to be hauled over the rails. The snag was that when a rope was thrown to a man, about six grabbed it and just hung on looking up blankly with the water breaking over their shoulders, and it was a hell of a job getting any of them to let go so that the rest could get pulled aboard.'

In this way some 3,000 troops passed over *Oriole* to safety. The ship was attacked at intervals throughout the day, frequently being straddled by sticks of bombs, but she was never hit, and in the evening, during another severe raid, Lieutenant Davies took *Oriole* off the beach with a load of 700 soldiers and nurses from the last of the field hospitals, and got safely back to England. There is a sequel to this action that is not without significance. Lieutenant Davies was too busy for the next couple of days to bother much about official correctitude, but on May 31st his official conscience finally pricked him to action, and he sent the following signal:

'Submit ref K.R. and A.I.1167. Deliberately grounded HMS *Oriole* Belgian coast dawn May 29th on own initiative objective speedy evacuation of troops. Refloated dusk same day no apparent damage. Will complete S.232 when operations permit meantime am again proceeding Belgian coast and will again run aground if such course seems desirable.'

There is a superb spirit in this message, a sort of blunt defiance of consequences that is the very essence of naval forthrightness. And in the official response there is much also of the essential spirit of the Royal Navy. Lieutenant Davies had deliberately hazarded his ship, a proceeding that is theoretically looked upon with much disfavour, but the reply that came to him read simply: 'Reference your telegram of May 31st. Your action fully approved.'

Deeds like this kept the flow of the evacuation moving but all the while the loss went on. The drifters had a bad day: *Comfort*, as has been described earlier, was rammed and sunk; *Girl Pamela* was sunk in collision off Dunkirk; *Nautilus*, after her sturdy work in the *Grafton* rescue, was sunk herself.

There were other collisions. From Southend the pleasure-boats *Shamrock*, *Princess Maud*, *Canvey Queen* and *Queen of England* had sailed. They had orders to make their 'utmost speed direct to the beaches eastward of Dunkirk'. In the darkness HM Skoot *Tilly* bore down on the little flotilla and sliced through the *Queen of England*.

Through collisions, gunfire, bombing and strafing the little ships worked on.

* * *

Behind this long story of sinkings and destruction was the fact that the Germans had now committed both air fleets in the west to the attack. The German Air Ministry situation report for the day says:

'. . . the full force of the air attacks was directed against the numerous merchant vessels in the adjacent sea area and the warships escorting them.'

Attacks on the perimeter line and on the retreating armies virtually ceased, and from noon onwards an endless series of raids developed on Dunkirk harbour, off the beaches and in the approach channels. The RAF decision to double the size of patrols (following the heavy losses of the 26th and 27th) meant the acceptance of very long intervals between each patrol. It was in these intervals that the heaviest loss was suffered by the ships. On the 27th twenty-three patrols had been flown, on this day there were only nine. When they were in the area the attacks were, for the most part, broken up, though even with the increased numbers there were times when the patrols were wholly engaged with enemy fighters and the bombers attacked unhindered. Nineteen RAF fighters were lost.

Once again very heavy claims were made for enemy aircraft destroyed. Disregarding the estimates made in the first flush of the enthusiasm of returning pilots, the official assessment of 11 Group was finally stabilised at sixty-five German fighters and bombers brought down. Four more were claimed as destroyed by ships' gunfire.

The Luftwaffe reports examined after the war recorded the loss of eighteen.

*　　　*　　　*

On the afternoon of the 29th it was decided at the Admiralty that the naval organisation off Dunkirk should be strengthened. It was not intended that Captain Tennant, as SNO, Dunkirk, should be in any way superseded, but Rear-Admiral W. F. Wake-Walker was appointed 'for command of seagoing ships and vessels off the Belgian coast'. The phrasing is odd in view of the fact that the major part of his duties was concerned with the French coast. He sailed in HMS *Esk* at eight o'clock that evening, with Commodore G. O. Stephenson and Commodore T. J. Hallett, who were appointed to take charge of operations off La Panne and Bray-Dunes respectively, and a beach control party of approximately eighty – made up of lieutenants from gunnery and torpedo courses, with petty officers and men.

While Admiral Wake-Walker was *en route* to his station the Admiralty came to the conclusion that the rate of loss had reached levels which could no longer be accepted. On this one day three destroyers had been sunk, and six had been damaged in varying degree. Coupled with earlier losses the casualty list had reached a level at which the whole question of future operations was endangered. The First Sea Lord had as his primary duty the protection of the sea life lines of Britain. The destroyer flotillas were a vital component of that protection. Desperately short at the beginning of the war, their losses had already been severe. Reluctantly Admiral Pound came to the decision that he must withdraw from Dunkirk the modern destroyers. All ships of the 'G' class were already out of action. He now ordered Admiral Ramsay to release all ships of the 'H', 'I' and 'J' classes from 'Dynamo'. There were left available fifteen destroyers of the older classes. Knowing that the loss crippled his effort, that the destroyers left to him could hope to lift no more than 17,000 troops in twenty-four hours and that already they had proved themselves the mainstay of the evacuation, Admiral Ramsay was none the less forced to agree.

Despite disaster, despite the crippling effect of the closure of Dunkirk harbour, despite the loss of the Mole, in these twenty-four hours 47,310 troops were landed in England. This is the day on which General Brooke saw fit to write in his diary:

'. . . found arrangements quite inadequate and of a most Heath Robinson nature. Saw Gort and asked him to get Admiralty to produce a few Marines and more landing craft.'

It is an entry whose arrogance is matched only by its lack of appreciation.

CHAPTER XI

Thursday, May 30th

We were robbed of the chance of claiming even a moral victory by unfavourable weather which made flying even riskier. Anyone who saw the wreckage over the coastal waters and the material scattered on the beaches or heard first-hand reports of what was happening from returning fighter, strafer and bombing crews can only have the highest admiration both for the performance of our airmen and for the superlative exertions, ingenuity and gallantry of the English. We had no idea in 1940 that the number of British and French who escaped was anywhere near the figure of 300,000 given today. Even 100,000 we believed to be well above the mark.

FIELD-MARSHAL KESSELRING

ON THIS Thursday the British Expeditionary Force and what remained of the French First Army made good their withdrawal into the defended perimeter of Dunkirk. There were left outside only the troops which held Bergues and the outskirts of Furnes, small mobile forces maintaining contact with the advancing enemy, and the dwindling stream of stragglers. The vast area of the Armies of the North that had encompassed all northern France from the Maginot Line, all Belgium to the Dyle, had shrunk now to this desperate flat of sand and marsh and dyke. West of Dunkirk the French held from the sea by the Mardyck Canal to the Bergues Canal and by that to the outskirts of Bergues itself, a distance of perhaps eleven miles. From there the BEF held the line of the Bergues-Furnes Canal through Furnes to Nieuport and from Nieuport by the line of the Yser to the sea, a total of 21 miles.

Along it the names of famous regiments read like a Roll of Honour of the British Army: the Loyals, the Sherwood Foresters, the East Lancashires, the Border Regiment, the Coldstream Guards, the Duke of Wellington's, the Green

Howards, the Yorkshire Regiment, the South Staffordshires, the Durham Light Infantry, the King's Own Scottish Borderers, the Royal Ulsters, the Grenadiers, the Berkshires, the Suffolks, the East Yorks., the Beds. and Herts., the Duke of Cornwall's, the Surreys, the Royal Fusiliers.

The line of their defence was the canal. It was narrow, in stretches it was scarcely more than an anti-tank ditch – but it was at least that. The high banks, the depth of the water made it impossible to rush the perimeter with armour. In front of it there were areas of marsh where the inundations had been carried out, but, owing to Command failures, the French engineers had left the flooding over large sectors until too late. Behind the banks the BEF dug in. Along them it established its machine-gun posts, and in the rear the artillery ranged itself out over the flat with what was left of its guns and what remained to it of ammunition.

How long could the perimeter hold?

In the first few minutes of the day the War Office received a telephone message from GHQ at La Panne to say that 'the perimeter cannot be held for long', and asking that as many boats and as much ammunition for Bofors guns as possible be sent over.

As the day progressed the troops of Army Group A and Army Group B moved up towards the line. The paralysis and indecision of Wednesday still held the German Command in its grip. Fourth Army was asked to attack through Bergues with mobile forces. On the previous day it had admitted that it could make little headway 'owing to very stubborn enemy resistance'. Now it protested that mobile forces would suffer heavy loss. Instead it ordered Kleist Group to close in and bring Dunkirk under fire from its 10 cm. guns. At three in the afternoon the OKH sanctioned an attack. Fourth Army retorted that it was ready but that Army Group B had pulled Sixth Army out to rest. Rundstedt then asked if it was not known that VIII Air Group was carrying out a full-scale attack on Dunkirk that afternoon. The operations officer at Fourth Army HQ complained irritably:

'There is an impression here that nothing is happening to-day, that no one is any longer interested in Dunkirk . . .'

It was discovered that the medium artillery had run out of ammunition. The bickerings and arguments of the day failed to resolve themselves until, late at night, the decision was taken to place all operations under Army Group B's

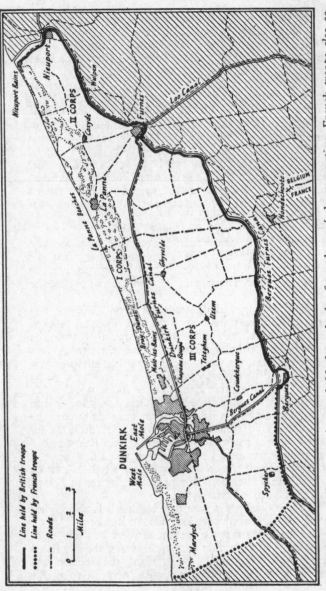

The Dunkirk perimeter as it was held through the first phase of the evacuation. French troops also co-operated in the defence of Bergues and manned the old fixed defences of the Franco-Belgian frontier. In the later stages they held the line through Ghyvelde, Uxem and Coudekerque to cover the final withdrawal.

Eighteenth Army. Army Group A was absolved of all further responsibility for Dunkirk. Rundstedt had at last got his way.

This day saw the end of his effort. In the darkness the last elements of the panzer divisions began their move to the re-grouping areas preliminary to the onslaught to the south against metropolitan France. Out of all the immense concentration of forces beyond the perimeter only one attack of importance developed on the 30th, when, after strong artillery preparation, an attempt was made to cross the canal north of Furnes. The attack was beaten off. At ten o'clock at night it was renewed and the Germans broke across the canal. The Coldstream Guards counter-attacked, drove them out of their bridgehead and restored the line.

*   *   *

At Dover Admiral Ramsay faced a position of tremendous difficulty. On the one hand he had the signal that had been made just after midnight that 'the perimeter cannot be held for long'. On the other hand he had the knowledge that the withdrawal of the big destroyers made a substantial increase in the lifting rate impossible. He was left with fifteen destroyers, mostly small and old. He calculated that they could lift approximately 17,000 men, the personnel ships 9,500 and all other vessels, including the small craft, 15,000, making a total lift of 43,000 for the day. On the estimates that he had been given of the men remaining a lift of 55,000 appeared to be essential.

In the early part of the day he did not know if the Mole was still functioning after the disaster of the previous evening. At dawn the destroyer *Vanquisher* was sent to investigate the situation and report. A little after six her signal said that though there were obstructions on the inside of the Mole, it was still possible to use it.

There were other items on the credit side. There had been no bombing since dusk the previous evening. The weather had improved, the surf along the beaches had gone down, there was a low cloud ceiling and the smoke of the burning oil tanks blowing off-shore screened a large sector of the anchorage – which partially justified Kesselring's excuses. Though part of the confusion of the German Command this day was based on the fact that the VIII Air Group was committed to a full-scale assault on Dunkirk, no major attack developed. Fighter Command operated patrols at three- and four-squadron strength and drove off enemy bombers encountered.

At least as important as any of these things, fresh small craft were beginning even in the early part of the day to reach the beaches. By nightfall they were streaming in – a fantastic armada of every shape and size. In addition, the Army, realising at last the immense difficulties that the crews of the small boats were meeting in getting the men away from the shallow water, began to build piers. Out of Bren-gun carriers, trucks, and ammunition wagons they constructed jetties running down towards the deeper water. They used pontoons elsewhere. At no time were these piers strong enough to take the larger craft, but to the small ships they were at the right states of the tide a godsend, and over them the flow from the beaches steadily increased.

At noon the responsibilities of Lord Gort and Admiral Ramsay were clarified. The Prime Minister called a meeting of the Chiefs of Staff and the Service Ministers. General Pownall, Gort's Chief of Staff, who had sailed from Dunkirk at midnight, attended, and the situation in the perimeter and at sea was reviewed in detail. In his own hand Mr Churchill wrote out the final orders to Lord Gort.

'Continue to defend the present perimeter to the utmost in order to cover maximum evacuation now proceeding well. Report every three hours through La Panne. If we can still communicate we shall send you an order to return to England with such officers as you may choose at the moment when we deem your command so reduced that it can be handed over to a Corps Commander. You should now nominate this Commander. If communications are broken you are to hand over and return as specified when your effective fighting force does not exceed the equivalent of three divisions. This is in accordance with correct military procedure, and no personal discretion is left you in the matter. On political grounds it would be a needless triumph to the enemy to capture you when only a small force remained under your orders. The Corps' Commander chosen by you should be ordered to carry on the defence in conjunction with the French, and evacuation whether from Dunkirk or the beaches, but when in his judgment no further organised evacuation is possible and no further proportionate damage can be inflicted on the enemy he is authorised in consultation with the senior French Commander to capitulate formally to avoid useless slaughter.'

Simultaneously, at Mr Churchill's urging, the meeting decided that French troops must be given an equal opportunity of evacuation not only in their own vessels, but also in British ships and boats.

While this conference was in progress in London another conference was being held at Dover between officers of Lord Gort's staff and Admiral Ramsay. Ramsay was told that Gort believed that it would be possible to hold the perimeter until early on June 1st and that by then he hoped to have reduced the BEF to a rearguard of about 4,000 men. The conference reached agreement on a scale of lifting for the next two nights which would cover this requirement. It was decided to build up reserves of small craft and tugs, and with these Admiral Ramsay planned a final lifting between 1.30 am and dawn on June 1st which would bring out the last of the rearguard and the naval beach parties. The final decision was to be made on Friday at 2 pm based on the progress of the lifting of the main body up to that hour.

*   *   *

Between the fighting on the perimeter and the policy-making in London and at Dover lay the whole complex of the evacuation.

Superficially there appears again on this morning to be a high degree of confusion. The lack of definite information as to the state of the Mole following the disasters of the previous evening, the general difficulty of communications, the great distances involved between the different beaches, and the serious weakness in the shore signalling arrangements led to a certain waste of effort, but at dawn Admiral Wake-Walker began to take control of the off-shore area and order was gradually brought out of the confusion.

It is easy to make that statement. To understand it properly a brief outline of Admiral Wake-Walker's movements is instructive. At four o'clock in the morning he transferred his flag from HMS *Esk* to the Fleet minesweeper *Hebe*, which had been acting as headquarters ship. In the early morning he entered Dunkirk harbour to make contact with Captain Tennant. *Hebe* filled up with approximately 700 men from the Mole. At 3.30 that afternoon Admiral Wake-Walker decided that he could no longer hold her and transferred his staff to HMS *Windsor*, going himself to MTB 102, in which he returned to Dunkirk. As the MTB's endurance was insufficient, he boarded the Fleet minesweeper *Gossamer* in which he went to La Panne, where he moved to HMS *Worcester*. As *Worcester* rapidly filled up with troops, he transferred his flag again shortly after 1 am to HMS *Express*. Few flags can have been transferred so frequently within the space of approximately twenty-four hours.

Despite all these changes his control was effective. If proof of that were needed, it lies in the record of the destroyers alone. On this day seven of them each landed more than 1,000 men at Dover. The ancient *Sabre*, though she had come under fire from the shore batteries, lifted 1,700 men in two trips; *Wolsey*, making amazingly quick 'turn rounds' at Dover, made three trips, lifting 1,677; *Vimy* lifted 1,472, *Express* 1,431, *Whitehall* 1,248, *Vanquisher* 1,204, *Vivacious* 1,023. The work of the destroyers throughout this day is beyond all praise. Their tasks were by no means confined to the lifting of men. Patrols were operated up to the latitude of the coast of Holland. A screen was maintained against the E-boats that had caused the heavy loss of the previous night, and anti-submarine patrols were extended. On either flank of the perimeter off Nieuport and off Mardyck destroyers carried out counter-battery fire as the German guns opened on the shipping. As enemy positions or even enemy formations on the road were spotted, they engaged them singly or in groups, fighting a strange, independent war of their own. All through the day in the reports of the masters and the skippers of the little ships their names recur – rescuing men from the water, towing broken-down craft out of danger zones, covering shipping in the anchorage and in the channels with anti-aircraft fire. Nowhere perhaps in the whole war until the bitter fighting off Okinawa were destroyers so continuously, so variously engaged.

* * *

French destroyers were also working vigorously this day. At dawn the five dispatch boats which had crossed the previous night, entered the harbour. A little later the torpedo-boats *Bouclier* and *Branlebas* were sent across, and at 9.30 am the destroyer *Bourrasque* was ordered to join them. At 2.15 pm she berthed at the Quai Félix Faure and an hour later, having picked up between 700 and 800 men, she sailed by Route Y. On her way out she passed the destroyer *Foudroyant* coming in. At half-past four, then off Nieuport, her captain

148

ordered her to 28 knots to slip through the shelling area as rapidly as possible. Almost at once, owing to trouble in the stokehold, speed fell to 15 knots, and the German guns began to get the range. Her engine-room managed to effect repairs and speed was increased to 25 knots; but her captain had already hauled out of the swept channel to avoid the fall of shot. His course took him into a minefield, and at 4.45 pm there was a violent explosion and *Bourrasque* began to sink by the stern. The troops on board were assembled in the bows in an effort to trim the ship, but gradually she heeled over to starboard and a quarter of an hour later she sank.

The *Branlebas*, following her a short distance astern, stopped and put her boats in the water. Already overloaded herself, she picked up 100 men. *Yorkshire Lass* and *Ut Prosim*, two of the Dover flare-burning drifters, closed and began to pick up many more, but as *Bourrasque* sank the explosion of her depth charges killed a large number of the men in the water. In less than two hours it was all over.

Bouclier, damaged in collision while loading, left some time later and limped back to Dover.

The major French lifting this day was made by the desperate expedient of sending in the supply ships which had been moored in the Downs. 3,000 French troops were embarked in the five ships sent over and were taken off in safety. Late in the night other destroyers began to cross, *Siroco* and *Cyclone* amongst them.

Unhappily the French Admiralty now decided to recall the dispatch boats. With their small size and their manoeuvrability they had been eminently suitable for working in the confined area of the harbour; but now they were ordered back to cover the convoys which were transporting the rescued Frenchmen from Southampton to Brest. Three of them made one last passage to Dunkirk this evening on their own responsibility, but by dawn all five were gone.

* * *

The personnel ships had been diverted from the Mole by the early reports of the blocking of the entrance. Four were in the area but, as Dover had no knowledge of their movements, the sailing of fresh vessels to Dunkirk was suspended until *Vanquisher*'s report came through. Despite that interruption a high rate of lifting was maintained. *St Helier* brought back one of the earliest loads. She had crossed in company with two

French troopships and picked up, according to her report, over 2,000 troops. She had the usual bombing attacks and claims to have brought down one plane. That night she was back in Dover.

Royal Sovereign, which had made two crossings the day before, completed her loading at 5.30 am. With a full load (and her master's laconic statements mean precisely what they say) she returned to Margate. No time was allowed for rest. At 11.35 am she was alongside Margate pier, disembarking; at one o'clock she was heading for Dunkirk; at 6.20 am she was anchored and once more embarking troops.

With the personnel ships the hospital carriers continued their admirable work. They suffered from the same disabilities as the personnel ships: their draught was too deep for the narrow shallows between the Dunkirk moles; they lifted up and down with the swell, with the wash of the ships outside, with the waves set up by bursting shells and bombs; their improvised gangways parted, broke as the ships ranged, carried away.

In the very early hours the *Isle of Guernsey,* which had had to return empty owing to the appalling bombing of the previous afternoon, reached Dunkirk again. Her master, Captain Hill, speaks of the area as being brilliantly lit up by fires. (There were many periods when the Dunkirk flames helped in the darkness of these nights, taking something of the confusion from the crowded harbour.) By 2.15 am she had taken 490 wounded on board,

'. . . although the ship was shaken every few minutes by the explosion of bombs falling on the quay and in the water. Just outside we found the sea full of men swimming and shouting for help, presumably a transport had just been sunk. As two destroyers were standing by picking these men up, we threaded our way carefully through them and proceeded towards Dover. It would have been fatal for us to attempt to stop and try to save any of these men, as we made such a wonderful target for the aircraft hovering ahead with the flames of the burning port showing all our white paintwork up. Everything was comparatively quiet on the way across, except that just before we got to Dover a patrol boat headed us off as we were heading straight for a recently laid minefield.'

This was the *Isle of Guernsey*'s last trip. In this and previous voyages she had sustained repeated minor damage. The sum of it was such that she had to lay off now for repairs. By the time her repairs were completed the evacuation was over.

These were the big ships. They made the outlines of the design that was Dunkirk. Between those outlines weaves the pattern of the little ships, growing firmer, stronger, more brilliant as the day goes on. In the early hours they were in the main the veterans of the previous day. *Shamrock*, for example, after the running down of the *Queen of England*, searched for her convoy mates and found *Canvey Queen* with her engine broken down again. She took her in tow and anchored for a little close to the *Clan MacAlister*. Allan Barrell of *Shamrock* said:

'Dawn soon came, we stared and stared at what looked like thousands of sticks on the beach and were amazed to see them turn into moving masses of humanity. I thought quickly of going in picking up seventy to eighty and clearing off, with the sun behind me I calculated I should find some East Coast town. We got our freight, so did the *Canvey Queen*, when I realised it would be selfish to clear off when several destroyers and large vessels were waiting in deep water to be fed by small craft, so I decided what our job was to be.

'We could seat sixty men and with those standing we had about eighty weary and starving British troops, some without boots, some only in their pants, but enough life left in them to clamber on board the destroyers with the kind hand of every available seaman. Again and again we brought our cargo to this ship until she was full, the *Canvey Queen* and the *Maud* were doing likewise . . .

'Navigation was extremely difficult owing to the various wreckage, up-turned boats, floating torpedoes, and soldiers in the water trying to be sailors for the first time, they paddled their collapsible little boats out to me with the butts of their rifles, and many shouted that they were sinking, we could not help them. I was inshore as close as I dare. "Stop shouting and save your breath, and bail out with your steel helmets," was the only command suitable for the occasion. Scores offered me cash and personal belongings which I refused, saying, "My name is Barrell, Canvey Island, send me a postcard if you get home all right." They have all forgotten – no wonder! . . .

'Later I took in two or three large Carley floats one behind the other. These were filled to capacity, about fifty men in each standing up to their waists in water in the net inside. My craft was well loaded too, we were just making for our destroyer when I was brought to a standstill; my engine stopped, the propeller had fouled, I believe a human obstruction. There were many in the shallow water . . . Naval men came down and tried to free the obstruction but without success. I was too weak to dive under the thick black oil which surrounded us, so rather than be left sitting on our useless craft I asked to be taken on HM ship. This was the last straw, having to leave my vessel which constituted my life savings . . . I took one more glance at the beach and sat down beneath a gun with my hands over my face and prayed.'

This is the stuff of epics.

With the veterans were the first of the new waves of little ships. *Tigris I* came from Kingston. She passed through Sheerness in command of her owner, Mr H. Hastings, who wrote:

'We arrived at Dunkirk but found we could not get in close enough to get the troops off the sands, so we got the *Lansdown* to go in and we pulled her off ground after the troops were aboard. We also used the *Princess Lily*. We were told to proceed to La Panne which is about nine miles further round the coast. Owing to the engines failing we had to leave with only a few troops. We proceeded back to Dunkirk where we took five more loads off the shore which we were now able to do owing to the rising tide. Whilst these operations were being carried out we were being bombed and we were under machine-gun fire. We took the troops off to the nearest vessels which were larger ships.

'On the fourth run back to the shore I was blown overboard by the blast from a bomb. After I got back aboard the vessel we proceeded to take more troops but our boat became disabled and I was told to abandon her as she was in a sinking condition. Eight hundred troops were taken off the beaches during the period and we were then taken back to Ramsgate in the same boat as the troops.'

Lieutenant Irving, RNR, took over *Triton*, a motor-boat, as leader of a convoy of eight small craft. He had lost three to engine trouble by the time he made the North Goodwin light. The convoy was ordered to a point between Bray-Dunes and the Moles. On the way across visibility was low with showers of heavy rain, and navigation became almost impossible. Just at dawn Irving fell in with a heavy destroyer, loaded with troops, and damaged by shellfire aft. She confirmed his course, and all five of the remaining boats reached the beaches safely near the cupola at La Panne. From five o'clock until noon *Triton* worked at the towing of small boats from the edge of the surf to the destroyers, the trawlers and the Dutch skoots. At midday she was hailed from a destroyer and boarded by Commodore Stephenson, who asked to be put ashore as he wished to make contact with Lord Gort. *Triton* dropped him as close in as she could, and the Commodore waded ashore up to his neck in water. He returned subsequently and carried on in *Triton* until the small hours, when she ran aground.

In the evening Admiral Wake-Walker himself went ashore and finally made contact with Lord Gort. He wrote subsequently:

'After dinner, Lord Gort and Brigadier Leese discussed the situation with Tennant and myself; it became obvious to me that they felt that they had successfully fallen back more or less intact on the sea in the face of great odds and that it was now up to the Navy to get them off but that the Navy were not making any real effort in the matter. Very early in the discussion I stressed the difficulty, slowness, and dependence on fine weather of any large-scale embarkation from the beaches and expressed the view that the bulk should move westward and come off from Dunkirk.

'This brought from Brigadier Leese a disparaging remark which included the words "ineptitude of the Navy". I could not let this pass and told him he had no business or justification to talk like that.'

*   *   *

In Sheerness the work of the Small Vessels Pool and of Admiral Taylor's staff was now in full spate. It is difficult to picture the complexity of it. Captain Docksey was making the converted motor-car engines of weekend yachts run well enough to take them to Dunkirk. Captain Coleridge of the base ship HMS *Wildfire* was producing stores and accommodation for a constant stream of officers and ratings out of reserves that were already extended to the utmost. The Chief Constructor of Sheerness dockyard, Mr S. R. Tickner, was building rafts small enough to be manhandled, large enough to carry men. The shipwrights of the yard were making ladders with which to load small ships from the high decking of the Mole or to pick up men who had waded out to ships grounded off the shallows of the beaches. The whole yard was working in a complete abandonment of official formulae, of paper work, of red tape.

Convoy after convoy was pushing out to sea: ships' boats and service boats, dockyard launches and 'X' lighters, Belgian and Dutch craft of one kind and another. The total of small craft sent out from Sheerness is extraordinary. There were more than 100 motor-boats, ten lighters, seven skoots, one oil tanker and six paddle-steamers in Admiral Taylor's division – quite apart from the naval craft under the Nore Command.

In the main the Sheerness effort was concerned with the handling of yard craft and motor yachts. But from every quarter fleets grew – fleets of ships of similar type and of similar capabilities. London River, for example, was swept clear of tugs. At the height of the evacuation only one tug capable of towing a deep-sea ship was left in the Port of London, the largest seaport in the United Kingdom. Dover, Newhaven, Portsmouth and Southampton sent their quota. The great towing companies – Sun, Watkins, Gamecock, Elliott, Gaselee – all made their contribution to this fleet.

It is impossible to detail their work and single examples must serve to illustrate the whole. The tug *Java* crossed on the 29th in company with three drifters and four motor-boats. At daybreak on the 30th she went as far in to the beach as she could go and lowered her boat. This was manned by the mate and one deck-hand, who rowed to and from the beach transferring troops to motor-boats, who again transferred them either to *Java* herself or to the drifters. After working in this way all the afternoon, she went into Dunkirk and berthed alongside the Mole, taking off a full complement of troops. Leaving Dunkirk, she moved up the beaches to La Panne, transferred her troops to destroyers, and returned to repeat the work all through the evening, loading a minesweeper as well as other craft.

The tug *Persia*, which had already done admirable work in bringing in a damaged destroyer, left Dover on the Wednesday, towing the dumb barges *Sark* and *Shetland*, loaded with food, ammunition and water, across the Channel. The supply situation was rapidly becoming critical in Dunkirk, and as an emergency measure it had been decided to strand barges laden with these commodities on the beach at high water so that they could be discharged by the troops themselves as occasion served and as need arose. With some difficulty *Persia* took her barges to a point 4 miles east of Dunkirk, arrived there at dawn on the 30th, and at 12.45 pm anchored the barges as close in to the beach as was prudent so that motor-boats could tow them in on the flood tide. 'Then,' said her master, H. Aldrich, 'left Dunkirk at 4 pm with soldiers and equipment, anchoring in the Downs at midnight.'

The most remarkable towage story of the day, however, belongs not to a tug but to an elderly river gunboat. Admiral Ramsay had at his disposal one sloop, HMS *Bideford*. She was a ship of the 'Shoreham' class with a displacement of 1,105 tons. She had been working off Bray beach close to HMS *Jaguar* in the later part of May 29th. While men were being brought off to her from the beach – she had already loaded something like 400 – a bomb hit on her quarter-deck. Forty feet of her stern was blown away; twenty-five of her crew and of the men who were crowding her decks were killed, fifty more were badly wounded. Surgeon-Lieutenant John Jordan, RN, her doctor, whose sick-berth attendant had been seriously wounded, dealt with the casualties, assisted by George William Crowther of the 6th Field Ambulance, who had embarked with the troops. The unwounded survivors were moved to another ship, but Crowther volunteered to stay with Lieutenant Jordan on *Bideford*, although by this time she had been run aground and seemed 'unlikely to reach England'.

The tugs *Lady Brassey* and *Foremost 87* were sent from Dover to see what they could do about HMS *Bideford*, but in the meantime the wreck had refloated and had been taken in tow by HM Gunboat *Locust*. *Locust* was half her size, a shallow-draught vessel built for river work, drawing only 5 feet of water, mounting two 4-inch guns, and looking rather more like a pleasure steamer than a man-of-war. She was theoretically capable of 17 knots, but not with an unwieldy tow like *Bideford* astern of her. The story of that voyage back is among the epics of Dunkirk. For thirty-six hours *Locust* towed the helpless ship – all through May 30th and into the 31st. The tugs passed them in the fog that came down at intervals during the day. Grimly *Locust* clung on to her damaged consort. All through the night they kept on, yawing wildly from side to side through the stream of traffic until on the following morning they were off Dover.

There was another 'fleet' – the boats of the Royal National Lifeboat Institution. The crews of the two ships nearest to Dover had already volunteered *en bloc*. Their record is magnificent, and the reports of the Ramsgate and Margate boats match the very finest traditions of their service.

The Margate lifeboat, *Lord Southborough*, left first at 5.30 pm on May 30th in tow of a Dutch skoot in order to save fuel. On arrival off Dunkirk the towing ship grounded, but with the help of the lifeboat an anchor was laid out to prevent the former from broaching to. In the event this proved to be a wise precaution, as later the wind freshened from the north-west, making a lee shore. The lifeboat repeatedly closed the shore and embarked batches of troops which she transferred to the barge and, when the latter was full, to a destroyer. The rising wind caused an awkward surf on the beaches.

'By this time things were getting bad,' wrote the coxswain, Edward Parker, in his report, 'troops were rushing out to us from all directions and were being drowned close to us and we could not get to them and the last time we went in to the shore it seemed to me we were doing more harm by drawing the men off the shore, as with their heavy clothing on the surf was knocking them over and they were unable to get up. The whaler from the destroyer which went in to the shore with us on our last trip was swamped, so was the motor pinnace that was working with the whaler, and so it was all along the sands as far as I could see, both sides of us and there was not a boat left afloat.'

This was the *Lord Southborough*'s first trip.

The Ramsgate lifeboat, *Prudential*, did similar excellent work, under her coxswain H. Knight, who wrote:

'. . . found naval ratings who manned wherries were not skilled at handling small boats under such conditions; members of lifeboat crew took their boats and places, and although an intensely dark night managed by shouting to establish communication with officer in charge of troops on beach; arranged for men to take to the water in batches of eight which was the capacity of the small boats, and each boat conveyed them to the lifeboat, thence to the awaiting craft in attendance: about 800 were safely transported on Thursday night and when the last three boatloads were being taken from the water, the officer called, "I cannot see who you are; are you a naval party?" He was answered, "No, sir, we are members of the crew of the Ramsgate lifeboat." He then called, "Thank you – and thank God for such men as you have this night proved yourselves to be." '

The Dover lifeboat volunteered also but was ordered to remain at Dover for service in the area. Fifteen other lifeboats from as far north as Great Yarmouth and as far west as Poole were concentrated at Ramsgate. They were not, strictly speaking, suitable vessels for the job. The modern lifeboat has developed a long way from the beach boats of tradition. Today they are heavy vessels, they draw a fair amount of water, they are motor driven, and they are not built to take the ground. The coxswains of the first outlying boats to reach Dover protested that on a falling tide they would inevitably be stranded and that their boats were not suited to the task. There was no time for argument. The Admiralty took over completely the first three boats which had protested, and manned them with naval crews, and then, to the considerable indignation of many of those who came after, took over the remainder, retaining only the services of the mechanics. The decision was a difficult one, but on May 30th there was little time for argument.

There were other 'fleets'. Pickfords, the great firm of carriers, sent five little ships built for the transport trade between the Solent ports and the Isle of Wight – *Bee*, *Bat*, *Chamois*, *Hound* and *M.F.H.* Their crews were small but, with only two exceptions, all insisted on going with their ships. *Chamois* was beaten back twice by air attack. Making a third attempt, she succeeded in getting within 2 miles of Dunkirk. There she encountered two ships being heavily bombed. She went to the rescue of the survivors – French and Belgian troops. The clothes of many of these were on fire and ammunition in their pockets was exploding, according to the report of her master, A. E. Brown, but she managed to rescue 120 men. *Bat* on her first trip picked up fifteen of the crew of the French destroyer *Bourrasque* and brought them back to Ramsgate.

There was a 'fleet' of fishing vessels too – Belgian ships, part of the great flotilla of 450 which left Belgium as the enemy swept down the coast, carrying refugees. They had passed through the Channel to Dartmouth, to Milford Haven, to Brixham and to the western French ports. When the signal to Admiral Darlan was made many of them turned back, in company with French vessels. Some of them were manned by the French Navy, some by their own crews. *Lydie Suzanne* was one; this day she lifted over 100 officers and men on her first trip. *Gilda*, with her, coming back heavily loaded with British and French troops, was attacked, and Commander Ghesselle, the Belgian naval officer in charge of her, was seriously wounded. Some of these ships were very small – they ranged from 23 to 217 tons. The *Maréchal Foch*, one of the smallest, lying alongside the quay in Dunkirk harbour sank under the weight of the men who crowded into her. Her crew refused to accept defeat. At low tide on the following day they salvaged their ship, reconditioned her and brought her back with 300 men.

All through the morning the lifting went on, and, as the figures came to the Dynamo Room, it was evident that despite the temporary suspension of work at the Mole, despite the difficulties of the beaches, the numbers were rising.

To Admiral Ramsay at Dover, however, the increase was not enough. Though the Royal Navy lost no destroyers this day – sinkings, in fact, were extraordinarily light – the French had lost *Bourrasque* and lesser damage to British vessels had put a number of ships out of action. The destroyers and the cross-Channel steamers were Ramsay's mainstay. The mathematics of their capacity made it clear that he could not hope to maintain the rate of lifting to cover the numbers that were involved.

In the early afternoon he spoke by telephone to the First Sea Lord in London. There must have been strange undertones of drama in that conversation. The First Sea Lord had ordered the withdrawal of the big destroyers for reasons that were beyond criticism. It was his duty to provide against the future. The destroyers were needed to preserve the balance of the Fleet, to cover the escort of the vital convoys in and out of Britain. It was Ramsay's duty to provide for the present. Overshadowing the possibilities of the future were the long columns of men stretching down into the shallows of the beaches, the stream that passed endlessly down the narrow planking of the Mole, the men who still lay in the inadequate rifle pits of the perimeter, and the mass of the French. But though his immediate concern was with the present, it also was linked indissolubly with the future. These were the men round whom the new armies would have to be built, the men who would have to defend Britain against the threat of invasion.

There is no record of that conversation. No one knows what arguments were used. Both its participants are dead and neither of them wrote down his words, but Admiral Ramsay made his point. At 3.30 pm the Commander-in-Chief, Nore, signalled *Harvester, Havant, Ivanhoe, Impulsive, Icarus* and *Intrepid* to return at once to Dunkirk.

As the destroyers crossed, the figures of men landed at the

British ports rose. The totals had reached the point now where senior officers were coming away as their work ended. Sir Ronald Adam, whose task was completed with the final withdrawal into the perimeter, embarked in a destroyer in the course of the day. At 7.15 pm General Brooke went down to the beaches and was carried out to an open boat and ferried to a destroyer. An entry in his diary shortly after says:

'We have been waiting till 10 pm before starting, rather nerve-racking as Germans are continually flying round and being shot at. After seeing yesterday the ease with which a dive-bomber can sink a destroyer, it is an unpleasant feeling.

'*Later.* – We never started till 12.15 am. At 3 am we were brought up short with a crash. I felt certain that we had hit a mine or been torpedoed.'

The destroyer, whose name General Brooke does not mention, had run aground in the shallows of Route X. She got off with slight damage to one propeller.

With every hour the tally of small ships working on the beaches rose. This above all was their day. The story of the *Constant Nymph* is typical of the work of the newcomers. She had left, as has been said, amongst the very earliest of the up-river boats from Isleworth. Dr Smith wrote:

'. . . there was some difficulty in getting signed on and I toured Sheerness Dockyard interviewing numerous people until late in the afternoon, and by 5 pm had formed a pretty accurate idea what the job was and was quite determined not to be put off, so I appealed to the Commodore himself, who was supervising the fuelling and victualling of the motor-boats at the basin. Within half an hour I was signed on and back at the basin, and by 6 pm was making my way out of the basin with a crew of two young ratings . . .

'We arrived at Dunkirk about dusk and turned along the beach eastwards for a few miles . . . At first we could find no life on the beach, but after a short time were hailed by Frenchmen and for a little while found Frenchmen only, and made one or two full journeys back to the ship with them. The procedure was to tow the whaler and cutter to the beach and swing them round and cast off tow in about 3 feet 6 inches (my draught being 2 feet 6 inches). The cutter then dropped her grapnel and went in as close as she dared without grounding the whaler, and troops waded out to board them. As soon as the two boats were full they called for the motor-boat and pulled up on the cutter's grapnel; I would come past and take the cutter's bow rope in passing and swing out towards the ship which had to lie about three-quarters of a mile to a mile out.

'While the whaler and cutter were loading I patrolled parallel with the beach . . . my job was to pick up any swimmers or waders and any odd craft which had put out from the shore. There were several of these. After the first few loads had been taken to the ship, all Frenchmen, a British officer waded out and was picked up by me and reported that a whole division of British were waiting to be taken off a little nearer Dunkirk town than we had been working.

'I took him aboard, went back and picked up the full cutter and whaler, and took them all back to the ship, reported to the captain of the *Jutland* that the British were further up the beach, and that I was going there, a big fire just inshore was my leading mark as the British were just to the east of this. From then on we worked to this point and the French came down the beach and mingled with the British: *Jutland* was filled roughly half and half British and French. . . .'

Bonny Heather was another of the up-river Thames motor-yachts. She left Ramsgate at 6.45 on Thursday evening, under the command of Lieutenant C. W. Read, RNR, as leader of a convoy of ten motor craft all towing ships' lifeboats. On the way across the convoy lost one boat, the *Wolsey*, a motor-yacht from Hampton Wick, which broke down owing to dirt in the carburettor and had to make fast for the night to the North Goodwin lightship. It is as well to record some of these failures. They were not failures of the spirit. The condition of these boats has been stressed earlier, but it must be borne in mind in considering the passages made by every single one of the little ships. *Wolsey* was a well-found, well-equipped craft, but Mr A. Malcolm, her owner, said in his account:

'In the meantime I had got the engine in running order, and the water-tank filled, but had no time to clear out the filters and carburettors or to attend to other details which would have been seen to in ordinary circumstances.'

Bonny Heather reached Dunkirk safely. This was the first of seven complete round trips which she made between Ramsgate and Dunkirk, in addition to incessant work in filling up transports and destroyers lying off the beaches. Normally she carried sixty men, once she carried eighty.

Side by side on the beaches with her were two of the ferry-boats from Sandbanks at the mouth of Poole harbour. At

June 1940: withdrawal from Dunkirk

Troops wade out to a Clyde river steamer

Part of the historic Armada

Arriving at Dover after the evacuation

Since the official route concerned itself as much with wrecks and mines as with what might be called normal navigational necessities, the remark is interesting. She experimented with a new berth well inside the outer harbour and embarked 'a full load of troops'. A thousand men with equipment, rifles and ammunition weighed very little under 100 tons. By the time she had her load aboard *Prague* was hard on the bottom. 'It took the combined efforts of two tugs (*Lady Brassey* and *Foremost 87*) and both engines working at full power to get the ship afloat', and this was done under shell-fire with 'several projectiles bursting in the water close to the ship'.

Royal Daffodil crossed about the same time and picked up 2,000 French troops.

Once again it must be remembered that these were not all the personnel ships which sailed for, or reached, Dunkirk on this day. It is improbable, even with these big ships, that every detail of the movements will ever be described.

Nor will it be possible with the movements of the hospital ships. *Dinard*, for instance, went in again under heavy fire. Shells falling and bursting close caused the ship to range, making it difficult to keep the improvised gangways intact. The tide was falling and when there was only a foot of water under her keel her master, Captain Ailwyn-Jones, decided to leave. Using an electric torch with which to identify the buoys and picking his way between the wrecks, he eventually reached the Downs with his cargo of wounded. In his report he gives particular praise to his engine-room staff. There is a special grimness about the duties of the engine-room in times like these. On the deck it is possible to see at least something of what is happening. There may be moments when to see is terrifying, but there is always at least the illusion of freedom and of space. The engine-room staffs worked deep in the ships at the bottom of long, frail ladders that had a tendency to jar off or to smash when bombs hit. They worked in absolute blindness for all the brilliance of their electric light, feeling only the shaking of the ship, the concussion of the bombs outside, the thud and clang of the splinters against the plating. There could be no illusion of shelter in their working place. No one knew better than the engineers the thinness of the skin plating, the ease with which those sides could open to the slash of steel, to the blast of high explosive. No one knew better than they the instant consequence of such opening: the furious anger of steam from the broken pipes, the crash of machinery wrecked at high speed, the rush of scalding water that overwhelms. Throughout the operation the courage, the self-sacrifice and the devotion of engineers and stokers is beyond praise, as it is beyond description.

There is one other point. In his report the master of the *Dinard* makes special reference to the stewardess. This was Mrs Goodrich, who had been one of the ship's stewardesses on the peace-time runs. Mrs Goodrich is the only woman whose name appears in the list of Dunkirk awards; she received a Mention in Dispatches. There were, however, other women at Dunkirk, notably the nurses of the hospital ships whose record throughout was magnificent.

Signs of strain began to show with some of the ships. The dry, dispassionate accounts of the masters indicate little of the pressure under which individuals worked. Except in the naval vessels, these men were civilians, untrained for war, unequipped for defence. With the hospital ships it was impossible to carry anti-aircraft guns even if they had been available. Inevitably there were failures among their personnel. Men broke down, men collapsed from sheer exhaustion, men went sick with the strain. At Newhaven on this day the crew of the hospital ship *St David* protested against sailing unless the ship were either armed or escorted. The Senior Naval Officer at Newhaven recommended at once that escort should be provided. From the Commander-in-Chief, Portsmouth, came a signal expressing his regret that he had 'nothing left' with which to escort them. Portsmouth had been swept clear of every naval vessel that could make the journey.

Delays, confusion, exhaustion and the malice of the enemy – all played their part upon this day, yet at midnight when the disembarkation totals of the landings were made up 53,823 men had been landed safely in England. Almost 30,000 of these had been lifted from the open, naked beaches. This was the triumph of the little ships.

CHAPTER XII

Friday, May 31st

*. . . a shell burst in between the last boat of them,
and us, we turned back, to go out, but the signaller
that we had on board, and had only been 'out' for
about six weeks, and never been under fire, said
'We've got to go in again' so we went in.*
Report of the Skipper of the cockle-boat *Letitia*

SHORTLY AFTER sunrise on this Friday the wind changed off
Dunkirk. First as a light air, then as a freshening breeze,
it blew in towards the shore, and in the long shallows the surf
rose. It was never a heavy surf, it was never a gale, but it was
more than the exhausted men of the small boats and the
weary soldiers could fight. Boat after boat broached to in the
shallows and grounded. The earlier ones were manhandled
head to sea and pushed off again, but, as the tide began to
fall, one after another they stranded until all along the coast
from the base of the Mole to the beaches of La Panne there
were small craft dry on the drying sand – and in the dunes the
men waited.

As the wind dispersed the haze and the smoke the German
artillery found the range in Dunkirk harbour. More and more
accurately the loading berths were brought under fire. At the
other end of the perimeter at Nieuport German guns, moving
up steadily to the line of the Yser as the morning progressed,
began to shell the La Panne beaches, controlled from an
observation balloon moored beyond the river.

At dusk the final withdrawal of II Corps from the eastern
sector of the perimeter began. It had been decided between
Lord Gort and Admiral Abrial at Dunkirk the previous evening that, with the pressure increasing in the Furnes area, it was
essential now to bring the line back to the old fixed defences
of the Franco-Belgian frontier. These defences had always
been considered as the switch line for this part of the operation, and they were manned by what remained of the French

12th Division. The decision meant that 9 miles of the coast-line would pass out of Allied control – it left only 7½ miles from the frontier to the base of the Mole still in Allied hands – Bray Dunes would be brought under shell-fire as the Germans followed up, and the beach at Malo-les-Bains would itself become vulnerable.

It meant also that Lord Gort's task was done. With that withdrawal and the evacuations of the day the force under his control would be reduced to the point where his orders allowed him no option: the time had almost come for him to hand over the command to a subordinate general.

He made a last visit to Admiral Abrial at Bastion 32 to 'co-ordinate plans for the evacuation of British and French forces'. In the course of this meeting he invited General Fagalde and General de la Laurencie to accompany him when he embarked for England. The invitation was declined. Gort now made a final request to be allowed to remain to the end. The request was refused, and he issued his last operations order. This was followed by his instructions to Major-General the Hon. H. R. L. G. Alexander, who had been appointed to command I Corps, which was to provide the rearguard. The operations order outlined the withdrawal of II Corps on the night of May 31st/June 1st, the perimeter to be abandoned by 11 pm on the 31st. The 50th Division was placed under I Corps from 6 pm to man the frontier defences in conjunction with the French troops already there.

*   *   *

At Dover Admiral Ramsay faced the dire news of the morning: embarkation from the beaches was breaking down, embarkation from the moles had become desperately dangerous. He had no news of the personnel ships that had been sent off through the night – none of them had yet returned to the United Kingdom to discharge. He could not risk the continued accumulation of valuable ships in the narrow waters off the beachhead. Though air activity had diminished the previous day, it would have been suicide to multiply targets, and there were already ten personnel vessels and three hospital carriers in the area and unaccounted for. A little after seven o'clock he suspended sailings.

The position was not actually as bad as it seemed at Dover. In fact, until dawn embarkation had progressed very rapidly. At sun-up, as the wind rose, large areas of the beaches were clear of troops. French soldiers, however, were coming down to the Mole and to the beaches near it in ever-increasing numbers.

Figures with regard to the French troops lifted are difficult to arrive at owing to the different methods of estimating adopted by the British and French authorities. According to Admiral Ramsay 9,271 had already been lifted by midnight on the 30th. During this morning he received a formal instruction from the Admiralty that the policy of the British Government was 'that both British and French troops be given an equal opportunity of being evacuated in British ships and boats'. The impact of this on his calculations must have been heavy. Logically it doubled the number of ship movements necessary to lift off the remaining British troops. It was accepted, as Admiral Ramsay accepted all the demands that were made on him, without comment.

There were two further problems. Through the night heavy enemy mine-laying from the air was reported, and at six o'clock the destroyer *Vimy* sighted a submarine close in to the English coast off the Goodwins and began a hunt.

General Brooke had arrived at Dover at 7.15 am. Writing after the war, he says that 'after a good wash-up, shave and breakfast' he went with General Adam to Dover Castle to see Admiral Ramsay. He had worked with him before at the Imperial Defence College.

'Had we not known each other as we did, it would, I feel certain, have been much more difficult to arrive at the changes in his dispositions that were necessary. He was planning for one more superhuman effort during the coming twenty-four hours and then to close down. I told him that this would not cater for all that still had to be moved, that he would have to endeavour to carry on with the effort for several more days . . . Providence was indeed kind that we should have known each other so well before this critical interview on which so much depended.'[1]

Admiral Ramsay makes no mention of this interview in his dispatch nor is there evidence of any change of plan as a result of it in the course of this morning. The evidence of the dispatch is, in fact, wholly to the contrary. During the formal conference with Staff officers from Lord Gort's headquarters on the Thursday morning, a plan had been agreed which involved the movement of Ramsay's special reserve of small

[1] *The Turn of the Tide* by Arthur Bryant.

craft from Ramsgate to make its main effort in the small hours of Saturday morning if progress justified it. The figures of the early arrivals this morning were excellent and, as the totals were added up, it became apparent that the plan agreed the previous day had now a fair prospect of success. Admiral Ramsay accordingly ordered the dispatch of this last reserve of small craft – it became known as the 'special tows' – at 1 pm from Ramsgate. It sailed on schedule.

Meanwhile Lord Gort, as has already been outlined, had found it possible to amend his original plan. In the course of the afternoon Admiral Ramsay received a signal informing him that the final evacuation of the rearguard of the British Expeditionary Force was postponed to the night of June 1st/2nd; that the troops of II Corps, withdrawing from the Nieuport end of the perimeter, were to fall back on the beaches, that troops already on the beaches at Bray and Malo were to be thinned out by a march westward to the Mole, and that the 'special tows' were to be used to lift II Corps from the La Panne area. At 7.20 pm all ships were informed by signal of the change of plan and 'that the evacuation of the French from Dunkirk and Malo beach would continue from 1st June by both British and French ships'.

*   *   *

These were the policy moves. As always the practical work of lifting went on without cease. It began in disaster, a French disaster. The destroyer *Siroco* had left Dover on the Thursday afternoon at three o'clock by Route Y – no information appears to have reached the French at that time as to the sinkings of the 29th. She embarked 750 men and the flag of the 92nd Regiment in Dunkirk harbour and sailed shortly before midnight. The night was clear and there was brilliant phosphorescence. A little after rounding the Kwinte Buoy enemy aircraft were heard overhead, and Lieutenant-Commander de Toulouse-Lautrec reduced speed to 7 knots in order to cut down the brilliance of the phosphorescence. Before *Siroco* picked up speed again she sighted two torpedo tracks. Avoiding action was taken, but shortly after two more torpedoes were sighted and she was hit in the stern. The watertight bulkheads held and for some time it was hoped that it would be possible to have her towed out. Enemy bombers, however, spotted the plume of steam from a ruptured condenser and the ship was heavily attacked. One bomb exploded the ready ammunition on her deck, two others hit in the vicinity of the bridge, and *Siroco* heeled over and sank.

The Polish destroyer *Blyskawica* was carrying out a patrol to cover this channel. A little before the attack on *Siroco* a torpedo was fired at her; it missed but exploded close to her bows. She at once began a search for the E-boat which had attacked her, and as this was in progress she heard an explosion some distance away and saw a high column of flame. Five minutes later she heard the engines of an E-boat, sighted her and opened fire.

It is important to remember in connection with this and other actions something of the handicaps under which the patrolling destroyers, and indeed all the ships of the movement, worked in the dark hours. The water was full of small craft sailing independently. Some of them were high-speed craft, almost any of them might have been E-boats. In the night darkness it is impossible to judge in the moment of sighting the precise size and shape of a small flat hull close to the water. The difference between an E-boat and a Thames pleasure yacht in the first instant in which she becomes apparent in the darkness – the critical instant in this tip-and-run warfare – is so small as to be negligible. All through the operations the destroyers and the other armed ships were sighting small craft and having to hold their fire until they could identify them. As has been said before, the swept channels were a potential paradise for the E-boat. The marvel is not that they sank ships like *Siroco* but that they sank so very few – that they did not disrupt the whole night sequence of the operation.

Blyskawica lost contact with her E-boat, which retired at high speed. She therefore turned in the direction of the explosion and sighted lights on the water. Steaming towards these, she began to pick up survivors of *Siroco*. The corvette HMS *Widgeon* had also reached the scene of the disaster. Oil fuel made rescue operations very difficult, and the loss of life was heavy.

Meanwhile the French destroyer *Cyclone* was in trouble. She had left Dover the previous evening after a delay due to engine defects. She had been informed of the new central route but, owing to the navigational difficulties connected with it, her commander chose to use the northern approach. Only able to make 16 knots, she reached the stretch between the West Hinder and the Kwinte Buoys at midnight and at twenty minutes past sighted the wake of a torpedo crossing her track.

It missed, but immediately after a second torpedo hit in the extreme bows. The damage was considerable but the watertight bulkheads held, and Captain Portzamparc, first manoeuvring his ship astern and then going slowly ahead at 4 knots, got back to Dover, escorted by two other French vessels, in mid-afternoon.

The loss to the French was heavy – three of their best ships in a little over twelve hours.

While these things were in progress the loadings went on. *Royal Sovereign* was one of the ten personnel vessels unaccounted for at daybreak. At 1.30 am she completed her loading and started back for Margate. On her way she picked up a handful of survivors from *Siroco*. Always her reports are remarkable for their brevity. Of this day Captain Aldis said:

'7.10 am Arrived alongside Margate pier.
8.30 am Anchored off pier.
6.5   pm Hove-up and proceeded towards Dunkirk.
10.10 pm Anchored off Dunkirk.
10.40 pm Ordered by HM ship to La Panne. Hove-up and
          proceeded.
11.15 pm Anchored off La Panne.'

St Helier cleared Dunkirk at dawn and she was in Dover by 7 am. One after the other the 'missing' ships came in.

Simultaneously ships were moving up from distant ports to take the place of those that had been lost in the preceding days. The Southern Railway steamers *Hythe* and *Whitstable* were brought from the reserve at Southampton. They had anchored in the Downs the previous day. Early in the morning the master of *Hythe* was given – there is a faint touch of indignation in his account – 'an army map to navigate on' and orders to proceed to No. 3 beach Dunkirk and take as many troops from small boats as possible. She received her orders at 2.15 am and she was under way at 2.30. One little descriptive phrase in Captain R. W. Morford's account conveys a curious gallantry of atmosphere: 'We passed the sunken *Normannia*, her flags still flying, only her mast and funnels showing. . . .

'The beach conditions,' he continued, 'were bad. Wind on shore force 3 making uncomfortable surf.

'I observed the difficulty the boats were having and as none could leave the beach I decided at 8 am to enter Dunkerque. Approaching the entrance a salvo of shells fell between the pier heads and as we steamed past this position another salvo fell astern. No damage suffered. I swung the ship and berthed on the stone jetty at the root of the east pier and soon the troops started to board carrying badly wounded men on stretchers. Shell-fire continued; shells falling on either side of the pier, one damaging the handrail on the east side abreast of the ship, the pier is about six feet wide at this point. Bombs fell at intervals from aircraft flying in the pall of smoke over the town and fires were observed to start in many places. . . .'

At ten o'clock *Hythe* sailed with 674 men.

'. . . Off the No. 3 beach in addition to many other craft sunk and aground our SS *Lorina* was observed, broken-backed and aground.'

Whitstable followed the *Hythe* an hour and a half later. At 8.20 am she anchored off Bray-Dunes in $2\frac{1}{4}$ fathoms and, on the falling tide, was compelled to move offshore and anchor again. She lay there all through the morning and not until 2.30 pm did a boat come alongside her with troops. Captain N. Baxter, her master, was a little aggrieved at this.

'The method used,' he said, 'for embarking the troops from the beach was that the soldiers rowed off in boats until they were in water deep enough for shallow draught launches to take them in tow. The launches then towed the boats to the ships at anchor, who in turn carried the troops to a home port. . . . It seemed to me very unfair that we merchantmen were kept waiting in a very dangerous position while ships armed to the teeth came in, loaded up, and departed again in an hour or so. . . .'

The criticism is an understandable one, but Captain Baxter was not in a position to see the whole picture. The destroyers were to a large extent using their own boats now in a desperate effort to make good the losses of the morning's tide. There were not enough of the survivors of Thursday's flotillas left to attend to all the ships, and the destroyers – old hands now at this gruelling work – knew where to lie for the small boats and how best to help them; inevitably they loaded more swiftly. But it is none the less possible to sympathise with a big ship lying in that place of bitter danger, to feel with Captain Baxter the frustration of those hours. At 3.30 pm the shellfire, which had been approaching the area with the gradual moving up of German forces during the morning, began to fall near the anchorage, and *Whitstable* hauled out.

This was one part of the pattern. On this day more than on any other the whole pattern comes together. The big ships were having difficulty in loading. What was happening to the little ships? As always, the personal accounts of their commanders paint the clearest picture. The motor yacht *Constant Nymph* worked through the night. Dr Smith wrote:

'About 7.30 am the captain of *Laudania* told me to come on board with all my crew to get some sort of meal . . .

'The whole of us who had been on the beach work then had our first stand-easy since 9.30 pm the day before, and my crew and I had not had anything to eat since 5.30 pm the day before, and nothing to drink since 3.30 pm, and had been continuously employed, as had the two naval ratings who remained on each of the naval rowing boats during the tow across.'

Dr Smith was an 'old hand'. The new hands were coming in rapidly now. At 3 am a convoy of four fast War Department launches – *Swallow*, *Marlborough*, *Haig* and *Wolfe* – left Ramsgate. They went across in line ahead at 18 knots, and despite damage to *Swallow* on the way over (she hit a piece of floating wreckage and lost a blade off one propeller), the whole flotilla was off Dunkirk very early. The other three launches entered the harbour and filled up with troops from a paddle-minesweeper, with the intention of returning direct with them to Ramsgate. Major J. R. L. Hutchins of the Grenadier Guards, who was in command of *Swallow*, considered this something of a waste of effort, and decided that his boat would be of more service ferrying men off the beaches to the larger craft. His account of the situation and of his subsequent work is of very great interest. He saw the circumstances of the army as a soldier, not as a sailor (despite very extensive yachting experience), and it was with a soldier's eye that he described the scene.

'The situation at 6 am was as follows:

'. . . There was a light onshore wind, which unfortunately freshened considerably later, and caused a ground swell which made embarkation more difficult. The tide at 6 am was setting fairly hard to the eastward. There was a heavy bombardment going on on shore, but the beaches were quiet except for occasional shelling and intermittent bombing which did not become heavy until late afternoon. . . .

'There was a Service cutter lying astern of a coaster, and I took it over for use in embarking the troops. . . . Crowds of soldiers immediately rushed into the water and clambered over the stern and quarters of the cutter. I instructed them by megaphone how to distribute their weight, and when I thought enough had been embarked, I went ahead so as to take the cutter out of reach of the remainder; subsequently stopping while hangers-on were pulled inboard. With the British troops the loading was easier, but in all cases the men were very weak and very helpless. . . .

'Each time after loading, I proceeded alongside *Impulsive*, which had a "jumping ladder" rigged. In order to avoid waste of time in shortening in my 80-fathom towline, I passed the end of it to *Impulsive* and requested her to haul the boats alongside, which was done by part of the ship's company doubling along her deck. After the first trip, I borrowed *Impulsive*'s whaler and two more hands, and made a number of trips from shore to ship, towing both boats. There were at this time very few boats working between the shore and the ships, but there were some boats full of troops broached-to on the beach and unable to get off. One motor-boat belonging to a destroyer, one whaler and a small motor-yacht were the only boats working on two or three miles of beach, and in view of the target presented to enemy aircraft by destroyers and other ships waiting to embark troops, I requested *Impulsive* to transmit a signal from me to Admiralty, repeated V-A, Dover, requesting more cutters and power boats to speed up the embarkation. There was some shelling on the beaches, and a good deal of AA fire from the ships as German aircraft appeared overhead at frequent intervals.

'At about midday, *Impulsive* hoisted two black shapes, and when I next came alongside she reported that she had struck some wreckage and damaged her port propeller (this happened, I think, while she was taking avoiding action during an attack by aircraft).

'As *Impulsive* had to proceed for docking, I returned her whaler and the borrowed ratings who had manned my cutter, and proceeded to work with *Winchelsea*. Up to this time *Impulsive* had taken some 400 soldiers, nearly all British. Before she left, I obtained from her fifty gallons of fuel for my boat. . . .

'In the early afternoon the wind lightened and conditions became easier. Observing that there were boats at the davits of a wreck (the Southern Railway Company's SS *Lorina*) close inshore, I borrowed some hands from *Winchelsea* to lower and man them, and ordered an RAF launch which was lying astern of a neighbouring vessel to take over these boats ex the wreck

173

and embark troops.

'Soon after this, on the suggestion of the captain of *Winchelsea* (Lieutenant-Commander W. A. F. Hawkins, RN), I boarded *Keith* to discuss with Rear-Admiral Wake-Walker the possibility of making all remaining troops march to Dunkirk for embarkation. The Admiral concurred in the suggestion and asked me to try to get into touch with the military commanders on shore and to give orders for the troops to march to the piers, in contradiction of previous orders. I landed for this purpose a young yachtsman (whose name I never learnt) who had come off in one of my boatloads and had asked if he might join me, his own craft having been put out of action. He succeeded in his mission.

'By 5.30 pm there were few troops waiting to embark at this part of the beach and the remainder were making their way along the beach to Dunkirk, and at this time *Winchelsea* signalled proposing that this should be the last trip; I concurred. In the last trip only about thirty soldiers embarked in the cutter, and I transferred them to the cabin and engine-room of my boat, handing over the cutter to the RAF launch. During this last half-hour several dive-bombing attacks were made on *Winchelsea*, which appeared to be straddled by the first salvo. A transport further to the eastward was hit about this time, and enemy air activity was intense. *Swallow* was hit by a few small splinters, presumably of anti-aircraft shell, but was undamaged.

'After the last trip inshore I proceeded direct to Ramsgate, and arrived there at about 9.50 pm. The engines of the boat had been running since 3.15 am, and when outside Ramsgate first the port, and a minute later, the starboard engine failed; the port engine was restarted.

'I estimate the total number of troops embarked from the beaches and transferred to HM Ships by *Swallow* as between 700 and 800.'

This admirable account is one of the most vivid that was written of the difficulties of the small boats. It explains something of the problems of the destroyer *Winchelsea*. It shows how off the beaches they arrived independently at the same conclusions as the Command ashore with regard to the necessity to move more men westwards towards the Mole. But it is in the essential colour of the detail that it illumines the extraordinary difficulty of ferrying exhausted men out of shoal water to ships in the deep off-shore.

174

The losses of the morning were made good with extraordinary speed. Long before the 'special tows' started out small craft were moving independently and in groups towards Dunkirk. With them were Thames barges. Amongst the loveliest survivors of the days of sail along the English coast, they were eminently suitable for one aspect of the work they had to do. Broad-beamed, shallow-draught ships, they carry for their sail area the smallest crews known to the sea. In harbour they are squat and chunky, but no one who has seen a line of them moving along the flat levels of the Thames estuary in the evening light, their canvas red against the eastern sky, their great spritsails soaring up like the point of a flame, can deny their beauty. It is the essential, fundamental beauty of craft absolutely suited to their task. On this day a fleet of them went in, many failed to return, but they went gallantly and their work is not least in the records of Dunkirk.

Lady Rosebery, loaded with stores, went over with the big convoy. The report of her journey says abruptly:

'Arrived Dunkirk 10.30 pm. Craft and tug blown up before stores could be unloaded. Ordinary Seaman Cook and J. E. Atkins missing.'

Atkins was a boy of fifteen. Her skipper was W. F. Ellis and her mate A. W. Cook.

Pudge picked up the survivors of the tug and of another barge, and was towed back to Ramsgate. *Glenway* was towed in to the beach with stores and beached on naval instructions. She was to have other adventures. *Duchess* somehow managed to ferry ninety soldiers out to a destroyer. On her last trip to the beach she had to be abandoned. *Ethel Everard* was loaded with small arms ammunition, food, and dynamite. She was sailed on to the beach but was knocked broadside by the surf, and was eventually abandoned and blown up. *Tollesbury*, which had worked in company with her, got most of her stores ashore, and finally came off heavily loaded with men. *Barbara Jean*, *Aidie* and *Doris* were all run ashore and abandoned. It was the only way to make certain that dumps of water, of food and – most vital of all – of ammunition, now dangerously low all along the line of the perimeter, should be got ashore. To discharge in the confines of the harbour was impossible; even to discharge on the beach was fraught with the very gravest difficulty and danger. But these barges took the ground upright. They were built to lie on the barge beds of the Thames foreshore, of the estuary banks, of a hundred creeks and mudflats in Essex; and, grounded, they became dumps that for a considerable proportion of the tide were available to working parties from the dunes. They and the Thames dumb barges and the lighters were sacrificed, but their sacrifice was by no means in vain.

Spurgeon was bombed on the passage over and damaged by splinters from a near miss. *Beatrice Maud* crossed and was anchored off the beaches. *Ena* was also anchored in deep water. The subsequent history of these two ships and of *Glenway* was remarkable, for *Ena* at the end of the evacuation came home by herself – she was found stranded on the Sandwich Flats practically undamaged and quite empty. *Beatrice Maud*'s career was almost more remarkable still, for on June 5th she was picked up in mid-Channel, long after the operation was over, with 260 men on board. *Glenway* was boarded by 190 soldiers on Malo beach, refloated, and on their courage and resource brought half-way across the Channel under sail. Here a tug found her and towed her to safety. *Lark* was abandoned on the beach. The motor barge *Seine*, under the orders of Lieutenant-Commander Filleul, on this day brought back 352 and on two subsequent trips brought back roughly the same number each time.

The tugs worked on throughout the day carrying out an almost endless variety of tasks. *Crested Cock* took over a lighter loaded with fresh water and food, together with an Army working party. Off the beaches she transferred the troops to a lighter and landed them. She was then ordered to the assistance of the destroyer *Basilisk*, which, owing to damage to one propeller, was unable to turn in the narrow channel. She worked *Basilisk* round and then, covered by the destroyer's guns past the danger area of Gravelines, returned to Dover.

At 5 am *Ocean Cock*, her sister ship, left with six motor-boats from Dover, reaching Dunkirk beach about 1 pm. Her master, A. V. Mastin, slipped his tow off the beaches and steamed back to Dover for orders. Towage, salvage – it was all the same to them.

In the same convoy the *Sun VII* was sent off with five RAF motor-boats in tow (these were tenders from the RAF station at Calshot). As a small indication of the difficulties of even a theoretically simple operation like this, G. Cawsey, her master, said laconically:

'Six times the boats broke adrift, and were picked up again, and eventually arrived at destination.'

Under command of Pilot Officer C. Collings they did excellent work on the beaches, ferrying troops out to deeper-draught ships. Two of them were lost in the course of the work – ST 254 and AMC 3. ST 254 became overcrowded and was caught by the swell, broached to and sank. AMC 3 damaged her propellers on the bottom and fetched up on the beach. But between them the launches rescued at least 500 men on this day, and the three remaining returned safely to Dover with the crews of the lost boats.

Sun XI left Dover at approximately ten o'clock with a barge loaded with stores and cans of water, with orders to beach it two miles east of the pier-heads. She was at Dunkirk by 5.30 pm. The account of her master, J. R. Lukes, is human in spite of its terse officialese.

'Got barge alongside and steamed in to 2 fathoms, a small motor-boat took barge and beached her. Jerry bombing beach and ships anchored off. Left Dunkirk 6 pm. 7 pm bombed by Jerry, two incendiary close to tug, one drifter went up. Tug *Contest* picked up crew. 7.30 pm passed *Sun XV, VIII* and *IV* going in, sorry for them, glad to get out.'

The French small craft were also coming into action. Forty-eight French vessels from destroyers to fishing boats worked the beaches and the harbour this day. The fishing boat *Triomphant* crossed under sail, her motor having broken down at Dover, and returned, still under sail, carrying thirty-three men.

In some ways, however, the most remarkable crossing of this morning was that of the hospital ship *St David*. It is remarkable not for any particular achievement but for the simple fact that it was made, for it was *St David* which had protested the previous evening against any further crossing without escort. In the signals and messages concerning this incident there is demonstrated a very genuine human sympathy on the part of the naval authorities, for the trouble with the men of the *St David* and their captain was sheer exhaustion. From the very beginning of the Flanders campaign the ship had been carrying wounded. As the flow increased with the increasing battle, her work became heavier but, as the enemy reached through to the coast, it became, like that of her sisters, almost intolerably difficult. They were supposed to be protected, these hospital carriers – protected by custom, protected by international law, protected by common decency. Now they suffered not only the attacks of high-flying aircraft, which possibly could not identify them, not only night shelling and the casual hostilities of the thick weather, but deliberate attack, deliberately pressed home, deliberately repeated. Yet it was not in reality these attacks which caused the momentary hesitation on the part of *St David*; it was the simple physical exhaustion of her people. Captain Joy at midday on the 30th was given a medical certificate to say that he was not fit to proceed to sea; early in the afternoon he collapsed completely. The second engineer disappeared from the ship and was found suffering from loss of memory. Yet at nine o'clock this Friday morning the ship sailed again – one night's rest was all that was necessary. She sailed again, unarmed and unescorted!

She was not alone in her difficulties. *St Julien*'s crew was also suffering from strain. To stiffen it, and to assist these inexpressibly weary men, additional personnel were put aboard. *St Julien* left very early in the morning.

'We proceeded,' said Captain L. T. Richardson, her master, 'using a different channel. By this time the crew were getting shaky and we arrived alongside at 8.58, and began loading under shell-fire (assisted by crew), shells falling about 50 feet away but no bombing.

'When we had completed our loading we left. . . . During the whole of this time the largest Red Cross flag was kept flying, and, no doubt about it, these were deliberate attacks on hospital carriers . . .'

The work of these tired men was supplemented by others. *Lady of Mann*, though not a hospital carrier, was sent over in the morning to embark wounded from the French hospitals. Berthing about 1.30 pm, she took on board a heavy load of casualties, many of them stretcher cases, together with a certain number of unwounded men. During this time she was constantly shelled and bombed. She had seven holes in the starboard bow close to the water-line, three of her lifeboats were damaged by splinters, and from her bridge they saw men killed by shellfire on the decking of the Mole 30 yards ahead of them. She left about 5 pm for Folkestone.

As has been described, the destroyers were picking up men off the beaches more rapidly than some of the personnel vessels. They were also, in spite of the increasingly accurate shelling, still picking up from the Mole. As the afternoon wore on the numbers increased. Signalling was much more satisfactory now. The large party of naval signalmen had accelerated ship-to-shore communications, and HMS *Wolsey* lay

throughout the day at anchor acting as wireless link with
Dover.

*   *   *

On the beaches the situation was improving. The wind had
diminished in the course of the afternoon, the surf had died
down. The makeshift piers of the Royal Engineers were paying
magnificent dividends, though they came in from time to time
for heavy air attack. New small craft were appearing everywhere. The contrasts between the various types of boat are
always one of the more extraordinary features of Dunkirk. In
the late afternoon there reached the beaches a 'flotilla' that
stood in the sharpest possible contrast to the swift, slender
RAF launches that had crossed at dawn. A little after ten
o'clock six cockle-boats sailed from Leigh-on-Sea, the familiar
old cutter-rigged cockle-boats of the estuary of the Thames
with their splendid names – *Renown, Reliance, Resolute, Defender, Endeavour* and *Letitia*. Off the Nore lightship it was
decided that the more powerful boats should take the weaker
in tow and, the little convoy having re-formed, they made for
Margate. Passing Margate pier, they received orders to shape
a course straight for Dunkirk, and off the Foreland they saw
the long line of that much-travelled sea road. By the evening
they were off Gravelines and at 7 pm they were attacked by
some forty German bombers. Ziz-zagging wildly, they escaped
the bombs and, moving independently, reached Dunkirk. As
the swell was too heavy for them to go in to the beach, they
began to ferry off troops from the outer end of the Mole. They
were working in conjunction with HM Skoot *Tilly* and swiftly
filled her. A. J. Dench, *Letitia*'s skipper, said:

'On going in for the third time, a shell burst in between the
last boat of them, and us, we turned back, to go out, but the
signaller that we had on board, and had only been "out" for
about six weeks, and never been under fire, said "We've got
to go in again" so we went in. . . .'

Letitia began the voyage home in tow of a trawler.

'Soon we saw another boat coming up behind us. It was the
Renown, and yelling that they had engine trouble, they made
fast to our stern and we towed them, about 3½ fathoms of rope
being the distance behind us. That was at 1.15 am, and tired
out, the engineer and seaman and signaller went to turn in,
as our work seemed nearly done. We were congratulating ourselves – when at about 1.50 a terrible explosion took place, and

179

a hail of wood splinters came down on our deck. In the pitch dark you could see nothing, and after the explosion we heard nothing. And we could do nothing, except pull in the tow-rope which was just as we passed it to the *Renown* about three-quarters of an hour before, but not a sign of *Renown*. . . .'

The story of the little ships and of the big at Dunkirk is underscored with many tragedies, but there is in this un-lettered, unadorned narrative a curious poignancy. These were fishing boats – only the day before they had been busy at their quiet task. They knew nothing of war; they went not to fight but to save. They had done their work, and now, suddenly, on the way home there came annihilation. It was a small tragedy in the great disasters of these days, yet it has in it a deep and humble bitterness. The crew of *Renown* consisted of W. H. Noakes, skipper; L. V. Osborne, mate; and F. W. Osborne, engineer. The tragedy was heavy, but these six cockle-boats between them rescued 1,000 men.

The skoot *Tilly* did excellent work in this period. The skoots, in fact, were one of the most successful pieces of previ-sion in the whole Dunkirk operation. Small, squat-looking ships, with their Diesel engines astern and living quarters for their Dutch captains and their families next to the engines, they were admirably suited to this work, for they were built for the coasts of the lowland sea. Throughout the operation until the very last night they worked strenuously and well. *Aegir*, for example, made six trips; *Reiger* made five. *Bornrif, Gorecht, Doggersbank, Java, Jutland, Pascholl, Besta, Twente, Princess Juliana, Hilda* – the names crop up endlessly. They were lucky ships too; only one was lost in the whole course of the opera-tions (*Horst*, which had to be abandoned after damage from a near miss) but a number of the others were damaged in varying degrees.

From Ramsgate about the same time went four hopper barges. By no means can a hopper barge be considered as a passenger-vessel. They are large, self-propelled steel barges, with a sludge hold amidships built to take the spoil of dredgers and capable of being opened to the sea. *Foremost 101*, the 'flagship' of the little flotilla, had been damaged already by a near miss and her sludge hold was full of water. Her maximum speed was about five knots.

Cadets of the RASC Officer Production Centre had been ordered to Ramsgate to take part in the defence of the harbour, and from this little force, some of whom were cleaning Bren guns and other weapons that had been brought back from France, twelve men asked permission to cross with the ships as gunners. They were told that no authority could be given, that if they went they might have to stay, and the officer who informed them ended his warning with the words, 'The school can accept no responsibility. Good luck!' The four naval officers who were in command of the hopper barges selected parties of three, and a little after ten o'clock the flotilla sailed. It reached Dunkirk in the middle of the afternoon, and motor-boats which had been towed were sent in to the beaches. For six hours the work went on, load after load of men being brought out. The hoppers were shelled and bombed during this time, and their improvised armament went into action against low-flying aircraft, but by 10 pm they were loaded. *Foremost 101*, the leader, started for home; her lifeboats were waterlogged and one of her motor-boats had to be left behind. In another of the hoppers the RASC gun crew was actually credited with a German plane. *Foremost 101*, after heading direct for Calais and being shouldered off by the watchful destroyers, reached Ramsgate safely with 400 British, Belgian and French troops. The rest of the little flotilla acquitted itself equally well.

From Ramsgate sailed three trawlers – *Kestrel, Tankerton Towers* and *Provider*. Walter W. Cribbens, skipper of *Kestrel*, paid an excellent tribute to the destroyers. Close to Dunkirk they were shelled by enemy batteries commanding the south channel. At once a destroyer covered them with a smoke screen and engaged the batteries with her guns.

'The destroyer went ahead, and as he passed us, we got a cheery wave from the officers on the bridge, and most of the crew. It was the cool efficiency with which those chaps were doing their job that drew the admiration of myself and crew. Their action made our work easier, and we filled up with troops in no time.'

Jack Hannaford, skipper of the *Tankerton Towers*, said in his report:

'During the afternoon of May 31st, after taking aboard some boatloads of soldiers, we decided to steam inshore to pick up some more, when we came across a motor-yacht disabled. This we took in tow. After about an hour her tow-rope fouled our propeller, which we could not free. I knew we should be seen by a patrol ship at some or other, so we went on with our work, getting as many soldiers aboard, which at this time proved a mixed lot, British and French. Every available space aboard was taken up by a soldier, cabin, fish hold, wheelhouse, decks, even in the engine-room. Some time in the evening, I cannot give the correct time, a patrol ship did arrive, and took us in tow.

'It has since occurred to me that no one thought of the predicament we were in, and the only concern of everyone was to get the troops aboard. In between times we were kept amused by the way our men of the navy were shooting down the dive-bombers, just like rooks.'

The Belgian fishing vessels were working in increasing numbers. *Lydie Suzanne* crossed again and brought back 105 men; *Zwaluw* brought back 58, *Cor Jesu* brought back 274, *Jonge Jan* 270, and the A.5. 234.

About the same time the ex-naval steam pinnace *Minotaur*, which had been converted to serve as a Sea Scout training craft, left Ramsgate. Normally she moored at Mortlake, ten miles above the London bridges. With a Scout crew she was brought down to Southend. Then, with a Rover Scout as engineer, she carried on to Ramsgate, took on stores and fuel, and, picking up two naval ratings, made her crossing. Her skipper, Mr T. Towndrow, Scout-master of the 1st Mortlake Sea Scouts, gives an interesting sidelight on the flow of rumour and what the lower deck calls 'buzzes' at Ramsgate during this time.

'Of the whole of our operations this six hours' crossing was the worst as we had nothing to do but contemplate the job ahead of us and had been foolish enough to listen to the idle talk of naval ratings in Ramsgate before we left, who assured us that very few of the boats that had gone across had come back and that, now that Jerry had captured the harbour and had mounted machine-guns covering the beaches, our chances of coming through were very slender indeed. Of course, such was not the position. The whole of Dunkirk was still very much in our hands, but we did not know this.'

She reached the beaches safely, and proceeded to ferry out troops and tow out loaded small boats to transports lying off the beach. She was working in a French area and all her troops were French soldiers, and Mr Towndrow said:

'We were astonished at the way they refused to discard any of their gear. We got some out of the water who still had their full uniforms on complete with blankets in a roll on their backs. It often required all the strength we had got to haul them on board.'

Pickford's fleet was carrying on. *Bat* returned for the second time. The report on her work said:

'. . . On this occasion they got on board in small boats about 100 men. These they brought safely back to England, having been without sleep for ninety-two hours, and the engines having been running continuously all the time.'

Bee reached Dunkirk on the 31st and

'. . . after lying three miles off the shore all one night, was placed alongshore and took 360 British troops aboard. These were later transferred to a tug. . . .'

Hound arrived there about six o'clock

'. . . and got alongside what remained of one of the little piers and took aboard about 100 French and Belgians.'

M.F.H. also crossed.

'Upon her arrival at Dunkirk there were about eighty German raiders overhead dropping bombs on the beach 40 feet away. Troops were picked up and disembarked on to a larger vessel. They then proceeded to the Mole, and took on board about 140 troops "including a colonel" and returned to England with them.'

The lifeboats were still working, both those manned by their own crews and those manned by naval parties. *Prudential*, the Ramsgate lifeboat, which had lifted superbly all through Thursday, continued throughout Friday and Friday night at the work of ferrying until she had taken more than 2,000 troops off the beach either by herself or in small craft which she towed off.

In the sector of the beach where the Margate lifeboat, *Lord Southborough*, worked, all the small craft from destroyers and other ships were lost in the early morning strandings, and as the beach in that area made it quite impossible for her to run herself aground to take men off, she decided to return. Coxswain Parker estimates that he transferred not less than 500 men to the destroyer *Icarus*.

The Navy does not pass compliments easily, but there is a letter from Lieutenant-Commander E. G. Roper of HMS *Icarus*, the destroyer with which *Lord Southborough* did most of her work, which reads:

'On behalf of every officer and man on this ship I should like to express to you our unbounded admiration of the magnificent behaviour of the crew of the lifeboat *Lord Southborough* during the recent evacuation from Dunkirk.

The manner in which, with no thought of rest, they brought off load after load of soldiers under continuous shelling, bombing and aerial machine-gun fire will be an inspiration to us all as long as we live. We are proud to be the fellow countrymen of such men.'

Charles Cooper Henderson, the Dungeness lifeboat, which worked this day with her sisters off the beaches, was found broken down with four naval ratings on board in the small hours of June 1st off Margate, and was brought in by Margate lifeboatmen. But on the whole the RNLI was fortunate in this period. The first boat to be seriously damaged was the *Thomas Kirk Wright*, which, as the result of a near miss, came back with 12 inches of water in her hold and one of the engines burnt out. The E.M.E.D. failed to return from her passage on June 1st and was believed lost, but reappeared on June 3rd. The RNVR lieutenant in command of her had been killed and her propeller was fouled by rope, but the servicing party at Dover cleared the trouble and got her back to Dunkirk. Many of the boats were stranded for varying periods. Sub-Lieutenant S. C. Dickinson, who was the Institute's inspector in Ireland, for example, found the *Mary Scott* on the beaches and worked her until she broke down and had to be abandoned again. She was, however, subsequently salved. At one time on June 1st three lifeboats were ashore but all eventually returned. The *Jane Holland* on June 2nd was hit forward by a French motor-boat and then aft by a British torpedo-boat and was abandoned, but came home, being found on June 6th drifting water-logged in the Channel. Only the *Viscountess Wakefield* of Hythe was completely lost. No news was received of her after her departure from Dover, and she disappeared without trace.

In the early afternoon one of the most remarkable of all the ships that took part in this most remarkable of all sea movements left Ramsgate – the Thames fire-float *Massey Shaw*. She was a floating fire-engine of the London Fire Brigade, built for short trips between the fire piers of the harbour areas of London River and the warehouses of the river bank or the shipping anchored off them. A shallow-draught vessel, built to take the mud easily, she was little more than a casing for gigantic pumps. She was sent to Ramsgate primarily in the hope that she might be of some service in fighting the huge fires in Dunkirk, but before she reached, for the first time in her career, the open waters of the Channel it was obvious that no good purpose could be served in attempting to fight the

Dunkirk flames.

At two o'clock this afternoon, when everything that could float and move was being sent across to make the floating bridge to England, the *Massey Shaw*, with her crew of firemen on board, was ordered out. She reached Dunkirk at seven o'clock. The harbour was full of personnel ships and her services were not required there, so she moved up the beaches three miles to the eastward of the Mole and, under Sub-Officer A. J. May, her crew of twelve London firemen worked to get men off the sands.

The beaches here were crowded now, in part with the increasing numbers of French who were coming down, in part with men who had moved westward as the shelling increased at La Panne. The farther end of the La Panne beaches was now untenable. Ships straddled over and over again by salvoes from the shore had been forced to move down towards the frontier line, but evacuation never wholly ceased and it was to build up at great speed again at nightfall.

With the increase in artillery fire there was an increase in air activity, and in the late afternoon and early evening there were three major attacks on the ships and the beaches. The RAF lost twenty-eight aircraft this day in the course of eight patrols. It claimed thirty-eight enemy aircraft destroyed, but that total must be considerably reduced in the light of subsequent examination of German records.

The most important share of the air effort this day was, however, a series of British attacks which was launched in the early evening. The withdrawals during the day had weakened resistance on the perimeter line from the frontier to Nieuport. Army Group B was moving up additional troops to take advantage of the situation. The possibility of a breakthrough before the retirement was complete was considerable, and six Albacores of the Fleet Air Arm and eighteen Blenheims bombed the enemy in Nieuport itself and the concentrations that were forming across the river. Bomber Command made other raids on enemy columns moving in from the east and the south, and no German ground attack developed until after the final abandonment of the perimeter line.

*   *   *

At dusk the 'special tows' closed the beaches. As they left Ramsgate they had made a continuous stream of ships almost 5 miles in length.

Lord Gort watched that procession of little ships move in from the minesweeper HMS *Hebe*. At noon *Hebe* had been forced to withdraw from La Panne by heavy shellfire. HMS *Keith*, which was the latest of Admiral Wake-Walker's flagships, made efforts to locate the batteries responsible. The German artillery called for support from their air, and *Keith* became the special target of numerous German bombers. She managed to avoid damage, but the respite she had secured was temporary only. The shelling increased in the late afternoon, and HMS *Vivacious* was hit twice off Bray and had a number of men killed and wounded.

It was during this shelling that Lord Gort was taken out to *Hebe*. In addition to the plans made by Admiral Wake-Walker Dover had sent over four MTBs and MA/SBs for the Headquarters party. A misunderstanding, however, arose over these ships. The remainder of the Headquarters staff was taken aboard *Keith*. *Hebe* continued to pick up men. At 6 pm GHQ of the British Expeditionary Force closed down and the end of a chapter in British history was recorded. In Gort's own cool words:

'. . . by this time there had been a general thinning out of the whole force, and I felt that, however the situation might develop, valuable cadres had been withdrawn which would enable the fighting units of the BEF to be quickly reformed at home.'

There is here a note of essential optimism in the very midst of disaster.

As Lord Gort was ferried out to *Hebe*, General Alexander took over the command. His first act was to consult with Admiral Abrial. At Bastion 32 he was informed that the French would hold 'from Gravelines to Bergues'. (It is difficult to understand this as Gravelines had passed out of French hands at the very beginning of the evacuation. Since the night of the 27th the western limit of the perimeter had been the old Mardyck Canal.) Alexander himself was to command a mixed French/British corps from Bergues along the canal to Les Moëres and through to the sea. Admiral Abrial proposed to maintain this perimeter 'till all the troops were embarked'. General Alexander said at once that in his view the plan did not take account of the realities of the situation, which he believed was deteriorating rapidly both at sea and on land.

A further element of the plan was a withdrawal to a line Bergues-Uxem-Ghyvelde. General Alexander believed that this would bring the German artillery so close in that it would not be possible to hold the perimeter after midnight 1st/2nd and that evacuation should be completed by dawn of the 2nd.

It is possible that had General Alexander been fully informed of the number of French troops available for defence he would have modified this opinion. The whole question of the number of French troops in the area is difficult to analyse at all times. On May 31st Admiral Ramsay's dispatch says:

'No firm information could be obtained from the French as regards:
   (i) The number of French troops to be evacuated.
  (ii) The nature and extent of French seaborne transport.
 (iii) The French military plan for the defence of the perimeter and the final withdrawal of French troops.'

In the event a line was held until June 3rd.

Meanwhile, through all these uncertainties the evacuation proceeded – French and British alike. From La Panne alone 5,000 men were lifted before midnight in a tremendous effort to get the beaches clear before the German follow-up came through. It succeeded. When in the small hours Lord Gort finally left for England in MA/SB6 the triumph of Dunkirk was assured. 68,014 men were landed in England by midnight – 23,000 of them from the beaches, the remainder from the harbour (of these over 15,000 were French). By dawn of June 1st Operation 'Dynamo' had landed 200,000 British, French and Belgian troops safely in Britain.

CHAPTER XIII

Saturday, June 1st

He that outlives this day, and comes safe home,
Will stand a tip-toe when this day is nam'd. . . .
                    SHAKESPEARE, *Henry V*

SWIFTLY THE drama of Dunkirk moved to its climax on June 1st. In the morning hours the Royal Navy was to suffer losses as heavy and as significant as those of some of the great sea battles of the past. There is in one of the accounts of the opening of this disaster a phrase that establishes its continuity with history, that links it irrevocably with tradition.

'We were setting our topsail to carry out this operation when a large number of German planes appeared overhead and immediately started bombing and machine-gunning us.'

This was the beginning of the heaviest air attack of the operation. Skipper H. Miller of the barge *Royalty* had been ordered to beach his ship opposite the first houses of Malo-les-Bains. 'We were setting our topsail' when the whole weight of two air fleets was unleashed for the second time against the crowded anchorage.

Up to this moment the embarkations of the first hours of the day had achieved new records. The paddle-minesweeper *Whippingham* had started loading about ten o'clock the previous evening under shellfire. By 1.30 am she estimated that she had loaded 2,700 men and, with her sponsons only about twelve inches above the water, she cast off from the Mole, worked her way out between the wrecks that now more thickly than ever studded the narrow channel, and got clear. Her commander, Lieutenant Eric Reed, RNR, says that her passage back was slow because she was 'very much over-loaded'. Again this is a classic example of understatement.

Royal Sovereign had been picking up off La Panne. She sailed at 2.30 am with a heavy load, and her master (usually very spare of words) wrote that the beach had come under 'terrific bombarding and shelling'.

One of the best accounts of the abandonment of La Panne is that of Captain R. P. Pim, RNVR, formerly Assistant Secretary to the Ministry of Home Affairs in the Government of Northern Island and at this time keeper of Winston Churchill's Map Room. Captain Pim had been on leave at the beginning of the evacuation. He volunteered and crossed with one of the tows. The report of his work says:

'By midnight all the troops which he could find were embarked and placed in ships which sailed for England. Just before midnight he went along some of the beaches to look for stragglers and was told by a staff officer that no more troops would embark from those beaches, but that it was anticipated that the beaches would be shelled and would probably be in German hands the following day. This was a correct forecast.

'He estimated that from the pontoons and beaches about 5,000 were embarked. He was impressed by the kindness that was shown to the tired soldiery in the various ships in which they were embarked and also by the fact that the military chaplains were always among the last of their respective parties to leave the beach.

'Anchorage had to be shifted during the night as shells meant for the beaches were ricocheting over HMS *Hilda* [which had towed them over] . . .'

Another tow of small craft was operating nearer to Malo-les-Bains.

The Belgian fishing boats were over again in this period. The *Anna Marguerite* lifted 120 French soldiers and on her return journey picked up thirty survivors of a French cargo ship which had been sunk by a magnetic mine. The *Georges Edouard*, which was commanded by a Merchant Marine officer, picked up nearly 500 men this day and, with an earlier trip, carried a total altogether of 1,007. The *Guido Gazelle* on two trips carried 403.

The destroyers *Icarus*, *Vanquisher* and *Windsor* carried 3,000 men between them. Despite the difficulties of the beaches the loads throughout were tremendously heavy. Minesweepers, Dutch skoots, trawlers, drifters, paddle-steamers – they all carried enormous numbers of men.

The sun rose and still they loaded. Through this night the Germans had bombed the harbour area intermittently, using brilliant flares. Now, with the sun, the raids redoubled. At five o'clock heavy bombing attacks developed over the whole area from La Panne to Dunkirk, and fighters began to make almost incessant strafing runs along the beaches. The first RAF patrol had been ordered to be over the area soon after 5 am. It was heavily engaged on arrival. A second patrol followed at 6 am and again met exceptionally strong opposition. Thereafter there was a gap until nine o'clock, and in this gap the Luftwaffe pounced.

The barge *Royalty*, as has been recorded, set her topsail under fire and ran herself ashore. She was loaded with food, water, and ammunition, and her job was to beach herself as high up the sands as possible so that the troops could unload her as the tide turned. Having carried out his operation immaculately, Skipper Miller rowed out to the tug *Cervia*, which had towed him across. On the way he picked up a launch, with twenty-five soldiers on board, that had broken down. When he joined her *Cervia* closed the barge *Tollesbury*, which had picked up 180 men.

'At 7.20 am,' said W. H. Simmons, *Cervia*'s master, 'we dropped our anchor and watched the barge. Soldiers began to run down the beach towards her, but guns started to bang away on the outskirts of Dunkirk, and an air-raid siren blew and the soldiers went back to shelter.'

The wail of that siren ushered in the attack which, had it been made earlier, might have been decisive in the history of Dunkirk. It is possible that this devastating raid was synchronised with the Germans' first assault of the day on the perimeter line. At 7.20 am a very heavy force of enemy bombers – predominantly Junkers 87 dive-bombers, but with the support of twin-engined Junkers 88s, elaborately escorted by fighters – made its appearance. There were no Allied aircraft in the air at the time, there was no escort for the ships in that narrow channel of destruction. The destroyers themselves, fighting against attack through almost every hour of the past days, were desperately short of ammunition. Many of them had had no time to re-ammunition in the brief spells at Dover. There was only time to discharge their troops, to take on fresh oil, to slip and put to sea again. *Keith*, after fighting all the previous day, had thirty rounds of AA ammunition left.

At once the attacks developed on the nearest ships. There is an appalling grandeur in that scene. From behind the beaches, from the harbour, from those ships whose guns could still answer the challenge of the air, the sky was filled with the pock-marks of bursting shells, with the thin trails of tracer bullets, with the whistle and roar of projectiles. Below the sea was flecked with small plumes as the splinters of the shells sang down into the water, between them lifted the monstrous, swirling fountains of the bombs.

Keith was heavily attacked by the first wave. Twisting, turning, at the utmost speed that she could manage in the narrow waters of the roadstead, she eluded the bombs. The account by the master of *Cervia* of these moments – cool, almost dour in its absence of emotion – conveys a graphic picture.

'A British destroyer outside of us began to fire at the enemy planes and bombs began to fall near her as she steamed about. At full speed with her helm hard to port nine bombs fell in a line in the water, along her starboard side, and they exploded under water, heeling the destroyer over on her beam ends, but she was righted again and a sloop joined in the gunfire, also shore batteries, and as the raiders made off over towards the land they machine-gunned us and we returned the fire with our Lewis gun.'

To avoid being rammed *Cervia* weighed anchor and got under way. She made towards the damaged *Keith* but, as she was doing so, a further air attack took place and the destroyer was again straddled by a stick of bombs. The tug *St Abbs* and a sloop were also going to the help of *Keith*, so *Cervia* turned round and picked up a motor-boat full of soldiers.

Actually *Keith* was damaged in the first attack, though she did not suffer a direct hit. A near miss jammed her rudder, and she turned in small circles for some time. In the second attack she was hit almost at once down her after-funnel and very near misses damaged her side severely. She was moving at high speed and turning at the moment of impact, and she at once listed heavily to port. Enormous clouds of steam came up through the after-funnel and boiler-room casings. Still turning, she lost speed rapidly as the steam went, and in a little her commander was compelled to bring his ship to anchor. Captain E. L. Berthon (he had won his DSC at Zeebrugge during the great attack on St George's Day, 1918) had taken the place of Captain D. J. R. Simson, Captain (D) of the 19th Flotilla, who had been killed at Boulogne on May 24th. By the time the anchor took hold *Keith* was listing almost 20 degrees to port and had no more than two feet of freeboard on that side. At this point, however, she seemed to steady up and sank no farther for the time being.

Close to her the Fleet minesweeper *Skipjack* was hit. She

had been embarking troops from Malo beach for some hours. Because of the incessant bombing and machine-gun fire most of the 275 men whom she had picked up were under cover below deck. The ship sank instantly, and only a very small handful of survivors reached the boats which went to her rescue.

The second destroyer, HMS *Ivanhoe*, was lying disabled west of the harbour. Badly damaged, she was taken in tow by the tug *Persia*. Within a few minutes fresh attacks took place, and a bomb, falling between *Persia* and the destroyer, cut the tow rope. Indefatigably the master of *Persia*, H. Aldrich, passed the tow again and a second time she moved off.

Though *Keith* was still afloat, she was clearly out of action. Admiral Wake-Walker, with his staff, disembarked into MTB 102, which had closed the destroyer immediately after she was damaged the second time, and headed down the roadstead to call up tugs. But the tugs had already turned towards the battered ship – the Admiralty tug *St Abbs*, the tug *Vincia* and the tug *Cervia*. Captain Pim, in HM Skoot *Hilda*, was also making his best speed towards the wreck. Before they could reach her she was hit in a third attack. This time the bombs dropped under the bridge, and she heeled right over and sank almost instantly. *Hilda* picked up fifty survivors from the water, including Brigadier Greenslade, the Deputy Quarter-master General, and other staff officers. The tug *Vincia* picked up 108 officers and ratings, including staff officers from both British and French headquarters, and *St Abbs*, which closed her just before she sank, took off Captain Berthon and more than 100 survivors.

All the while there was no cessation in the fury of the Luftwaffe's attack. Farther down the water the dive-bombers were peeling off at 10,000 feet and coming down with a terrifying snarl of their motors to within a few hundred feet of the water. While the work of rescue was in progress the destroyer *Basilisk*, which had been held ready to give supporting fire in the event of the enemy attack along the beach, was bombed. *St Abbs*, under the orders of Captain Berthon, turned towards the spot to rescue survivors. Aircraft were flying overhead continuously and a Junkers 88, at high level, let go a single bomb. By a thousand to one chance it hit the hurrying tug amidships. She disintegrated and sank, leaving Captain Berthon and the comparatively small number of men who now survived, a second time in the water.

Shortly after, the destroyer *Whitehall* on her first trip – she made two trips this day – found the still-floating hulk of HMS *Basilisk* and sank it. She was herself dive-bombed and suffered damage from near misses. HMS *Worcester* was also damaged by bombing and was to be in collision as she struggled back to Dover.

The gunboat *Mosquito*, which had done magnificent work now for many days, was hit in the same period, badly damaged, set on fire, and had to be abandoned. The Fleet minesweeper *Salamander* was damaged and tugs were sent in search of her. There were other naval casualties, other ships damaged in this period. Admiral Wake-Walker, hurrying to Dunkirk itself in the MTB which had picked him up, was dive-bombed but not hit. All up and down the long, narrow channel of the roadstead there was havoc and the thunder of the bombs. All up and down the roadstead were the long and lamentable pools of oil which marked the new ship graves; and with them, floating on the tide, was the pitiful wreckage of smashed boats and empty rafts, of battered furnishings and splintered planks.

Within little more than an hour the Royal Navy had lost three destroyers, a Fleet minesweeper and a gunboat, and four destroyers had been damaged.

Nor was this the end of disaster. At 1 pm the French destroyer *Foudroyant*, the last surviving ship of the 2nd Destroyer Flotilla, came in through Route X. Four miles from the West Mole she was 'submerged in a cloud of Stukas', according to a French account. The channel at that point was narrow and manoeuvring was impossible. In less than a minute she was hit by a number of bombs and capsized instantly. Small craft and the minesweeper *Sainte-Bernadette-de-Lourdes*, herself damaged by splinters from near misses and listing heavily, picked up her survivors.

The naval losses were desperately serious but the personnel ships suffered in the same period almost equally heavy loss. *Prague*, coming in by Route X, reached Dunkirk at the very height of the first attacks. Her armament was one Lewis gun and one Bren gun, but she closed the entrance and went inside. She berthed at the western side of the outer harbour, close outside the locks, and loaded about 3,000 French troops. On the return voyage towards the Downs the ship was shelled off Gravelines and dive-bombed off No. 5 buoy. Although not actually hit on either occasion, she suffered severe internal damage and the starboard engine was put out of action. Captain Baxter reported:

'From the time of the explosion (10.25) the ship was kept going ahead as fast as it was possible to do on the port engine which was the only one left in service, craft in the vicinity were warned and several naval auxiliaries agreed to stand by us and the ship slowly progressed homewards. It was evident, however, that the water was gaining, and such measures as getting as many troops as possible forward to ease the weight on the after part of the ship were giving only temporary respite, so I decided to try to transfer the troops while the ship was still under way so as to lose as little time as possible. HM Destroyer *Shikari* and a sloop and paddle minesweeper whose names I was unable to obtain came alongside in turn and very skilfully managed to transfer all except a handful of troops while the ship was steaming as fast as possible towards the Downs. . . .'

HMS *Shikari* transferred under way 500 men. She then called the *Queen of Thanet* to come alongside in her turn. Commander S. P. Herival, RNVR, asked how many troops were left on board and was told 2,000. He embarked most of these – remember both ships were moving at the best speed *Prague* could make all the time – and took them in to Margate. The corvette *Shearwater* then transferred approximately 200 of the remainder and took them to Sheerness.

It was a rescue that in time of peace would have held the attention of the world. There is a tremendous drama, a tension, in the race to beach the ship before she sank under them. There is a desperate excitement in the transfer of those 3,000 exhausted men.

As *Prague* came out from the Dunkirk roadstead through the bombing another railway steamer, the *Scotia*, went in. She was a coal-burner, and in addition to the exhaustion and difficulty of the work that she was doing was the necessity to coal ship. There were no proper facilities. For the oil-burning ships there were tankers from which they could take their oil by pipe line direct. *Scotia* and the other coal-burners had to be supplied with bags and shovels and work their own coal aboard from colliers or hulks. She herself shipped 90 tons from the coal hulk *Agincourt*, then moved to Margate roads and finished bunkering from the coaster *Jolly Days*. Her whole crew took part in the work, filling bags and manhandling them to the bunkers. On the way across a homeward-bound destroyer signalled to her: 'Windy off No. 6 buoy'. The humour was grim. Off No. 6 buoy she was attacked. In the course of the attack British aircraft came in and the enemy disappeared, to reappear again as soon as the RAF patrol had gone.

Scotia returned to Dunkirk under air attack, being near-missed off the entrance. She berthed at the West Mole. 'We found Dunkirk quiet except for a few rounds fired from shore batteries,' wrote Captain Hughes, and she embarked about 2,000 French troops. As she reached No. 6 buoy on the return voyage she was attacked by three formations of enemy aircraft in groups of four. The ship was hit abaft the engine-room on the starboard side and on the poop deck, and in the final attack one bomb went down the after-funnel. *Scotia* was heavily damaged and began to sink by the stern, heeling steadily over to starboard.

'We carried ten boats, but three of them had been smashed by the bombs. The troops, being French, could not under-stand orders and they were rushing the boats, which made it very difficult to man the falls – the port boats being most difficult as the vessel was heeling over to starboard. The chief officer had been given a revolver to use by a French officer, threatening to use this helped matters a little. However, they obeyed my mouth whistle and hand signs and so stood aside while the boats were being lowered.

'Commander Couch of HMS *Esk* had received our SOS. He was lying at Dunkirk at the time; he came at full speed to the rescue. By now the boat deck starboard side was in the water and the vessel was still going over. He very skilfully put the bow of his ship close to the forecastle head, taking off a large number of troops and picking up hundreds out of the sea. Backing his ship out again, he came amidships on the starboard side, his stem being now against the boat deck, and continued to pick up survivors.

'The *Scotia* had by now gone over until her forward funnel and mast were in the water. Two enemy bombers again approached us dropping four bombs and machine-gunning those swimming and clinging to wreckage. The *Esk* kept firing and drove the enemy away. Commander Couch again skil-fully manoeuvred his ship around to the port side, the *Scotia* having gone over until the port bilge keel was out of the water. Hundreds of the soldiers were huddled on the bilge and some of them swam to the *Esk*, while others were pulled up by ropes and rafts.'

While the work of rescue was in progress a fresh bombing

attack developed, but the aircraft were driven off by gunfire and the rescue continued uninterrupted until finally only three men were left lying against the bilge keel of the *Scotia*. Captain Hughes fastened ropes round each of these men in turn, they were hauled up to the deck of the *Esk*, and eventually he himself reached the rescue ship. Thirty of *Scotia*'s crew were killed or died subsequently, and Captain Hughes estimated that between two and three hundred Frenchmen were lost. The sinking of the *Scotia* was a tragedy; but for the coolness of Captain Hughes and the brilliant work of the rescue ship it might have been a very great disaster.

HMM *Brighton Queen*, one of the paddle-minesweepers of the 7th Flotilla, which had come down from the Firth of Forth in reinforcement the previous day, made her second trip in the early afternoon. She picked up 700 French and Moroccan troops, and stood out on the homeward passage. At the end of the narrows she was made the target of a concentrated attack by dive-bombers. For some while she dodged the rain of bombs, but eventually she was hit in the stern and badly holed. The minesweeper *Saltash* was the first ship to reach her. She reported that 'the French troops behaved steadily and intelligently though nearly half of them were killed by the explosion'.

Amongst the small ships the loss was equally heavy. The trawler *Jacinta* cleared with 200 Chasseurs d'Afrique, was attacked by Stukas but survived, and when 2 miles from Ramsgate and safety spiked herself on an uncharted wreck. All hands were saved. A French convoy of four ships – *Denis Papin* and the auxiliary patrol boats *President Briand, Venus* and *Moussaillon* – reached No. 6 buoy about 4 pm. They passed through heavy fire from a 155 mm. battery, which had been established a little inshore from the beach at Clipon, and immediately after were systematically attacked by eight Stukas. The *Denis Papin* went down in thirty seconds. She was followed shortly after by the *Venus* and a very little after by the *Moussaillon*. Only the *President Briand* remained afloat.

* * *

Four destroyers had been sunk in a matter of a few hours, four had been seriously damaged. Two of the largest of the cross-Channel steamers and a paddle-minesweeper had been lost. Up and down the roads small ships were on fire and sinking. New wrecks studded the narrow waters of the Channel from No. 6 buoy across the banks. The time had come for a change of plan.

At noon the Commander-in-Chief, Nore, signalled the Admiralty to suggest the 'discontinuation of the use of destroyers by day off the French coast'. At 6 pm a signal from Dunkirk to Admiral Ramsay said:

'Things are getting very hot for ships; over 100 bombers on ships here since 0530, many casualties. Have directed that no ships sail during daylight. Evacuation by transports therefore ceases at 0300. If perimeter holds will complete evacuation tomorrow, Sunday night, including most French. General concurs.'

The Admiralty made up its mind. Independently Admiral Ramsay came to similar conclusions. Signals from London and from Dover crossed. The Admiralty directed the suspension of evacuation from Dunkirk at seven o'clock the following morning. Admiral Ramsay's message stated that he had ordered all ships to withdraw from Dunkirk before daylight – the ships could no longer accept the danger of the day. As Admiral Ramsay, considering the problem, wrote:

'In these circumstances, it was apparent that continuation of the operation by day must cause losses of ships and personnel out of all proportion to the number of troops evacuated, and if persisted in, the momentum of evacuation would automatically and rapidly decrease.'

But at dusk the ships would go in again – this was not yet the end.

* * *

This day criticism of the RAF reached its height. It is not easy to balance the scales in this matter. On June 1st the RAF was asked to provide patrols from 5 am onwards. Eight fighter sweeps were made in the course of the day, varying in strength from three to four squadrons. Smaller sweeps, as has been outlined, had been found impracticable early in the operation. On May 27th twenty-three sweeps had been flown, but the weakness of small patrols invited strong enemy reaction. On this Saturday a second sweep followed at 6 am. There was then a three-hour gap until nine. There was another gap through the middle of the day. It was in these two gaps that the heaviest loss took place.

In addition to these fighter operations Coastal Command

and the Fleet Air Arm flew patrols over the approach channels and the open sea, and an astonishing variety of planes was used – Hurricanes, Spitfires, Defiants, Ansons, Hudsons and Swordfish. Three Ansons, reconnaissance aircraft of Coastal Command, engaged nine Messerschmitt fighters at one period of the day, flying almost at water level. They shot down two of them, possibly two more, and drove the rest away. Three Hudsons found 'a patch of sky black with Jerrys' – Junkers 87s and 88s ready to dive on transports, with a dense screen of Messerschmitts above them. In thirteen minutes three dive-bombers had been shot down, two had dived out of control, and the formation had been driven off. Spitfires claimed twelve German bombers and fighters during a morning patrol, and in the afternoon went up again and claimed another six.

The airman's view was totally different from that of the seaman. A Spitfire pilot wrote:[1]

'Nieuport slowly appeared beneath my wings, and I turned to run back down the coast. I had just turned again at Dunkirk, and was heading back once more, when something moving on my left caught my eye. I looked round in time to see an aircraft diving down towards the shipping off the harbour. Coming hard round I dived after it, the rest of the squadron chasing after me. The aircraft flattened out over a destroyer for a moment and then turned, climbing towards the coast. As I followed there was a terrific flash below and a huge fountain of water was flung high into the air, to fall slowly back into the sea. As the disturbance subsided I saw that the destroyer had completely disappeared. So the aircraft in front of me was a Hun. A blind fury gripped me.'

The bomber got clear in the cloud cover but almost immediately afterwards the fighter pilot found a new target, attacked and damaged it, and again lost it in the cloud. After three dog-fights he turned for home short of petrol, coming down to sea level.

'A mile ahead I recognised a cross-Channel steamer. I smiled to myself, remembering the long hours I had spent on her in happier days, crossing to the Continent. She would take a good two hours more to get home now, whereas I would be there in ten minutes.

'Just as I came abreast of the ship the whole sea suddenly erupted immediately behind her, and only a few hundred yards away from me. I nearly jumped out of the cockpit with

[1] *Spitfire!* by Squadron Leader 'B. J. Ellan'.

fright! I had been rudely awakened from my dreaming by a Dornier sitting at about 2,000 feet, nearly over the top of me. As I looked, four little black objects left the belly of the bomber and came hurtling down towards the ship. I turned sharply and began to climb as hard as I could, feeling absolutely wild that the Hun had given me such a fright. He looked so insolent, sitting up there throttled right back, and letting his eggs go in that deliberate fashion. Luckily for me it hadn't helped him to aim accurately, but I felt like ramming him. I was not, however, forced to dwell further on this suicidal measure, for the Hun then turned back towards the French coast and climbed away as hard as he could, pursued by bursts of AA fire from a cruiser a mile or so to the north-east. Looking at the cruiser I watched the flickering stabs of flame from one of her "Chicago Pianos". Though it certainly looked a wicked and deadly performance enough, I couldn't see whether the Dornier was hit or not.'

At the end of the day the RAF claimed seventy-eight enemy aircraft destroyed. It was believed that a new record for the war had been established. A more sober analysis of claims brought the figure down to forty-three. In actual fact, German returns examined since the war show that ten fighters and nineteen bombers in all were lost in the course of the day's operations. Of this total a number must be credited to ships. Naval vessels claimed thirteen 'kills' during daylight hours. On the other side of the ledger thirty-one British aircraft were lost this Saturday. The legend of qualitative superiority that was built up over Dunkirk rested on perilously slender foundations.

*   *   *

At sea and in the air the battle had reached points of crisis. What was the position on the land?

At 8 am, while the Luftwaffe attack against the ships was at its height, General Alexander met Admiral Abrial and General Fagalde again. It was obvious by now that there was no question of a successful completion of the evacuation by the dawn of Sunday. General Alexander agreed to a modification of the original plan. The line was to be held as before until midnight. Thereafter it was proposed that he should withdraw to what is described as 'a bridgehead round Dunkirk with all available anti-aircraft and anti-tank guns and with such troops as had not yet embarked'.

Already heavy German attacks were developing against the

'Canal Line'. At Bergues the 1st Loyals were forced out of the town and took up new defensive positions on the canal bank on its outskirts. At Hoymille, a little to the east, the enemy penetrated a position held by the Warwickshires and secured a foothold across the canal. The position was restored late in the afternoon by the Loyals in a vigorous counter-attack. The Border Regiment was also pushed back, and at dark the last of the British troops were withdrawn through the French on the intermediate line, which ran through Uxem and Ghyvelde. The Canal des Chats at Uxem was less than 4 miles from the beaches. The end was very close.

*   *   *

Thirty-one ships in all were lost and eleven were seriously damaged between midnight and midnight. It was a major disaster, and yet such is the strange quality of Dunkirk that through it all the loading went on, hardly losing its rhythm. Though it was interrupted as the Stukas raided the open beaches, though ships withdrew under attack or were turned back from the approach channels, though the Mole was almost incessantly under fire now, it never ceased. Through it all the small craft worked, pausing sometimes to rescue drowning men from the water, helping to tow a damaged ship, standing by a sinking one.

Five small wooden drifters had crossed first on the 29th. They had been requisitioned for work in the magnetic mine campaign and were known as '*Vernon*'s Private Navy'. One of them, *Silver Dawn*, had been damaged this night and another, *Lord Cavan*, was sunk by shell fire, but the remainder took full loads. They were on their way home when *Scotia* sank, and in spite of their loads they went straight to the work of rescue, picking up a large number of survivors. The record of these small ships is amazing: through the whole operation they brought back 4,085 men – *Silver Dawn* once crossed with 312. Their safe complement was said to be 100 men.

Even when the news of the disaster filtered through to Ramsgate the little ships continued to sail. All that night the windows in Ramsgate and along the Kentish coast had shaken with the thunder of the Dunkirk guns and the crash of the bombing. The men who went this morning had no need of the news of the eight o'clock disasters to convince them of the dire necessities of the situation or to warn them of its heavy dangers. Not many men went to Dunkirk without the knowledge that they were thrusting into the most dangerous area of water that the sea had known for a generation. There were few who shirked that thrusting, few who turned back.

About this time in the naval records there begin to creep in brief phrases: 'Sub-Lieutenant So-and-So, against orders, attempted to go over.' . . . 'Yacht So-and-So, though told she was too slow, started out and was turned back by the drifters.' News of the morning disasters, as it filtered through to the serried boats in Ramsgate harbour and along the quays and piers of Folkestone, of Dover, of Deal, of Margate and Sheerness and Southend, seems only to have raised the temper of those who waited for fresh orders.

At dawn from Ramsgate a convoy of eight boats, including *Westerly*, *Naiad Errant* and *White Heather*, moved off for Dunkirk. The description of Able Seaman Samuel Palmer is perhaps the best individual account by any member of the lower deck who took part in the beach work through this time. Palmer was a 'Westoe'. He came to Ramsgate with a draft from the Royal Naval Barracks, Devonport, where he had been serving for some time past as a member of the Plymouth City Patrol. He was a 'stripey', a three-badge man, and held the Long Service and Good Conduct medals, but he was still an Able Seaman. His narrative is simple and graphic with the simplicity of the 'Old Navy'.

'The adventure began with a sudden draft from Devonport to Ramsgate. For one night at Ramsgate I was billeted with other seamen in the Fun Fair Ballroom, and the next day action began. I was told off with another seaman, two ordinary seamen and two stokers, to take over two motor-yachts, the *Naiad Errant* and the *Westerly*. Being the senior hand, I detailed one seaman, an ordinary seaman, and one stoker to take charge of the *Westerly* and took the remainder on board the *Naiad Errant* with me. I thought she looked the better of the two boats. . . .

'About 3 miles outside Dunkirk I saw a French destroyer doing about 25 to 30 knots [this was the *Foudroyant*], making her way into Dunkirk. I took my eyes off her for a minute or two and then glanced back, but there was nothing there. She must have had a direct hit from a bomb and sunk within a few minutes. I made my course over to where she had gone and picked up her survivors, which altogether numbered only about twenty. Those I picked up I put on board a French tug which happened to be in the vicinity, and once more carried on into Dunkirk.

'Eventually I arrived off the beach where the swarms of soldiers were gathered, and at the same time one of our big ships came and anchored close inshore. Three of our little convoy of eight had arrived. The first immediately filled with soldiers and carried on back to England. The second went aground. My first job was to ferry soldiers from the beach to the big ship, and I made a number of trips. Then I tried to tow the boat that had run aground off the beach but the young seaman with me got the tow rope around my propellers, the result being that I had to give the job up and that my own ship ran aground. All around there was ceaseless activity and, jumping over the side, I gave a hand carrying the wounded soldiers to the big ship's skiff which had been launched. . . .'

Naiad Errant's crew was ordered aboard the 'big ship', but in turn she ran aground. In the interval soldiers got *Naiad Errant* clear again, and Palmer, after securing enough petrol for the return journey, started back. Shortly after *Naiad Errant*'s engines failed.

'With no engineer on board, and me without the slightest knowledge of engines, I had to hope that the soldiers could get her going again. The engineers among them got to work. The others I ordered to break up both the cabin doors and use the pieces as paddles in order to keep a little way on the boat and prevent her from running on to the pier. Although they were dead tired they put all they knew into it and so we managed to keep a little way on the boat and keep her in a safe position. About this time I began to shiver and got very cold as it got dark, for I had on the same togs that I had been swimming in. I was still wet through. Then one of the soldiers tapped me on the shoulder. He handed over a flask, asking me to drink. I did. It was rum, and it certainly put warmth and fresh life into me.

'The soldiers tinkered with the engine in the darkness and it must have been between ten and eleven o'clock at night when there was a clamour of excitement. They had got the starboard engine going! I told them to "drop everything" and leave the port engine and I would get them over to England all right on the one engine, which gave me about 5 to 6 knots. I counteracted the pull of the one engine with the wheel. . . .

'Just after dawn I struck Dover dead centre and then followed the coast up to Ramsgate, arriving there at eleven and I put the soldiers ashore on the pier.'

White Heather was abandoned. *Westerly* was damaged and her people were rescued later.

Another convoy left Ramsgate about 9.30 am. Between the two there were a number of individual sailings. In the convoy were the tugs *Prince, Princess* and *Duke* with the Isle of Wight ferry *Fishbourne* in tow. The *Sun III* had four barges astern of her – *Ada Mary, Haste Away, Burton* and *Shannon*. She had great trouble with barges breaking adrift, and *Duke* was detached from *Fishbourne* to pick up *Haste Away* and *Ada Mary*. By 2.30 pm they were close in to Dunkirk. Air attacks were heavy again by this time, and it was eventually decided that *Fishbourne* should return to Ramsgate. The barge tows meanwhile had got well ahead of her and in the middle of the afternoon reached position a little north of Dunkirk during the inevitable air attack. The master of *Duke*, B. P. Mansfield, records, however, that this attack was split up by our own fighter aircraft.

Half an hour after they had left Ramsgate the yacht *Sundowner* began her crossing. *Sundowner* belonged to Commander C. H. Lightoller, RNR (Retd), who, as senior surviving officer of the *Titanic*, had been the principal witness at the inquiry into that disaster. She was a biggish craft, approximately 60 feet with a speed of 10 knots and, with the assistance of his son and a Sea Scout, Commander Lightoller had taken her out of Cubitt's Yacht Basin at Chiswick on May 31st and had dropped down the river to Southend as part of a big convoy of forty boats which had mustered at Westminster. At dawn on June 1st he left Southend with five others and, reaching Ramsgate, was instructed in the casual manner of those days to 'proceed to Dunkirk for further orders'. His charts were somewhat antiquated, and he was fortunate enough to be able to obtain a new set. At ten o'clock he left by the route laid down.

On the way across Commander Lightoller picked up the crew of *Westerly*, originally one of Able Seaman Palmer's flotilla. She was broken down and on fire. Finding no more men on the beaches, and successfully dodging several air attacks, he headed up for Dunkirk harbour, where he berthed alongside a destroyer and started to load troops. With great foresight every bit of unnecessary gear had been removed from *Sundowner* before leaving Cubitt's Yacht Basin. Commander Lightoller wrote:

'My son, as previously arranged, was to pack the men in and

use every available inch of space – which I'll say he carried out to some purpose. On deck I detailed a naval rating to tally the troops aboard. At fifty I called below, "How are you getting on?" getting the cheery reply, "Oh, plenty of room yet." At seventy-five my son admitted they were getting pretty tight – all equipment and arms being left on deck.

'I now started to pack them on deck, having passed word below for every man to lie down and keep down; the same applied on deck. By the time we had fifty on deck, I could feel her getting distinctly tender, so took no more. Actually we had exactly 130 on board, including three *Sundowners* and five *Westerlys*.

'During the whole embarkation we had quite a lot of attention from enemy planes, but derived an amazing degree of comfort from the fact that the *Worcester*'s AA guns kept up an everlasting bark overhead. . . .

'Arriving off the harbour I was at first told to "lie off". But when I informed them that I had 130 on board, permission was at once given to "come in" (I don't think the authorities believed for a minute that I had 130), and I put her alongside a trawler lying at the quay. Whilst entering, the men started to get to their feet and she promptly went over to a terrific angle. I got them down again in time and told those below to remain below and lying down till I gave the word. The impression ashore was that the fifty-odd lying on deck plus the mass of equipment was my full load.

'After I had got rid of those on deck I gave the order "Come up from below", and the look on the official face was amusing to behold as troops vomited up through the forward companionway, the after companionway, and the doors either side of the wheelhouse. As a stoker PO, helping them over the bulwarks, said, "God's truth, mate! Where did you put them?" He might well ask. . . .'

The old stagers were still carrying on. HMM *Medway Queen* was over again, having left for Dunkirk at 9.30 am. With the ships' boats which she towed again was Mr R. B. Brett. Writing subsequently, he said that he saw one of the crew of the *Medway Queen*, a Royal Naval pensioner, calmly fishing over the stern while the *Medway Queen* was lying off the Mole waiting for her turn to go in.

'When told that there were no fish about and that, if there were, they were dead, he sang out, "You never can tell, sir. I might catch a bloody Boche helmet." '

Brett took his boat in until she had almost grounded and then, being the tallest man on board, he waded ashore, calling out, 'I want sixty men!' For some time he received no reply. Then, he wrote:

'I sighted a causeway about eight feet wide heading out into the water. To my surprise I found it to be a perfectly ordered straight column of men about six abreast, standing as if on parade. When I reached them a sergeant stepped up to me and said, "Yes, sir. Sixty men, sir?" He then walked along the column, which remained in perfect formation, and detailed the required number to follow me.'

A footnote to the stoicism of Mr Brett's 'human pier' is his account of a blinded man. His hand was placed in Mr Brett's and he was led to the boat and told that he was being taken to safety. He said, simply, 'Thanks, mate,' and followed patiently and wordlessly into the deep water.

The personnel ships too, despite their heavy loss, carried straight through. *Maid of Orleans* lay alongside the Mole for six hours acting as a floating landing-stage so that men could get more easily from the high plankway to the decks of the smaller ships. Two destroyers loaded across her with more than a thousand men apiece. In her turn she picked up 1,400 British and 400 French, and reached Dover safely.

At ten o'clock in the morning, though she must by then have heard the news, *St Helier* sailed from Dover. She reached Dunkirk in the middle of a violent air attack and loaded wounded. At six o'clock she shifted berth from the Mole and was hit by shell fire. Altogether she was alongside for seven hours, then, with every inch of space filled with troops, she sailed at 10.15 pm, continuously shelled by the Clipon batteries.

Royal Daffodil brought back 1,600 Frenchmen. *King George V* returned, loaded.

At 1.15 pm *Royal Sovereign* left for Dunkirk for the second time this day. In the darkness she had been picking up men off the beaches under heavy fire, within less than twelve hours she was on her way over again. At 3.20 pm she was under attack once more and was bombed by enemy aircraft. Thirty minutes later she was again attacked from the air, violent avoiding action just saving her. Immediately after she came under heavy fire from the enemy positions at Gravelines. It was Hobson's choice now whichever channel the ships attempted. *Royal Sovereign* turned back. The measure of the

German opposition lies in that fact. Her record was one of the finest of all those of the personnel ships throughout the operation – but she turned back. Her master said, tersely, 'As two ships appeared to be blocking channel returned to Margate for instructions.'

* * *

Admiral Wake-Walker, after the bombing of *Keith*, ordered MTB 102, which had picked him up, to proceed into Dunkirk. Landing near the naval dug-out headquarters at the base of the Mole, he was informed of General Alexander's intention to continue the evacuation during the night from the western beaches and Dunkirk, the rearguard retiring at dawn on Dunkirk itself. Fearing the results of a second attack such as the one that had just been experienced, Admiral Wake-Walker returned to Dover for direct contact with Admiral Ramsay. He crossed in the MTB, bombed and machine-gunned on the way. At 7.45 pm he was off Dunkirk again to take charge of the embarkation operation for the night, and at a conference at Bastion 32 with General Alexander and Captain Tennant the last details of the night's operations were agreed. At that conference he was informed that the French were holding a line in rear of the British positions through which the British rearguard would withdraw.

The whole emphasis had been changed to night loading. Admiral Ramsay's plan provided for all minesweepers, paddle-steamers, skoots, and small craft to work the Malo beach for a mile and a half from Dunkirk. The harbour itself was to be served by eight destroyers and seven personnel ships. Drifters and smaller craft from Ramsgate were to go up into the inner harbour. French ships were to use the guiding jetty and the West Mole, and very small ships the Quai Félix Faure. French fishing craft and drifters were to work with the British on the Malo beach.

The night was very dark. At times as many as six or seven ships were attempting to use the wreck-studded entrance to the harbour at once. Collisions and obstruction were incessant. The confusion of other days seemed to be redoubled, yet again the confusion was apparent rather than real. The sense of individual masters, the seamanship of their crews, the determination of everyone concerned in the operation was such that this vast concentration of ships moved in and out with astonishingly small loss.

Yet loss there was. *Maid of Orleans* was one of the earliest of the personnel ships of the night flight to leave. In six trips she had lifted 5,319 men. The utter disregard that this unarmed vessel showed for the almost intolerable dangers of the work and the limitless endurance of her people give her a high place in the record of famous ships.

At 8.30 pm she moved out from the Admiralty Pier and within ten minutes was in collision with the destroyer *Worcester*. *Worcester* had been damaged by bombs earlier in the day. She had been towed most of the way across the Channel and then engineers, working in the crippled engine-room, had managed to get her under her own steam again. She was slipping thankfully into port now when the two ships met with a tremendous crash. There were many tugs and small craft available; men thrown into the water were picked up, and both ships were towed into harbour. *Maid of Orleans*, however, was so damaged as to be unable to continue her voyage. She had done most gallant work. *Worcester* also was finished as far as Dunkirk was concerned, and she too had matched the very highest traditions of her Service. In the six trips which she had made, two of them under very heavy attack from the enemy, she had brought back 4,350 men.

Even endurance has its inevitable limits. The personnel ships had been working now, some of them, for a full week. They were civilian ships – before everything this must be remembered. They were not trained to the necessities of war, they were not moulded to its disciplines. Now, as their weariness grew, there were failures. *Tynwald* should have sailed from Folkestone at this time. She had completed three hard voyages, bringing away 4,500 men, but on this evening she failed to sail. Her master stated that his men had been continually on their feet for a week, that his officers were completely exhausted, and that he himself had had only four hours' rest in the whole course of the week and was unfit for further duty. *Malines* and *Ben-My-Chree* were in the same condition.

Exhaustion was beginning to show amongst the naval vessels as well. It was found possible in certain instances to put fresh captains on board. With the personnel ships Admiral Ramsay now took the necessary step of putting a naval commander or lieutenant-commander on board with a party of ten seamen. Relief crews were ordered up for *Ben-My-Chree* and *Tynwald*.

* * *

In the previous chapters, for the sake of clarity between one day and another, midnight was accepted as the end of each day's operations. It is more convenient here to carry through until dawn, for the new decision telescoped the whole work of loading into the dark hours and made each night an entity.

As this night went on what was left of the 46th Division, the 1st Division and the 126th Infantry Brigade were taken aboard the ships.

The destroyers still were lifting the greater share of the total. HMS *Whitshed* had made good the damage that she had received at Boulogne. This night she came back to service. She berthed at one o'clock against the concrete of the outer nose of the Mole.

As she made fast her ropes the Mole was empty. Commander Conder left his ship and walked along the Mole. A little way down it he found a bicycle lying up against a post and on this he rode down to the town. There was damage at various points. At one place the decking of the Mole had gone completely and the gap was bridged by a ship's gangway. At other points there were shell holes patched with any material available. At the far end there was another area of damage, and he had to dismount to circumvent it. Just beyond this he met a naval pier party and was told that troops would be coming at any moment. He went on past the pier party and in a warehouse a few hundred yards farther down found a number of exhausted French and Belgian troops. These he stirred into wakefulness and sent down the pier. There was an air attack on at the time but he was busy hunting. A little farther he found a party of British troops in command of a sergeant – their officers had brought them down as far as the pier and gone back to round up more men. These he took back with him.

The destroyers were taking incredible risks in stowing the vast quantities of men they lifted. It is recorded that *Whitshed* had first unshipped her mess tables and cleared all possible movable gear on the lower deck; now she opened compartments that normally were shut in danger areas, leaving the watertight doors open throughout the ship in order to make 'living spaces'. Having taken approximately 1,000 men on board by these heroic measures, *Whitshed* sent a berthing party to take the ropes of the succeeding destroyers as they came in and, as soon as these were berthed, pulled out stern first between the breakwaters, listing heavily with the weight of men, and got clear.

Her commanding officer's search is typical of many of the efforts made by naval officers at this time. Whenever there was a break in the flow a party from the ships would search. *Malcolm*'s navigator marched through the streets of Dunkirk playing a set of bagpipes as a summons to the weary men – there is no evidence on record as to the skill with which he played them.

At 2 am a signal from Dunkirk read:

'C.-in-C. says it is essential that rearguard BEF embarks from the beaches east of Mole on account of French congestion on Mole. Considerable number British troops still on Mole. Military are expecting further arrivals there. Rearguard expects to arrive at beach at 0230.'

This was an hour and a half after *Whitshed* had re-started the flow. It seemed obvious that large numbers would not arrive until after the time set for the close of operations. The reaction of Dover was immediate and forthright. It is embodied in a signal which said: 'Endeavour to embark rearguard from beach remaining after 3 am if necessary.' The wording is simple. It was, however, the acceptance of a challenge. The events of the previous morning were still very vivid in the minds of Admiral Ramsay and the Dover Command. Yet, if the men could not be got down to the beach before dawn, the Navy was still prepared to wait until after dawn to take them.

The tugs *Crested Cock*, *Ocean Cock*, *Sun VII*, *Sun XI* and *Sun XII*, which had been sent out the previous evening at 9.55 with the grim orders 'proceed over as far as possible to Dunkirk and pick up anything', searched widely through the approaches to the channel. Visibility on this night was bad. The normal signals of distress could not be used. Ships for the most part went in darkness or switched on dim navigation lights only when the press of traffic threatened disaster. There were no rockets to call them up, no flares were burned except in the last, most dire necessity.

Most of the rescue tugs found nothing, but at 2 am *Sun XI* broke out of line. Her master said:

'I saw small lights and someone with a very dim Morse light. Put tug hard a-starboard and found large Government lighter broken down full of wounded and troops. Two-thirty took lighter in tow, arrived 6.30 am. Berthed lighter, terrible sight.'

He had picked up the last of the survivors of HM Tug *St Abbs*, who were the last survivors of HMS *Keith*. Captain Berthon, with about sixty men in all, had got clear of *St Abbs* as she disintegrated after the bomb hit. He swam for a long time, and in that period the group was passed by a small camouflaged yacht which failed to see the men struggling in the water; otherwise nothing that floated came near them. This was at the very worst period of the air attack. Eventually Captain Berthon got to shore. The lighter in which he essayed to bring home some of his people broke down, and he was drifting helplessly when *Sun XI* saw that faint Morse light and ended his odyssey. Of the crew of *Keith* three officers and thirty-three men were lost. There is no record of the soldiers drowned.

Through this period the small boats worked steadily. They worked in circumstances of rapidly increasing difficulty. The language problem, now that the French predominated along the beaches, was almost impossible. Amongst certain units discipline had broken down, and it was equally hard without an absolute command of the language to stop men from rushing the boats and settling them firmly into the sand. Latecomers could not be prevented from jumping into overloaded boats. There were not a few cases of small craft that left the beach and sank as soon as they reached deep water and the tumultuous wash of the destroyers.

With the Babel of tongues, there was a Babel of order and counter-order, of rumour and counter-rumour. It was believed in the Dynamo Room that some of this was due to fifth column activity. Signals were sent out stating that false information and false orders to return were being given to the inshore units. It is possible that this was so, but it is also possible that in the awful confusion of those dark hours rumour flooded upon exhaustion, apprehension crowded upon lack of knowledge. Every possible effort was made by Admiral Wake-Walker and his staff to keep ships and boats and men and beach parties informed; but it would have required a dozen police boats, a hundred staff officers, to have kept that navy of the improvisation ordered and orderly. The small-boat work at Dunkirk succeeded upon the initiative of individuals. Where it failed – as in some cases in all those hundreds it was bound to fail – it failed upon the initiative of individuals. That was a part of the price that had to be paid for triumph.

The great bulk of those of the small boats that still floated and were still capable of progressing under their own steam left in accordance with orders at zero hour. The French continued loading a little later than the British ships. A battalion of the BEF, which had marched from Bergues through the night, reached the end of the Mole as the last of the British personnel ships, already fully loaded, cast off for home. The battalion turned and marched off the Mole against the line of the French who still marched down to their own ships. In a little that line ceased also. Those who were left dug themselves into the canal banks and the dunes on the outskirts of the town and lay there till night.

The last ships had held on until sun-up. In full daylight they pulled out to join the end of the long stream that was headed back to the English coast. Over the waters of Dunkirk channel a silence fell. At midnight, when the list for June 1st closed, 64,429 men had been brought safe to the English shore. With all the destruction, with all the loss, this was another Glorious First of June.

CHAPTER XIV

Sunday, June 2nd

To VA DOVER from SNO DUNKIRK
BEF EVACUATED.

2330/2

A LITTLE AFTER sunrise on June 2nd a chaplain of the British Expeditionary Force celebrated Holy Communion in the Dunkirk dunes. John Masefield, who tells the story, says that five times before the service ended the congregation of men of the weary rearguard was scattered by low-flying aircraft.

Between 3,000 and 4,000 of the BEF remained ashore this day. Detachments of these men, with seven anti-aircraft and twelve anti-tank guns, worked with the French throughout the day on the 'intermediate line'. The French figures were still uncertain. At Dover Admiral Ramsay recorded that the estimate as to 'the number of French troops remaining was increasing from the 25,000 quoted the previous evening to figures in the region of 50,000 to 60,000'. This uncertainty made planning almost unbelievably difficult. One factor harshly simplified it – the capacity of the embarkation facilities that remained. There was left now only the harbour – almost continuously under shell fire – and a bare mile and a half of beach – equally within range of the German guns.

It was estimated that 25,000 men could be moved during the hours of darkness provided a rapid flow of troops to the embarkation points could be maintained. The night's operation was, therefore, planned on the basis of a lifting of 25,000. Thirteen personnel vessels, two large store carriers, eleven destroyers, five paddle-minesweepers, nine Fleet sweepers, one special service vessel, nine drifters, six skoots, two armed yachts, one gunboat, and a number of tugs towing small craft and freelance motor-boats were ordered to sail from five o'clock onwards. The French sent altogether forty-three ships, including the Breton fishermen who had worked well the previous day. It was possible for most of the ships' companies this day to get some rest.

*   *   *

There was, however, one aspect of the evacuation for which at this time no provision could be made. The outward flow of wounded virtually ceased this morning. One Casualty Clearing Station remained – 12 CCS at Rosendaël. The difficulties which had faced the hospital ships and the accumulating disaster of the morning of June 1st had stopped the movement of stretcher cases. The staff of 12 CCS had abandoned all hope of returning to England.

Late in the morning, however, orders came from I Corps HQ to say that one officer and ten men were to be left for every hundred casualties and that the remainder of the medical personnel of 12 CCS was to proceed to the Mole for evacuation. The order led to one of the most remarkable ballots in army history. At two o'clock in the afternoon the names of all medical personnel remaining were placed in a hat. There were by now 230 stretcher cases at Rosendaël, and three officers and thirty men had to be chosen to stay with them. It was decided that 'first out of the hat' was first to go, and there were left at the end an officer who had been separated from his field ambulance, another who had been sent over from England for beach duties at Dunkirk, and the surgical specialist of the unit. At ten o'clock at night the remainder of the personnel of 12 CCS moved to the Mole and after an interminable journey reached three destroyers at the end of it.

The wounded, however, were not yet abandoned. At 10.30 am Captain Tennant made a signal in plain language directed to the German Command. It read:

'Wounded situation acute and hospital ships should enter during day. Geneva Convention will be honourably observed and it is felt that the enemy will refrain from attacking.'

The Southern Railway steamer *Worthing*, which had been taken over at the beginning of the war for service as a hospital carrier, was lying in the Downs. Two hours after the broadcast she received her orders and at 12.55 pm she left for Dunkirk at 20 knots. At 2.32 pm she was attacked by twelve enemy aircraft. Nine bombs were dropped, two of which fell within three or four feet of her despite drastic avoiding action. This attack was carried out in good visibility and regardless of the fact that the ship was carrying all the marks and signs of a hospital ship as required by the Geneva Convention. The Convention had been repeatedly flouted throughout the evacuation as it had been flouted on countless occasions before. On this day, however, the attack was more despicable even than upon these earlier occasions. It was made in flagrant, open contempt of the appeal that had been sent out.

Simultaneously with the orders to *Worthing*, *Paris* of the same line received orders to sail at three o'clock. At 2.30 pm the wireless operator of *Paris* received *Worthing*'s attack message and, immediately afterwards, the message saying that she was believed to be making water and was returning at full speed. The master of *Paris* made a signal to the shore asking if, in view of this attack, he was to carry out his previous orders. At 4.48 pm he was instructed by radio message to proceed. 'I at once weighed anchor and proceeded to Dunkirk.' This simple sentence in Captain Biles' report represents perhaps the whole spirit of Dunkirk – the spirit of gallantry, of defiance of known and obvious danger that possessed and lifted up the men who did that work. The *Paris* was also attacked, two aircraft dropping bombs close alongside which burst steam pipes in the engine-room and put auxiliary machinery (including the lighting system) out of action. As the ship was out of control, Captain Biles ordered the lifeboats to be slung out and lowered to deck level, and a distress signal was sent out on the emergency radio set. Fifty minutes later fifteen more enemy aircraft approached and dropped a number of bombs, one of which went through the bows of an outturned lifeboat and caused further internal damage to the ship, which ultimately had to be abandoned.

While these attacks were taking place the Navy also suffered loss. Though all movements in the area of Dunkirk itself had ceased, the patrols on the approaches had to be maintained. Destroyers, anti-submarine trawlers, drifters, and minesweepers worked throughout the day to safeguard the channels for the night flow. Early in the afternoon the anti-submarine trawler *Spurs* was bombed and badly damaged. The destroyer *Vanquisher*, working near her, went at once to the rescue. *Spurs*, however, managed to get away under her own steam.

As the time for the evening flow approached the patrols were pushed farther and farther to the east. At 4.15 pm the anti-submarine trawler *Blackburn Rovers* was hit, apparently by a torpedo from one of the small coastal submarines which intermittently worked through the area, and sank. An hour and a half later the anti-submarine trawler *Westella* was hit in turn – possibly by a torpedo from the same U-boat – and also sank.

*   *   *

The diminished perimeter about Dunkirk held. To the west of the town no serious attack had been made on the sector line which ran down to the sea in the vicinity of Mardyck, though a number of batteries had been positioned in the vicinity to harass shipping. From Mardyck it held firm along the course of the old Mardyck Canal to Spycker, then along the main canal to Bergues, and from Bergues diagonally across through Uxem and Ghyvelde to the old fortifications on the Franco-Belgian frontier and so back to the sea.

The normal approach to Dunkirk from the south, as has been said, is by the main road which passes through Bergues and, running parallel with the broad Bergues–Dunkirk Canal, moves almost due north into the suburbs of the town. The successful defence of the junction of this canal with the Bergues–Nieuport Canal had so far held the Germans from any attempt at a direct assault, but attacks to the eastward of this road over the level ground which led towards the village of Teteghem had placed the new line there in jeopardy.

At six o'clock in the morning, therefore, the French launched a counter-attack in this area. Though it began vigorously, it was brought to a halt by two successive air attacks, each by more than fifty aircraft, and it was finally stopped at the hamlet of Notre Dame des Neiges. At 9 am it was decided to fall back on the Canal des Moëres opposite Teteghem. Throughout the day this position was maintained.

On the other side of the main approach road pressure now increased steadily in the area of Spycker and, as evening fell, the line was penetrated there and a general withdrawal took place. The strength of the holding position in the complicated junction between the canals and roads which led to Dunkirk from the outskirts of Bergues had evidently dissuaded the Germans from a direct frontal assault, and they were plainly endeavouring to find an indirect approach. At nightfall, however, they suspended operations.

Throughout the defence of the perimeter night attacks were rare and hardly ever strongly maintained. The explanation of this lies almost certainly in the nature of the terrain, cut up, as it was, by a complex of navigable canals with, between them, an endless succession of large and small drainage dykes.

As the ships of the night flow approached Dunkirk the position was, therefore, that the perimeter had fallen in but that the line, threatened on either side of the main approach road, still held.

*   *   *

At 3.30 in the afternoon Commander Clouston, who had returned to Dover for a brief rest, left with an augmented pier party in two RAF motor-boats, Nos. 243 and 270, to make the necessary arrangements at the Mole to receive the first ships of the night. Off Gravelines the boats were attacked by eight Junkers 87. No. 243, in which Commander Clouston had sailed, was near-missed early in the attack and became waterlogged. As the attacks continued, both with small bombs and machine-guns, the crew of 243, with Commander Clouston, took to the water. No. 270 was also damaged but managed, by zigzagging and high speed, to avoid the worst of the attack. Ten minutes after 243 had been hit she returned to the waterlogged wreck. Commander Clouston, who was in the water, waved to her to get clear. Some of his crew had been killed, but with one officer and some of the survivors he set out to swim to a boat that could be seen about two miles away, while the RAF men endeavoured to swim to shore. The water was cold. Commander Clouston, who had for the past week worked almost without sleep and without rest, rapidly became exhausted. He decided finally that he could not make the distance and turned to swim back to the waterlogged wreck of 243. He was not seen again.

The officer with him, after swimming for nearly three hours, reached the boat and found her deserted. With great difficulty he boarded her and was eventually picked up by a French trawler, which had lost her way and which he navigated back to Ramsgate. One of the aircraftmen also turned back to the wreck, reached it and was picked up eight hours later by HMS *Whitshed*.

This is one of the great tragedies of Dunkirk. Commander Clouston was responsible for the traffic of the Mole from the beginning of the operation. Under his guidance 200,000 men had passed down its narrow plankway to safety. It is impossible to exaggerate the importance of his achievement. It was carried out under conditions that could have been surmounted only by a strong spirit. Darkness, wind, sea, enemy shellfire, and incessant bombing conspired always against those who tried to control the traffic of the Mole. The plankway itself was wrecked by direct hits. The loading berths were blocked by sunken ships. The flow of troops was irregular, and the difficulties of dealing with men unaccustomed to the sea and heavy with the exhaustion of defeat were indescribable. Throughout it all Commander Clouston maintained the very highest traditions of the Royal Navy. His service to the BEF and to his country is not to be measured in words.

No. 270 followed her orders and went on to Dunkirk. It had been intended that she should police the fairways and direct traffic. She was, however, so damaged that this was now impossible. Sub-Lieutenant Wake, who commanded her, landed at the Mole and, in the tradition of the Navy, took over the task which Commander Clouston had set out to perform. The inherent difficulty of persuading the inland *poilu* to embark upon an unfamiliar element now reached its height. Coupled with the ordinary language difficulty and the macabre setting of the Mole at night under shellfire and air attack the problem of maintaining the flow was enough to daunt much older men. Sub-Lieutenant Wake kept it going by methods that were at times empirical.

Admiral Wake-Walker, still using MA/SB 10 as his 'flagship', crossed at 8.30 pm, accompanied by Admiral Somerville. At this hour the main flow of the night was on its way. The small craft left first, the organised flotillas moving at five o'clock. Once again heavy loss was sustained. The Belgian fishing vessels, many of which were manned by the French, lost the *Getuigt vor Christus* in collision with a patrol boat in Dunkirk. *Onze Lieve Vrouw Van Vlaanderen* was sunk by shellfire with a cargo of munitions and supplies on board. But to offset these things the *Lydie Suzanne* lifted ninety-eight men; the *Pharailde* (which had sailed from Dover with food and munitions) discharged her cargo, picked up forty French soldiers, and then went to help two British ships that had been bombed and sunk, and saved eighty-two British soldiers and three seamen; the *Zwaluw* picked up 255 soldiers together with ten from a destroyer, and on the way home rescued three French soldiers from a canoe and seven from a pontoon.

The motor-boat *Blue Bird* crossed under the command of Lieutenant-Colonel H. T. B. Barnard, who had made two previous attempts to get across. This day, however, he left Sheerness with a mixed crew of yachtsmen and ratings. *Blue Bird* closed the eastern end of the beaches but found no troops and, moving down the beach towards the base of the Mole, discovered that water had been put in the petrol tank. This last mishap was a common one through the greater part of the evacuation. Water, as has been described, was being taken over for the use of the Army. The available water cans of the Southern Command – and indeed of the south of England – were used up early, and as a substitute petrol cans were filled and taken over. The petrol for the small craft was also stored in ordinary two-gallon cans. These were appropriately marked, but dumps got mixed on occasion – especially when refuelling was done at night – and the mixture proved disastrous to many ships. *Blue Bird* was towed home by HM Skoot *Hilda*.

The 20-tonner *Rosaura* had a long previous history. She had crossed first on the Thursday, being brought back on the Friday by Sub-Lieutenant W. B. L. Tower (of HMS *Somali*), and on the Friday and Saturday had crossed again under his command. On the Sunday night she reached Dunkirk a little before midnight and worked, as she had done previously, ferrying men from the Mole to ships outside. During this period her propeller was fouled. It was cleared temporarily just as Sub-Lieutenant Tower received orders to leave. He decided that he had still time to fulfil a promise to some men who had been left on the jetty and, going in for the last time, picked up thirty-three French troops and three officers. At four o'clock in the morning he set out for Ramsgate, but when *Rosaura* was barely clear of the harbour the engine began to race and it was discovered that the propeller-shaft had broken. Efforts were made to repair it, but these failed and Tower decided, as it was almost light, to attempt to swim across to a small boat a mile away and try to get assistance. He reached the boat and started in towards the harbour but was not seen again. Efforts were made by his crew to make a sail of waterproof capes but these were unsuccessful, and *Rosaura* drifted helplessly all through Monday, through Tuesday, and through most of Wednesday, until that afternoon she was sighted by an RAF speed-boat searching the Channel, and her passengers and crew were taken off and brought in to Ramsgate.

Sea Roamer, a 40-foot motor-cruiser owned and commanded by Mr J. E. W. Wheatley, also crossed this Sunday evening, with a naval party on board. They towed over a boat to work the beaches and made an independent course across the shallows of the off-lying banks. Outside the harbour they were told to investigate the beaches but, though they closed to within 50 yards of the shore, they could see no signs of life in any part of the area which they examined. While they were doing this the Casino and the Kursaal were hit by incendiary bombs and went up in flames. They searched to two and a half miles north-east of Dunkirk and then, abandoning hopes of picking up anybody from the sands, decided to inspect the wrecks offshore. Circling the first one and shouting, they were rewarded by a head popping up over the side and demanding, 'Etes-vous Allemands ou Français?' They replied that they were English, and picked up a number of French soldiers who had reached the wreck the day before. These men said that they had seen nobody on the beach for the past twenty-four hours. As she was nearing the next wreck Sea Roamer's people sighted a low, fast-looking vessel carrying, apparently, a heavy gun. There was for some little while considerable exchange of anxiety between the two ships until the newcomer turned out to be the Massey Shaw with her powerful fire-fighting monitor on the foredeck. Continuing the search, they worked finally down to the Dunkirk entrance, where they were in collision with a destroyer. Sea Roamer herself was slightly damaged, but the boat she was towing was reduced to splinters and the tow-rope, suddenly freed, fouled her propeller. She was able to move slowly with the auxiliary engine, but she was eventually picked up and towed home by a paddle-steamer.

Sea Roamer, incidentally, recorded one of the better stories of the operation. Discussing the difficulty of persuading French troops to entrust themselves to small boats, her owner said:

'The French, it seems, were not always prepared to wade out and clamber into the dinghies in the surf. A story was told me of a French officer who steadfastly refused to do this. Finally he sent a note to the anxious yacht skipper. It read, "I have just eaten and am therefore unable to enter the water." '

The Massey Shaw had left Ramsgate at 6.40 pm under the command of Lieutenant G. Walker, RNVR, but with eight of her own crew still on board. She found no troops on the beach and Walker took her up the harbour, leaving finally at 3.15 am.

Admiral Taylor, having dispatched from Sheerness everything that would float and move, went to Ramsgate in the middle of Sunday afternoon. Discussing the conditions with military officers who had just arrived, he was informed that a pocket of men who had not been able to get into Dunkirk was holding out near Malo-les-Bains, and a special party was organised to get these men away. Three skoots and a dozen fast motor-boats were selected, and sailed late in the afternoon. Commandant Anduse-Faru of the French Navy undertook to arrange for a paddle-steamer and a French ship to be off the beach, and for a number of French fishing vessels to co-operate with Admiral Taylor's boats and ferry off troops to them and to the skoots. He was taken out to the fishing vessels to make arrangements. They had lovely names: *Ciel de France*, *Ave Maria Gratia Plena*, *Jeanne Antoine*, *Arc en Ciel*. They had done good work already and they were very tired but, after argument in the French fashion, they went over again.

The personnel ships moved out later and met with trouble at once. *Royal Daffodil* was off the Ruytingen buoy just before eight o'clock when she was attacked by six enemy aircraft. It is probable that this was a portion of the same bomber sweep which accounted for *Paris*. She had just passed the boats of the *Paris* when the attack developed. Six heavy bombs (Captain G. Johnson of the *Royal Daffodil* described them as 'aerial torpedoes') were dropped.

'Five of these missed, but the sixth hit the ship, passed through three decks, entered the engine-room, and went out through the starboard side before exploding just clear of the ship. The collar of the missile went through the bilge. The engines stopped and the aeroplanes machine-gunned the ship with tracer bullets, which started small fires. The ship began to make water through the hole made by the bomb and listed to starboard. Gear was shifted to the port side and the port boats were lowered to the deck and filled with water. This raised the starboard side enough to lift the hole just clear of the water line. Mr J. Coulthard, the chief engineer, and Mr W. Evans, the second engineer, took all the beds they could find and used them to plug the hole. Mr Evans stood up to his neck in the water in the engine-room holding open the bilge valve while Mr Coulthard kept the pumps going. With a diesel-engined ship this was a great risk; but the *Royal Daffodil* managed to get back to Ramsgate, with the engines running very slowly, as they had three parts of water to one of oil in their system, and was able to land all the troops she had taken on board.'

It is difficult to speak too highly of this feat. The sheer seamanship of it is beyond praise. The bravery of her engineers who, with the almost pathetic inadequacy of mattresses and planks, stanched the great hole in her side is superb.

Royal Sovereign, *Lady of Mann*, *Autocarrier* and *St Helier* crossed in succession. In the morning the naval authorities had informed Captain Pitman, *St Helier*'s master, that they considered that he had done enough and that they were prepared to put a naval officer in charge. Captain Pitman refused relief, but a commander and ten ratings were put on board to assist his tired crew and to help work the boats in case she was needed to take troops off the beaches.

With that flight went *Tynwald* with her chief officer, J. Whiteway, as master, her second officer, purser, W/T operator and carpenter of her old complement, the relief crew, and a naval officer and ten ratings. She completed the round trip, making another heavy lifting.

Ben-My-Chree, with some of her own people and a relief crew, sailed about the same time. Unfortunately, very shortly after she took her departure *Ben-My-Chree* was in collision and the trip was abandoned.

Malines had left the area in the course of the afternoon without orders, and returned to Southampton.

Manxman, which had made three trips already, lifting 2,300 men, should have sailed at 9.15 pm but failed. A new crew was put on board – her engineers stayed with the ship – and she left but did not reach Dunkirk.

Amongst the French personnel ships that crossed this time were *Rouen* and *Newhaven*.

Admiral Taylor, who had completed his work ashore, decided to proceed to Dunkirk to supervise the lifting of the pocket from Malo-les-Bains in person. I had at that time stolen a small twin-screw Thames motor cruiser and was ordered to stand by to take the Admiral over. Her name was *White Wing*, she was about 30-foot in length and she had a speed of approximately 12 knots but, owing to trouble with the starboard engine, did not make this speed all the way across. We reached Dunkirk with only minor difficulties and our work for the night is covered in an account that I wrote at the time.

'Having the Admiral on board, we were not actually working the beaches but were in control of small boat operations. We moved about as necessary and, after we had spent some time putting boats in touch with their towing ships, the 5.9 battery off Nieuport way began to drop shells on us. It seemed pure spite. The nearest salvo was about twenty yards astern, which was close enough.

'We stayed there until everybody else had been sent back and then went pottering about looking for stragglers. While we were doing that, a salvo of shells got one of the ships alongside the Mole. She was hit clean in the boilers and exploded in one terrific crash. There were then, I suppose, about 1,000 Frenchmen on the Mole. We had seen them crowding along its narrow crest, outlined against the flames. They had gone out under shellfire to board the boat, and now they had to go back again, still being shelled. It was quite the most tragic thing I ever have seen in my life. We could do nothing with our little dinghy.

'While they were still filing back to the beach and the dawn was breaking with uncomfortable brilliance, we found one of our stragglers – a Navy whaler. We told her people to come aboard, but they said that there was a white motor-boat aground and they would have to fetch off her crew. They went in, and we waited. It was my longest wait – ever. For various reasons they were terribly slow. When they found the captain of the motor-boat, they stood and argued with him, and he wouldn't come off anyway – damned plucky chap.'

The white motor-boat on the beach was *Singapore*. She had run aground at 1.30 in the morning. She eventually refloated on the rising tide and left with three French officers in addition to her crew. On the way Sub-Lieutenant J. W. Pratt, RNVR, who was in command of her, picked up two British soldiers who were 'floating around'. Wine from the Frenchmen's water-bottles brought them back to consciousness. Subsequently he took in tow three lifeboats which he found in mid-Channel, but eventually his engines broke down and he was himself taken in tow by *Kitcat*.

Commander Troup, who had accompanied Admiral Taylor from Sheerness, took over the War Department fast motorboat *Haig* with *Marlborough*, *Wolfe* and *Swallow*. With him was the French Naval Attaché, Captain de Rivoyre. The four boats crossed in company, with orders to act together on the other side ferrying until dawn and then to bring a final load back to England.

Commander Troup, with *Haig*, himself went into the harbour and, after ferrying a number of men and being twice rammed, was eventually obliged to abandon his craft. Badly damaged as she was, *Haig* was subsequently salved and got back to Ramsgate.

The rate of flow through this early part of the night was admirable. Steadily the last of the British element of the rearguard was marched to the Mole and embarked, French troops came down in a continuous stream, and the prospects for the night looked excellent.

One important mishap marred the proceedings. The French cross-Channel steamer *Rouen*, with a number of men on board, stranded on the mud inside the harbour as she was turning. The tug *Foremost 22* went to her assistance, but ran aground herself and only just got clear. The tide was ebbing fast, and she left the area so that a tug of lesser draught could make the attempt. The *Sun X* then closed the *Rouen*, but 200 feet away she found only 10 feet of water and it was obvious that it would be impossible to move her until the next high tide. Both tugs loaded with men, some of them from the *Rouen*.

General Alexander, with his staff, was picked up by Admiral Wake-Walker in MA/SB 10. He was subsequently transferred to a destroyer which was attacked and machine-gunned when close to Dover.

By eleven o'clock the last of the British Expeditionary Force was moving on to the ships. *St Helier* claims the honour of the final lifting, an appropriate finish to a great record. At about 11.30 pm, fully loaded, she slipped her ropes for the last time and felt her way out of the harbour, down by the head and leaking badly in her forepeak.

So ended a chapter in the story of the British Army, a story that had begun a bare three weeks before, as the British Expeditionary Force moved through the barriers of the Belgian frontier and raced into Belgium with lilac on their hats. So ended the story of a great retreat, one of the greatest in military history. So ended, though no man knew it on that day, Hitler's opportunity to break the power of Britain.

At 11.30 pm Captain Tennant, Senior Naval Officer, Dunkirk, made the simple signal: 'BEF evacuated.'

* * *

So far this had been the smoothest and the swiftest embarkation of the whole evacuation. French troops had been lifted in large numbers while the last of the BEF was getting clear, but now the movement faltered.

It is not possible even today wholly to explain this failure. At Dover it was believed that the French had been held back for a counter-attack which was proposed for the late afternoon.

Elsewhere it was suggested that the reluctance of the inland Frenchman to embark in the circumstances which prevailed and the difficulty in persuading units to split up in order to go aboard had also slowed the flow. The French naval historian Jacques Mordal discounts both these suggestions. He states that the troops which had already reached the Mole and the area immediately behind it when evacuation was suspended at dawn on June 2nd had scattered widely into the sand dunes beyond Malo-les-Bains and dug themselves in. Liaison failures, coupled perhaps with bad estimates as to the time necessary to get these men back to the Mole, resulted in this breakdown.

No one of these explanations appears to be adequate. The broad and lamentable fact is that there was a complete cessation of embarkation a little before midnight. At 12.30 am Admiral Wake-Walker signalled Dover saying that four ships were alongside the Mole but that there were no French troops coming down. Again at 1.15 am he signalled: 'Plenty of ships, cannot get troops.'

On the far side of the harbour there were troops, particularly at the base of the West Mole. This was the area allocated to the French vessels. It was not possible in the circumstances which prevailed to alter the careful plan that had been made to keep the movements along the East Mole going, and ship after ship waited beyond her scheduled time, slipped her moorings finally and put to sea empty. Ten thousand places were lost in these hours. At dawn the movement ceased. Only a handful of French troops had come down the East Mole. The paddle-minesweeper *Medway Queen* lifted one of the largest loads during this time, a total of 723 men.

It appears impossible to ascribe the failure to anything other than that general breakdown in French Command organisation which is the most lamentable feature of the whole of this campaign. One important aspect of this breakdown was the lack of knowledge of the condition and morale of troops in general and at specific points. There was no inherent difficulty in bringing men to the loading points at this period. The night was in no way worse than all the nights that had preceded it, the damage was hardly greater; nor, as was made painfully clear on the following night, was there a shortage of men. The explanation lies in the omission to produce a logical plan for the movement of units, to make certain that orders reached the units, that the organisation existed to guide them to the proper points, and that the necessary discipline was enforced.

There is no excuse for the fact that 10,000 men who could have been brought back, failed to reach safety.

This break in the rhythm does not affect the figures for June 2nd. The total number of men evacuated was roughly half that of the previous day, the fall in numbers being due entirely to the fact that during the daylight hours no loading was possible. At midnight the total landed in the twenty-four hours amounted to 26,256.

At twelve minutes past three a signal from Dunkirk said that all ships were leaving and that the blockships had entered.

CHAPTER XV

Monday, June 3rd

De toutes les caves, de tous les trous sortaient des
hommes désarmés. 'Des ruisselets humains qui
sortaient de partout et convergeaient vers la jetée, y
formant par leur réunion un fleuve immense im-
pressionnant, presque figé sur place. . . .'

JACQUES MORDAL

THE SUNRISE of June 3rd was hard and brilliant. The black
smoke that swirled up from the blazing oil tanks drifted
with a light north-east wind parallel with the coast past Gravelines towards Calais. Nothing moved in the Dunkirk channel.
In the harbour there were only wrecks and the French personnel ship *Rouen*, still aground, still waiting with a desperate
patience for the rising tide. On the Malo beach the motor-boat
Singapore waited also. The last small boat to move from Dunkirk that morning records that the water was silent and 'terribly
lonely'. Stukas soared out from above the smoke cloud, flying
very high, but she was not attacked. Nothing else moved on the
sea.

On the land the Germans mounted their last assault. From
Spycker a strong force thrust down the angle between the
Bergues Canal and the canal of Bourbourg, heading for the
suburb of St Georges. The reconnaissance group of the
French 68th Infantry Division met it and held it. On the
other side of the Bergues Canal a strong French counter-
attack was launched, headed by the last of the tanks. It had
a weight of about four battalions and it moved off at 4 am.
It was unable to penetrate deeper than the cross-roads at
Galghouck and was thrown back from there to Teteghem at
eleven o'clock by markedly superior German forces strongly
supported by artillery. Of the 1st Battalion of the 137th
Regiment, which bore the brunt of the fighting, only fifty men
were left.

The Germans followed up the retreat rapidly. Urgent SOS

messages to General Barthélémy brought only the answer that there were no reserves and that the position was to be held at all costs even if it were surrounded, as the defence of Teteghem was essential to the plans for the final embarkation. At four o'clock the enemy forced a passage to the west of Teteghem village and came round in rear of the area. The defenders in the houses held on until they were killed or captured one by one, but the resistance lasted long enough for the 2nd Battalion of the regiment to establish a new holding position under Commandant Miquel at the bridge of Chapeau Rouge over the Dunkirk-Furnes Canal. At 6.30 pm the line was stabilised and the Germans were halted less than two and a half miles from the base of the East Mole.

In the centre, on the main approach to Dunkirk, a subsidiary attack developed. It was directed principally against two heavy guns manned by naval forces, which had previously been operating one on either side of the old Fort Vallières. These had been driven from their position following the destruction of the fort in a prolonged air attack and had re-established themselves near the bridge of Sept-Planètes. They opened the day with a bombardment of the bridges to the east of Bergues and on the enemy columns. They fired their last sixty rounds and their crews then established a road block across the main road with tractors and lorries. They held this barricade until finally they received orders to retire to the level-crossing at Coudekerque-Branche and held there to the last man. To the right of the new position Fort Castelnau, the last of the out-lying fortifications on the main approach to the town, still held out.

So, as the evening drew on, the final line outside Dunkirk was established. It ran from the dunes to the bridge of Chapeau Rouge, from Chapeau Rouge through the level-crossing at Coudekerque-Branche by the old Fort Castelnau, past the holding position outside St Georges, and so round the outer houses of Dunkirk to the beach beyond the burning tank farm. It was desperately close but it held, and at a conference between Admiral Abrial, General Fagalde and General de la Laurencie it was decided that the final evacuation should take place that night. The long agony of Dunkirk was almost over. The stage was set for the last macabre tragedy, the tragedy of the rear-guard.

*   *   *

At Dover Admiral Ramsay made his plans for the night. He had received no assurance that this would be the last crossing.

The condition of the crews of the ships was giving rise now to considerable anxiety. The accumulated effects of exhaustion were beginning to show themselves in the destroyers as well as in the personnel vessels. The number of destroyers available had diminished with sinkings, with collision damage, with bombing, and shell fire, and stranding until only nine ships were left of the forty which had successively been placed under his command. The personnel ships were similarly reduced – ten out of thirty remained, and their crews had reached the ultimate point of exhaustion. This was not cowardice, it was not self-interest, it was not even lack of will. No man who did not see that grim congestion between the moles of Dunkirk can judge properly the failures that took place. On the destroyers, on the personnel ships and on the smaller vessels men were driven to the extremes of human capability.

In the course of the afternoon Admiral Ramsay informed Admiralty that in his view 'the continuance of the demands made by evacuation would subject a number of officers and men to a test which might be beyond the limit of human endurance . . .' He asked that if the evacuation had to be continued after the coming night, fresh forces should be drafted in the full knowledge of the delays that that would entail.

Even while he made that declaration the preparations for the night went on. All his destroyers were placed under orders to cross and nine of the ten cross-Channel steamers, with one waiting in reserve. Four paddle-minesweepers, seven Fleet minesweepers, two corvettes, the gunboat *Locust*, nine drifters, and a number of motor-boat flotillas (mostly towed by tugs) made up the fleet. The French Navy organised its greatest effort this night. The official figures record that sixty-three French-manned vessels, including a large number of fishing-boats, set out. The lifting capacity of the combined forces was substantially over 30,000 men, but it was still held that the facilities which remained at Dunkirk were not capable of handling more than 25,000 in the hours of darkness available and then only if the most rapid rate of embarkation were maintained.

'In the evening,' said Admiral Ramsay in his dispatch, 'the Vice-Admiral was informed by the BNLO Marceau[1] that it

[1] The British Naval Liaison Officer at French Naval Headquarters.

was estimated 30,000 French remained and that the French Admiralty agree that evacuation should be terminated that night if possible.'

This figure is of the first importance. From the beginning of the operation French official estimates as to the number of their troops within the perimeter were unreliable and misleading. Admiral Ramsay, as has been said, was informed on the Saturday night that a total of 25,000 French remained. On the Sunday a new estimate reached him to the effect that, notwithstanding the very large numbers lifted since the previous estimate, between 50,000 and 60,000 were still in the area. Now on this Monday night the new estimate of 30,000 appeared to tally with the Sunday figure. In the twenty-four hours of June 3rd 26,746 men (of whom over 20,000 were French) had reached the English coast in safety. The difference between this and the Sunday evening estimate was a little over 30,000.

It was in accordance with this figure, which had previously been arrived at by the Dynamo Room staff and which now was confirmed from official French sources, that the night flight was prepared. Enough ships were sent to lift 30,000 men provided they could be got to the embarkation points within the hours of darkness. It is necessary to underline this point in view of accusations that were made subsequently by the Vichy Government.

The tug *Racia* was the first ship to sail. She left Ramsgate at 2.30 pm with a naval party on board. At four o'clock the skoot *Pascholl* took departure with four others. At 4.30 Admiral Taylor moved a convoy of motor-boats in tow of tugs; he himself sailed with *Mermaiden*, the leading boat; *Letitia II*, *Madame Sans Gêne* and the Clacton lifeboat were with the party. At 5.15 the tug *Sun IV* left with four more small craft and a party of naval officers and ratings. Shortly afterwards the remaining fast launches of the War Department, headed by *Marlborough*, took off.

At 6.15 pm the first of the cross-Channel steamers, *Autocarrier*, cleared. She was followed at once by *Lady of Mann*. *King George V* sailed at 6.30, close astern of her were the French vessels *Côte d'Argent* and *Rouen*. *Canterbury* had completed temporary repairs following her bombing on May 29th; she sailed at 6.45. *Manxman* failed to sail and was replaced by *Royal Sovereign*. *Princess Maud* and *Tynwald* were amongst the last to leave.

Simultaneously the destroyers began to cross. Admiral Wake-Walker went over in MTB 102. He reached the Mole at ten o'clock and as *Whitshed*, the first of the destroyers to arrive, had difficulty in berthing alongside the Mole in the fresh north-easterly breeze which was now blowing, he sent 102 to ferry off the naval pier parties from her. *Whitshed* had already been in trouble in Dover harbour earlier in the day when she was rammed by a small vessel and holed in a fuel tank. Making a second attempt, she got her ropes ashore.

Once again her account underlines the difficulties of dealing with the inland French. Though this was the last night and German machine-guns could already be heard on the outskirts of the town, her people found it necessary to 'push, pull, cajole and bully the *poilus* on board'. With very considerable effort she picked up 800 Frenchmen, took on one of the last of the small British Army parties that had remained ashore, and backed out of the harbour.

Lady of Mann was the first personnel ship to arrive. A number of French fishing vessels had reached the harbour. They had been ordered to go right into the town to lift men from any point at which they could get down to the water, but most of them appear to have made fast to the Mole on arrival. *Lady of Mann* found it impossible to berth until late because of this. They were eventually shifted by Admiral Wake-Walker himself, who used the MTB, which was the last of his flag-ships, to magnificent effect in bringing order out of the chaos of the last hours.

A strong easterly wind and a fast-running tide made attempts to come alongside the Mole exceptionally hazardous. *Autocarrier*, however, found a berth outside the Mole, almost at the pierhead, and made fast at eleven o'clock. She picked up 712 men and left at once. *Canterbury* berthed and picked up 659. *Côte d'Argent* got alongside at high water and was away by 12.30 am with 1,000 men.

Princess Maud arrived just before midnight, and Captain Clarke's account gives a vivid picture of the urgency and congestion of this last night.

'We arrived off Dunkirk breakwater at 11.57 pm, very close to our appointed time. We entered the pier-heads, and looked for a berth. The narrow fairway was crammed to capacity, with all varying types of ships bound in and out. Wrecks dotted the harbour here and there. The only light was that of shells bursting, and the occasional glare of fires . . .'

'At 12.55 we proceeded alongside a vacated berth at the extreme end of the eastern jetty. Troops then clambered aboard all ways, no gangways available. Dogs of all kinds got aboard somehow. There was no confusion whilst a steady line of men was directed along the jetty by several members of the crew.

'At 1.40 am the flow of troops thinned out, only stragglers came along. I was told that the port was going to be blocked at 2.30 am. At 1.50 we were fairly well packed, so I cast off after being told that was the last of the troops, although one other steamer was ahead loaded. Whilst swinging at 2.5 a shell fell in the berth we had just vacated. . . .'

Lady of Mann, which had been backing and filling inside the harbour waiting for a berth for nearly two hours, got alongside at 12.30 am and picked up a heavy load. *King George V* took a full load and got clear a little later. *Tynwald* got out with 1,500 men.

Royal Sovereign, after a slight collision on the way across in fog, berthed at the West Mole. At 2.55 am 'overladen with troops we left the pier, cutting our own forward ropes. Heavy gunfire continuously; leaving harbour saw crew of unknown vessel being rescued by small boats'. *Royal Sovereign* in her six completed crossings had carried, according to Admiral Ramsay's official record of the work of the personnel vessels, 6,585 men, almost exactly a tenth of the total carried by all the cross-Channel steamers in the operation.

Princess Maud and *Royal Sovereign* were the last of the passenger ships to leave, and with their departure a great chapter in the history of the British Merchant Navy came to its magnificent close.

Across this pattern the small boats worked endlessly. They were penetrating deep up into the harbour now, searching for stragglers, rescuing men from isolated points, ferrying them to the tugs or to the ships outside. HMS *Locust* lay off the moles as a receiving depot for these small liftings. The motor-boat *Letitia II*, which had picked up forty French troops well up the harbour, came out to her and was sent away again with a demolition party to the wreck of the gunboat *Mosquito*. Two depth charges were manhandled on board the wreck and fused. *Letitia II* withdrew, and with a tremendous explosion HMS *Mosquito* disintegrated. *Letitia II* was damaged as she returned to *Locust* and had to be abandoned on the way home.

Admiral Taylor, who had transferred to the fast launch *Marlborough* on the way across, went up the harbour to the Quai Félix Faure. Arrangements had been made to pick up a party of French naval personnel at that point. Though they met with difficulty in identifying the quay since none of the French ashore were familiar with the harbour, they made contact with their party and eventually got it away. On the outward passage *Marlborough* was following a French trawler when the Frenchman slewed suddenly across the channel. *Marlborough* headed for the gap at her stern. The quay at this point had been bombed, and she scraped over a patch of rubble and concrete and ripped off her unprotected propellers and rudder. Admiral and crew improvised paddles and attempted to get her out, but without success. A little later MA/SB 7 tried to take her in tow but, owing to engine trouble, rammed her instead. Finally she was picked up by the motor-yacht *Gulzar*, which was commanded by a Dominican monk, and towed back to Dover.

Admiral Taylor's assistant, Commander Troup, who had gone over with *Swallow*, another of the fast War Department boats, went alongside the West Mole at 10.30 pm. Finding considerable confusion there, he appointed himself piermaster and took control. Again he found trouble in inducing French troops to board small craft or to break their units in order to accommodate themselves to the ships available. Occasionally, he reported, if a small boat could not take a whole company or sometimes even if a ship could not take a battalion, men already on board insisted on being put ashore again.

To the West Mole came *Pascholl* with her flotilla of skoots. *Horst* ran aground in the shallows here and was abandoned. The others lifted full loads and got clear. *Pascholl* herself was wedged against the quay by a destroyer which was loading. Lieutenant J. N. Wise, RNVR, her commanding officer, described the scene as chaotic, but eventually she sailed with 300 men.

Finally Commander Troup, with the help of Capitaine le Comte de Chartier de Sedouy (a French liaison officer), succeeded in persuading French troops that they would meet again in England and eventually had the flow moving rapidly. From this one battered stretch of pier some thousands of troops were evacuated in the course of that night. Commander Troup had arranged for a boat to come in to collect him at three o'clock and to take off a French general and his staff. His picture of the final scene is among the dramatic moments of Dunkirk. She was the last boat out of that sector of the harbour and there were still about 1,000 men remaining on the pier. They stood at attention along the length of it. The general and his staff stood about 30 feet away from them, facing them, in the faint light of the dawn with the flames bringing faces and helmets into sharp relief. The general saluted, the men returned the salute; then he turned about, climbed down into the boat, and Troup put out to sea.

The last of the personnel ships had left. Now the paddle-steamers, the Fleet sweepers, the trawlers, the drifters, and, finally, the destroyers made their last departures.

HMM *Medway Queen*, whose name has appeared so often in the accounts of previous nights, made her seventh run. Shortly after she came alongside a shell-burst threw a destroyer astern of her against her lines, cutting them. Both ships swung out from the Mole. *Medway Queen* lost her brow, and the men who were coming aboard at the time flung themselves on to the ship as it fell. Her captain, Lieutenant A. T. Cook, RNR, rapidly regained control of his ship and nursed the destroyer back into position. Immediately after she was rammed by a cross-Channel steamer but escaped with slight damage. At the end of it all she picked up 367 French troops and sailed.

The destroyer *Malcolm* made her last passage. She had made six runs in all, having had one day off on the direct and personal orders of Admiral Ramsay. In these six trips she had carried 6,400 men.

Sabre completed her last venture. The oldest destroyer in the flotillas, she had the honour of bringing the first full cargo of men from the beaches. On this night she had the additional honour of carrying one of the last. With it she established the Dunkirk record of ten round trips. In all she lifted over 5,000 men.

At 3.18 am the destroyer *Express* backed out of the harbour. She had completed six runs, two to the beaches and four to Dunkirk, lifting in all 3,500 men.

* * *

At seven o'clock in the evening preparations for the evacuation of the staff of the *Force Maritime Nord* and the headquarters staff began. At this hour Admiral Abrial took leave of his officers, and at eight o'clock they moved down towards the East Mole. They were eventually embarked in *Autocarrier* and *Newhaven*. At the same time the men of the *Police de la Navigation*, who throughout the embarkation had handled the traffic of the West Mole and the inner harbour, left in their three remaining boats, two of which were in tow. The majority of the staff were clear by midnight.

At two o'clock Abrial himself embarked. As with Gort, he had been given final orders which admitted of no compromise and, accompanied by Admiral Platon, Admiral Leclerc and General Fagalde, he sailed with the motor-torpedo boats VTB 25 and 26, which had been sent across earlier in the evening by Admiral Landriau. In the roadstead, after being involved in a minor collision, he waited, watching the final embarkations, and at three o'clock he took departure for Dover.

General Barthélémy's final plan provided for the rearguard to disengage after dark and to move inwards towards the Mole and the harbour between eleven and midnight. Along most of the front the disengagement was successfully executed. Only the battalions holding the bridges across the Furnes Canal at Chapeau Rouge had difficulty in getting clear. At 10.30 pm the last retreat began. The troops of the rearguard had been told that ships would be provided. The ships were sent, but now, as darkness fell, out of the cellars, the ruined houses and the shelters of Malo and Dunkirk arose a monstrous army. The French historian Jacques Mordal described the scene.[1]

'General Barthélémy's hopes were not to be realised. As he approached Malo with the rearguard, he saw a vast crowd of troops materialise suddenly as the news of the last departure spread. Out of the cellars and the holes streams of unarmed men appeared, emerging everywhere, converging on the Mole, until they became an immense river of men frozen almost solid at the approaches. These hidden heroes, these warriors who for days had not left their shelters, had no intention now of giving up their chances of escape to those who had been fighting for them. Barthélémy's column marked time, waiting, watching, as these men of the army train, these transport drivers, these men of the auxiliary services filed past in thousands under its nose.

'Dawn came early at this time of year. As it broke, the rearguard saw the last ships leave. A few small boats came along-

[1] *La Bataille de Dunkerque.*

234

side and went in their turn. Then, when no one believed that another ship would come, the British destroyer *Shikari* slipped in. She took on board 600 men of the *Secteur fortifié des Flandres*. The rest of the rearguard of the beleaguered area, the men of the west, of the south and of the east, remained in the hands of the enemy.

'No episode in the epic of Dunkirk caused more heartbreak.'

So, held off by a hopeless army, the rearguard waited for the light. It is a lamentable story – lamentable for the evidence of the breakdown of morale, lamentable for the failure of Command which is implicit. In the circumscribed area of Dunkirk it should have been impossible for 40,000 men to hide.

The figures are clear, bitterly clear. At dusk the Command estimate was that 30,000 men remained in the area. In the course of the night 26,175 were lifted. According to German accounts 40,000 were captured. There must, then, have been more than 66,000 men in Dunkirk as the first ships of the night flight came in. Dunkirk was a major French base, it was the headquarters of an important area. It had a full staff organisation, and in that organisation it had its full share of police. How were 40,000 men able to hide – and stay hidden – through nine days of battle?

There was one other tragedy that night. The large French minesweeper *Emile Deschamps* sailed with 500 men on board. In the early morning she sighted the North Foreland, and the English coast was already in clear view when she detonated a magnetic mine and sank within a few seconds. With her went down a number of the survivors of the French destroyer *Jaguar* (which had been lost before the evacuation began), who had fought gallantly on the line of the Aa Canal as infantrymen. Some eighty men were picked up by the British minesweeper *Albury* and the two French drifters *Sainte-Elizabeth* and *Anne-Marie*.

At the end of the Mole *Shikari*, the last ship of Dunkirk, waited while the dawn broke. She was one of the oldest destroyers in service in the Royal Navy – small, battered, not particularly beautiful – but to her goes the honour of being the last ship from Dunkirk. At 3.40 am, with the sound of the German machine-guns close at hand, she pulled out, deeply loaded, and set course for England. It was no little glory.

Astern of her, as the dawn brightened, the valiant rearguard waited, hemmed in between the broken men, the deserters, the stragglers, the cast-offs of their own army, and the advancing army of the enemy. At nine o'clock in the morning Dunkirk surrendered.

338,226 men had been brought back in triumph to the English shore.

This was Dunkirk.

To each of the four nations which played a part in it it presented itself in a different way. Yet there was a common factor which linked its aspects. Basically Dunkirk was an opportunity. It was important not so much in itself as in what it made possible.

To the Germans it presented the opportunity to destroy the British Expeditionary Force in the general destruction of the Armies of the North, and with it the British will to resist.

To the Belgians it represented no more than an opportunity to continue a battle which they judged already lost.

To the French it was an opportunity to retrieve something of the disasters consequent upon the breakdown of the High Command.

To the British it was the traditional opportunity to withdraw in order to fight again – at a time and in a place of their own choosing.

Because of these basic differences it is necessary to examine separately the mistakes and the achievements of each of the four nations.

CHAPTER XVI

Germany's Triumph and Failure

Für den Angriff werden dann alle zu Gebote stehenden Kräfte eingesetzt mit dem Zweck, möglichst starke Teile des französischen Heeres und seiner Verbündeten auf nordfranzösischem und belgischem Boden zur Schlacht zu stellen und zu schlagen. . . .   Army Group A War Diary

THE PRINCIPAL object of Plan Yellow, according to the War Diary of Army Group A, was 'to engage and defeat as strong a portion of the French and Allied Armies as possible in Northern France and Belgium'.

A third of a million men of the Armies of the North escaped through Dunkirk. Why did the Germans fail?

A study of the handling of the three arms of the forces of the Reich after the astonishing triumph of the thrust to Abbeville is a fascinating exercise in the consequences of military indecision. Its origins lie in the period of the reconstruction of the German Army. Though her new forces were based upon the tank, though she had developed and perfected the combination of armour, of air support and of speed, the High Command had never wholly accepted the new philosophy of war. Despite the fact that Guderian and other generals had fully proved its possibilities in Poland, it was left, as has been described, to Manstein, to Rundstedt and, finally, to Hitler himself to force it upon Brauchitsch and the General Staff as a practical plan for the attack in the west. Because of that fact the High Command viewed the speed and depth of the first breakthrough with apprehension. The armoured divisions were halted again and again to consolidate in their race across France. Rundstedt was reminded endlessly and incessantly of the weakness of his flanks.

This was the first cause. There was a second.

Because the High Command had not believed its achievement possible, there was no plan for the immediate further use of the armoured columns once they had reached the sea. Quite literally Abbeville was the end of German thinking. General Guderian wrote of May 20th:[1]

'On the evening of this remarkable day we did not know in what direction our advance should continue; nor had Panzer Group von Kleist received any instructions concerning the further prosecution of our offensive.'

These two factors were drawn together by the British clearance operation to the south of Arras – the so-called 'Arras counter-attack'. To Rommell, then only a divisional general, knocked off balance by the first real fighting that he had come up against since the crossing of the Meuse, the Arras attack was demonstrably the beginning of the reaction of the Armies of the North. This – the first appearance of well-handled enemy armour – seemed as if it must be the beginning of the thrust against the northern flank, which would inevitably be matched by another thrust from the south designed to cut off the armoured columns from the main body of the following army. His fears communicated themselves to Rundstedt. They coincided with the decision to turn the leading armour north along the coast and they delayed that movement.

That brief delay, which enabled the British to take action at Boulogne and Calais, was, however, only a small part of the effect of the Arras attack. Throughout his handling of the armour thereafter Rundstedt clearly shows himself almost as apprehensive as the General Staff. He counted his losses: fifty per cent of his armour and his vehicles by the 23rd, substantial losses in men. To the north, it will be recalled, he was moving against an area that was unsuited to tanks – the ditch-seamed marshy line of the Aa Canal and the low-lying, dyke-bedevilled country of the Flanders Plain. A combination of factors weighed on his mind. He had to prepare, on the Führer's orders, for the resumption of the attack to the south – the attack against metropolitan France. He still believed (because it was militarily impossible not to believe) in the strength of the French armies. He knew that the French had had more tanks at the outset than he had possessed. He knew that all well-conducted armies have a properly disposed reserve. He looked, then, to the north with its unsuitable terrain; he looked to the south with its new responsibilities and its fresh dangers: and at 6.10 on the evening of May 23rd

[1] *Panzer Leader.*

he halted the armour on the line of the Aa Canal and gave Gort the time he needed to consolidate his desperate, piece-meal defence.

On the following day Hitler confirmed Rundstedt's order. He confirmed it in the midst of a high confusion of military opinion on the part of the German leaders. Brauchitsch considered that the encircling attacks should proceed without pause and that Bock should command all the forces engaged. Halder thought that this order would lead to trouble and publicly washed his hands. Jodl in his normal jackal manner recorded that Hitler was very happy about Rundstedt's measures. Rundstedt felt that the situation was under control, the armies were encircled, and that his armour had done enough. Hitler himself considered that the Allied armies would be smashed between the anvil of Rundstedt's armour halted along the Aa Canal and the hammer of Bock's armies smashing down through Belgium. Goering was convinced that the Luftwaffe could deal with everything.

But Bock himself had diverted his hammer blow. Ordered to attack to the south, he had instead decided to exploit the weakness that had been discovered at the point of junction between the British and the Belgian Armies. He was correct about the weakness, triumphantly he forced a gap between the British and the Belgians – and fatally he failed to utilise it. He failed because in the swift success of the thrust to Abbeville the High Command had suddenly overdone its enthusiasm for the new theory of war and had taken away the three divisions of armour that he had had with him at the start. When the gap opened he had nothing to hurl through it. Whether he could have done more with the force at his disposal is debatable. His handling of his troops throughout was conventional, slow-thinking, and uninspired. The hammer never struck the anvil. The Armies of the North were not cut off from the sea.

Those, in brief outline, are the main reasons for the failure of the German Army, but there was yet another factor which closely influenced the considerations both of Hitler and of his generals – the pot-valiant offer of Reichsmarschall Goering to destroy the Armies of the North with the Luftwaffe. This was bedevilling action as early as May 24th, when Guderian records the receipt of an order embodying the proposal. 'We were,' he says, 'utterly speechless.'

So, apparently, was Field-Marshal Kesselring, the officer

responsible for executing the task.[1]

'I was all the more surprised when my Command – perhaps as a reward for our late achievements? – was given the task of annihilating the remains of the British Expeditionary Force almost without assistance from the army.'

The Luftwaffe by the 27th had flown seventeen days of ceaseless missions. The contribution of the tactical arm of the German Air Force to Rundstedt's advance, to the invasion of Holland and to the breaking of the Belgian frontier line is of the very highest importance. It was the full expression of the technique which was first displayed against Poland, and it achieved its results. But it achieved them at a considerable cost in aircraft and an important cost in pilots, and behind all these things were the physical exhaustion of the front-line squadrons. Kesselring's view was that his own force was quite unable to accomplish the task which Goering had claimed for it. Even with the addition of the VIII Air Group he believed the operation to be completely impossible. Was he correct in his assumption?

The docks and loading facilities at Dunkirk had been put out of action long before the evacuation started. It is highly doubtful if any heavy equipment could have been handled after May 24th. Yet throughout the operation a very substantial share of the Luftwaffe's effort was expended on Dunkirk town and docks. A second and almost equally substantial share was expended on the long straight lines of the dunes and beaches. The effort was almost wholly wasted: in the dunes the soft sand blanketed the effect of bombs, in the town shelter was adequate. The total of casualties to personnel was quite incommensurate with the scale of the German effort. It had no major effect on the evacuation.

There was here a fundamental failure in the thinking of Goering, of Kesselring, and of the staff of the Luftwaffe as a whole. In part it was due to the general German failure to grasp the essentials of sea-power. Added to that was the failure of the airman's mind to appreciate its potentialities and its weaknesses. To put it in its simplest possible form: one bomb in the soft sand dunes of La Panne might kill five men; one bomb dropped on a crowded destroyer might bring death to 500. The failure of the Luftwaffe at Dunkirk was its failure to concentrate from the very first on the shipping. An army, reasonably dug in and properly dispersed, waiting for evacua-

[1] The Memoirs of Field-Marshal Kesselring.

tion, is not seriously vulnerable to the type of attack that was possible at that time. Ships, partly because of the lamentable state of seaborne anti-aircraft gunnery at the beginning of the war, were intensely vulnerable.

If Kesselring from the outset of the operation had concentrated on shipping, he might well have fulfilled Goering's boast. As early as Wednesday, May 29th, losses amongst the destroyers, it will be recalled, forced an important change in policy – that Ramsay managed to reverse that change is beside the point. On June 1st the proof was clear for all to read. Ramsay himself was forced to abandon daylight operations. The loss in destroyers and in personnel ships on that grim morning was equivalent to the loss of a naval battle. Had it occurred earlier in the week, had it been repeated as it should have been, the consequences to the evacuation are clear and obvious. Ramsay could not have afforded the loss of more destroyers, he could not have afforded the loss of more personnel ships. If, in addition, Dover, Ramsgate, Folkestone and Sheerness, crowded with shipping and ill-protected, had been attacked even by night, the evacuation might well have collapsed in the first days.

If to a properly directed air effort had been added a properly directed naval effort, it must have collapsed.

The reasons for the German naval failure also lie far back in time. With the Z Plan, the definitive outline for the re-establishment of the German Navy, Admiral Raeder had evolved a scheme which would have given Germany a powerful and balanced fleet of modern ships in 1942 and overwhelming strength by 1948. In 1939 the German admirals entered the war unwilling and with forebodings. The relative sizes of the fleets involved gave them no reasons for confidence. When the plans for the attack in the west were drafted Germany had, none the less, strong forces, which were capable of playing a substantial part. The famous Directive No. 6 laid down that:

'The Naval Staff is to apply all its resources to the direct and indirect support of the Army and Air Force during the period of the attack.'[1]

Directive No. 6 was issued in October 1939. A month before Plan Yellow was put into operation in May 1940, Hitler overran Denmark and invaded Norway. The whole available strength of the German Navy was at once diverted from any

[1] *Sea Warfare 1939–1945*, by Vice-Admiral Friedrich Ruge.

consideration of support on the right flank of Plan Yellow to the necessities of Norway. Admiral Raeder, who prepared the naval plan, was fully aware that:

'The operation in itself is contrary to all principles in the theory of naval warfare. According to this theory, it could be carried out by us only if we had naval supremacy. We do *not* have this.'[1]

For this very patent reason he made certain reservations. They resulted in a brush with Hitler at a meeting on March 29th. Hitler wished to leave naval forces in Narvik. Raeder said:

'In Narvik destroyers are helpless, since they are exposed to the danger of being destroyed by superior forces.'

The last paragraph of his report read at one of the more famous and acrimonious of the Führer Conferences, says:

'The Führer gives up the idea of leaving ships behind in Narvik . . .'

It was simple to take decisions in conference, it was not as simple to carry them out. Ten of the largest and newest of the German destroyers were dispatched to cover the Narvik operation. Their fuel endurance was such that it was essential for them to be re-fuelled immediately on arrival at the port. Two tankers were sent for this purpose. One of these, the *Kattegat*, was intercepted by Norwegian patrol vessels and sunk in the Vestfjord, and the re-fuelling of the Narvik destroyers was delayed. Because of this Warburton-Lee's flotilla was given time to attack them and begin the work of annihilation which *Warspite* and her destroyers completed. The destruction at Narvik, added to the tally of loss and damage in the other operations of the Norwegian invasion, wrecked the precarious balance of the German Navy.

On May 10th, when the German Army crossed the Maastricht bridges, there was nothing whatever to spare for co-operation with the attack in the west, nor to the German admirals did the opportunity for such co-operation appear to be imminent. No more than the German General Staff did they believe in the possibility of a triumph as swift as the race to Abbeville. When the Allied Armies of the North were finally cut off from metropolitan France there were no German naval vessels in the home bases capable of serious interference either with the supply of the armies in the early stages or with the beginnings of evacuation.

[1] Führer Conferences on Naval Affairs – March 9th, 1940.

Mining operations in the Scheldt and off the western harbours, which had been one of the principal items in the original plan, had been handed over to the Luftwaffe. The responsibility for interference fell to four coastal U-boats, which were operating in what the Germans called the Hoofden – the southern sector of the North Sea and the entrance to the Channel. Not until May 21st was the first aggressive step taken by recalling the two motor torpedo-boat flotillas which were operating in Norwegian waters to the German Bight for operations in the area of the Hoofden. The only other ships available up to this had been the depleted local minesweeping, anti-aircraft, and coastal protection vessels of the Heligoland Bight.

A further complication arose in connection with this movement. The mining operations undertaken by the Luftwaffe had been carried out with a certain lack of discrimination. The opening of the Dutch ports, which gave access to the Dunkirk area, was delayed until mine clearance could be undertaken, and the operations of the flotillas were postponed thereby.

While it was possible for Admiral Ramsay's ships to use Route Z, the short route which ran past Calais, the opportunities for effective action by German MTBs were comparatively limited. When the approach was switched on May 28th to Route Y, the whole situation altered dangerously. The turning point for Route Y was well out to sea off Ostend. Ostend is little more than 30 miles from Flushing, less than an hour's run by MTB. But, in addition, Ostend itself passed into German hands on May 28th. The opportunities for the two flotillas which had been sent from Norway thus became virtually unlimited. The constant stream of traffic during the hours of darkness through Route Y was intensely vulnerable to attack. Because of the very large number of small craft in the area Allied naval vessels were under direct orders not to fire until they had definitely established the hostile identity of strange ships. Every chance, then, lay with the resolute commander of an MTB. Not until May 29th were those chances exploited – and then it was by a U-boat commander. The destruction at midnight of the two destroyers *Wakeful* and *Grafton* represented an important victory to the Germans, for it caused the partial abandonment of Route Y and it forced the necessity to establish a new route of approach.

But to develop the victory it was necessary to press home

the attacks. In this the German torpedo-boat flotillas failed signally. For three nights they appear to have been unaware of the diversion of traffic to the new approach route – Route X – and the major casualty during this period was the French destroyer *Siroco*, though there was also loss to personnel ships and small craft. It is probable that the lack of destroyer support for these operations contributed to this irresolution. The U-boats operating in this area had also very little success.

The explanation of these failures seems to lie – as it does with the operations of the Luftwaffe – once again basically in the failure to appreciate the possibilities of sea-power. It is strange that this criticism should have to be made with regard to the decisions of admirals, but it is implicit in the memorandum from Admiral Schniewind, Raeder's Chief of Staff, to the Supreme Command (Air), Führer Headquarters, quoted at the head of Chapter VII. In it he confesses bluntly the Navy's inability to interfere.

That memorandum is a confession of weakness – moral weakness and mental weakness. It seems to have affected all concerned in such measures as the Navy did undertake. The hold-ups in mine clearance, the delays in bringing the Dutch ports into use, the lack of determination in pressing home the attacks even after substantial success had been achieved, speak with the utmost clarity of inadequate Command.

The blame for the German failure is shared by all three Services. Its consequences were to be decisive. It was an opportunity thrown away.

CHAPTER XVII

The Belgian Effort

The cause of the Allies is lost. Soon, within a few days perhaps, France will, in her turn, be obliged to abandon the struggle, for the disproportion of forces precludes any hope for her. No doubt, Britain will continue to fight, not on the Continent, but on the seas and in her colonies. The war may be a long one. But it will be one in which Belgium will have no opportunity of intervening, and, therefore, the role of this country is finished.

KING LEOPOLD OF THE BELGIANS
at the Château of Wynendaele, May 25th, 1940

To THE Belgians evacuation, had they considered it possible, could have meant two things only: the certain abandonment of their country, and the doubtful opportunity of resuming the battle at the side of France.

In any consideration of this situation, the character of the King of the Belgians is the first essential. King Leopold, as *de facto* Commander-in-Chief of the Belgian Army, played two roles in the story. With the first of these roles it is not necessary to deal in detail here. Belgium had decided upon a policy of armed neutrality. The impracticability of that decision is obvious today, but at that time both the Belgians and their king believed in it, and it was maintained through the various threats between September of 1939 and May of 1940. Not until the Germans crossed the frontier was a call made upon the Allies for assistance, nor were any proper arrangements made for co-operation.

The Belgian Army, as Leopold told Gort through Sir Roger Keyes, 'existed solely for defence, it had neither tanks nor aircraft and was not trained or equipped for offensive warfare'. Its defects were much the same as those of the French. It was committed to the static defence of a frontier which, though it was not based upon a Maginot Line, was at points defended by strong modern fortifications.

When on May 10th the Germans seized vital bridges by treachery, destroyed the great fortress of Eben Emael by a brilliant airborne operation, and broke through the fortified zone, the Belgian Army had been informed of the outline of Plan D. How much the knowledge that the Allies were moving to a defensive position behind them contributed to the timing of their initial withdrawal it is impossible to estimate, but it seems evident that the Belgian Army was already looking over its shoulder when Eben Emael fell. The retreat to the Antwerp-Louvain line was accomplished at speed and long before the French High Command anticipated it. After the necessary readjustments to that line, however, the Belgian Army equated itself to the general Allied scheme with remarkable efficiency. It must be remembered that, as an army of fixed defences, its transport and supply arrangements were sketchy in the extreme, but when on the 16th the retreat from the Dyle position began it kept pace, despite its lack of transport, with the rate of the Allied withdrawal. There were, inevitably, misunderstandings; touch was lost on occasion; but these things are part and parcel of allied operations. The Belgian Army came back by stages to the line of the River Lys as an efficient part of the Allied fighting machine. On the night of May 23rd it was finally established along a front of roughly 60 miles from Menin through Eecloo to the sea – approximately one and a half times the length of front that it had held under Plan D at the beginning of the campaign.

Though it had been in contact with the Germans during most of this period, fighting, it will be remembered, was not heavy. As the line stood on the Escaut, it began to grow in intensity. By the 24th, following the final withdrawal to the Lys, the southern portion of its sector was under very heavy pressure and at the point of junction with the British Expeditionary Force the Belgians suffered considerable punishment.

Lord Gort was fully aware both of the qualities and the weaknesses of the Belgian Army and of the weight of the German offensive against it. On the 20th Sir Roger Keyes, who represented the British Government at Belgian Headquarters, had reported on its situation. It had already yielded more than three-quarters of the territory of Belgium, including the capital and the principal cities, with all the inevitable consequence to morale. It had fallen back not on a firm base, but

247

on a seaboard barren of all military production. Ammunition supplies were, therefore, reduced to a minimum. It had no alternative sources of supply and it had no sea-power with which to organise them. Finally, on the last fragment of Belgian soil were compressed the hordes of refugees that had fled ahead of the retreating armies. It was estimated that at the most only fourteen days' food supply remained in the area.

The attitude of King Leopold was commendably reasonable. He declared that:

'He did not feel that he had any right to expect the British Government to consider jeopardising perhaps the very existence of its ten divisions in order to keep contact with the Belgian Army.'[1]

In a measure this may be said to be the first warning which Leopold issued. At the Ypres meeting on the following day that warning was elaborated. At the conclusion of the meeting Gort had no illusions as to the strength of the Belgians and no confidence in their army's ability to withdraw to the Yser line in conformity with Weygand's requirements.

The influence of General van Overstraeten on King Leopold has been the subject of much criticism. As the King's military ADC his position was ill-defined. He seems to have exercised very much more influence in counsel than the Chief of the Belgian Staff. His personal attitude appears to have exacerbated many of those who made contact with the King during this period and his 'defeatism' occupies a prominent place in all the memoirs. At this meeting his opinion and his method of delivering it was the subject of particularly acrid comment, yet it is doubtful if in actual fact he went much beyond the realities of the situation.

Long before the meeting took place King Leopold appears to have made up his mind that the French Command was not, in reality, exercising command and that the French Armies were not, in fact, able to produce an effective plan for resistance against the German thrust. He seems to have reached that opinion on a dispassionate reading of the evidence and the application of cool common-sense, and he was perfectly correct in his assumptions. He was equally correct in his assessment of Weygand's vagueness and indecision.

Looking at the position of the Belgian Army from his point of view, the situation was relatively simple. Whatever the Allies did after this moment the Belgian Army was bound to

[1] *The War in France and Flanders* by Major L. F. Ellis.

suffer. If the thrust to the south or Ironside's plan for a withdrawal to the Somme could be mounted and were to succeed, the British Expeditionary Force and the French First Army must inevitably draw away from the Belgians, in which case whether the Belgians shortened their line to the Yser or whether they remained upon the Lys their fate was in every respect identical. They had no hope of fighting out a prolonged resistance on the coast. They had no hope of providing for their own evacuation, no object in continuing the fight after the loss of their entire country, no faith in the ability or even in the intention of France to carry on the battle, and very little belief in the capacity of Britain to do so. In all these things except the last the Belgian assumptions were correct. None the less, so long as the Belgian Army was in a position to fight it went on fighting.

For three days after that conference it sustained the increasing weight of Bock's attack. At midnight on May 24th the Needham Mission – the British Army liaison at Belgian Headquarters – sent the signal to Gort which read:

'Position serious Belgian front between Menin and canal junction NW of Desselghem . . . Enemy penetration on this front everywhere exceeds one mile. Belgians are NOT repeat NOT counter-attacking this morning but may later in day . . .'

This was the beginning of the end. On the 25th the penetration had developed into an open breach. On the 26th General Michiels, the Belgian Chief of Staff, sent Gort a note which declared:

'. . . the Belgian Army is being attacked with extreme violence on the front Menin-Nevele, and since the battle is now spreading to the whole of the area of Eecloo, the lack of Belgian reserves makes it impossible to extend our boundaries, which were notified yesterday, farther to the right. We must therefore, with regret, say that we have no forces available to fill the gap in the direction of Ypres.'

On the 27th Lord Gort received from Sir Roger Keyes a message which said:

'The King wishes you to know that his army is greatly disheartened . . . The knowledge that the Allied armies in this sector have been encircled and that the Germans have great superiority in the air has led his troops to believe that the position is almost hopeless. He fears a moment is rapidly approaching when he can no longer rely upon his troops to fight or to be of any further use to the BEF. He wishes you to realise that he will be obliged to surrender before a débâcle . . .'

At three o'clock in the afternoon the Needham Mission sent a signal: 'Situation still very confused but indications are that the Belgian front may be crumbling.' Just before six o'clock it sent a final message: 'Belgian front has broken under ceaseless bombing. King asking for an armistice now.' This last message failed to reach Lord Gort: none the less it was sent. A duplicate of the message reached London.

Similar signals were sent to French Headquarters and reached Weygand. Throughout the period of the decline of the Belgian Army, in fact, the same information, the same warnings were available to the French. Yet Weygand says of the surrender: [1]

'This news fell like a bolt out of the blue. There had been no warning, no indication which might lead me to anticipate such a step.'

It is unnecessary to comment on this except to say that Weygand had found his third scapegoat.

Was the Belgian surrender the irremediable disaster that Reynaud, Weygand and a host of other critics claimed it to be? Did it wreck the Weygand Plan? Did it cause the loss of the French First Army? Did it jeopardise the general position of France on the new line of the Somme? The answer appears to be that except perhaps in regard to time – and only very doubtfully there – it made no major difference to the inexorable progress of the defeat of the Armies of the North.

The BEF was the formation most directly affected by it. Three full days before Leopold sent his emissaries to ask Bock for terms Gort had 'written off' the Belgians. Because of the breach which had developed between Menin and Desselghem it was quite obvious to him that his left flank was already open. The retirement of the Belgians northwards instead of to the line of the Yser was forced by the weight and direction of the German attack. Nothing that the BEF could do with the reserves it had left could restore contact. When at six o'clock on the evening of the 25th May Gort finally abandoned the Weygand Plan, it was because of the military defeat of the Belgian Army, because of the inability of the BEF to restore the front, and because the utmost he could now hope for was to build up his left flank enough to cover his withdrawal to the sea.

[1] *Rappelé au Service* by General Weygand.

By the Saturday evening evacuation was finally determined upon, by Sunday afternoon it was ordered, by Sunday evening it was already in progress. The British took unilateral action and took it first. Leopold was not informed – officially, at any rate – of the decision to evacuate until the Monday. He took his own unilateral action to capitulate twenty-four hours *after* Operation 'Dynamo' had begun.

That the final news of Leopold's surrender came as a shock to Gort in the circumstances in which he received it – away from his Command Post and separated from communications – is undeniable. Yet he had already made not only all the necessary dispositions, but all the dispositions it was possible to make to counteract its results. He had no further reserves to throw into the battle. There was nothing more that he could do. It is true that had the Belgians continued to fight for a few more days they would have continued to draw a large portion of the weight of Bock's army on to themselves and away from the flank of the retreat to Dunkirk, but the British Expeditionary Force was, in fact, evacuating – clearing out. It had made its decision without reference to the Belgian Army. The Belgian Army made its decision to surrender without reference to the British. These are hard truths, but it is necessary that cold common sense should be injected into the irrational controversies which have surrounded this matter.

To the Belgians Dunkirk was an opportunity without significance.

CHAPTER XVIII

Collapse of the French Army

If you had seen, as I have done this morning, the broad smile of General Gamelin when he told me the direction of the enemy attack, you would feel no uneasiness. The Germans have provided him with just the opportunity which he was awaiting.

M. JACQUINOT, Controller-General of the French Army, May 10th, 1940

TO THE French Dunkirk, for reasons which are apparent and logical, could not and did not have the importance which it assumed in British eyes. Yet the Command, both military and political, was striving desperately to establish a new line on the Somme. Every man who could be brought out of the north was not saved merely from a German prison camp, but was a trained and tested reinforcement for the battle of the south. That this was either not realised at all or realised too late is a part of that general collapse of French military thought which is the underlying cause of the disaster of the north.

It is not possible here to examine in detail all the causes of that collapse but they extend back far in time. Three men are primarily responsible for the disaster – Pétain, Gamelin and Weygand: Pétain who directed French policy to the defensive, Gamelin who readied the armies of France for war and directed the opening of the campaign on the basis of that policy, Weygand who commanded the final débâcle. That the politicians played their part behind these three men, that the pressure of the industrialists of the Lille area had its influence, that the man in the street contributed to the general breakdown of the French body politic is beside the point. These were the soldiers, these were the men professionally dedicated to the defence of France.

The origins lie in Pétain's *Note sur l'organisation défensive du territoire* in 1921. Then Commander-in-Chief, ignoring

252

completely the implication of the invention of the tank, he committed France to a 'continuous frontier battlefield' similar in principle to that of the trench systems of 1914–18. To defend the northern frontier, he claimed, it was necessary to advance into Belgium.

General Gamelin became *Ier Sous-Chef de l'État-Major de l'Armée* in 1930. In 1931 he became Chief of Staff. For the nine years which preceded the war, therefore, he held a succession of appointments of increasing importance until in 1938 he became *Chef d'État-Major Général de la Défense Nationale*. In 1937 he was instructed to devise a four-year plan for the army. He asked for an expenditure of 9,000 million francs. Daladier increased it to 14,000 million, Parliament added twenty per cent, and in 1938 and 1939 a further 23,000 million was voted. The French Army of 1939, therefore, was largely his creation and its military policies are entirely his responsibility.

It is painfully evident on any analysis of events that the French Army was wholly inefficient as an instrument for the defence of France. It had armour qualitatively and quantitatively sufficient for its task but it had no concept for its use. It had the Maginot Line but it allowed secondary considerations to drain off forty divisions of men to an area which was designed to be held with steel and concrete. It had an air force but it was too out of date to make a significant contribution to the land battle. Its infantry formations, with a few magnificent exceptions, proved to be ill-trained, ill-disciplined, and inadequately led.

In all these things Gamelin, by virtue of the role he had played from 1930 onwards, has a major responsibility, but for the policy for the use of this *matériel* the responsibility is his alone. He was the Supreme Commander, he was not in any way bound to the twenty-year-old theories of Pétain – yet he implemented them. In course of doing so he committed the two cardinal errors of a supreme commander in time of war: he wholly misread the enemy's intentions and he failed to provide the reserve with which to meet the vicissitudes of the encounter battle to which he dispatched his main forces – the Armies of the North.

On May 9th Reynaud decided to force his dismissal, if necessary by resigning and reconstructing the Government. The launching of the German attack on May 10th made the change impossible. Gamelin, reprieved, professed himself

253

completely satisfied with the course of events.

'If you had seen, as I have done this morning,' said M. Jacquinot, the Controller-General of the Army, 'the broad smile of General Gamelin . . .'

A daily précis of events is illuminating. On the 11th Gamelin considered it proper to order Giraud to be very careful. The thrust into Holland (which had taken away the best part of the reserve of the Armies of the North) had already manifestly failed. On the 12th the German panzer divisions reached the area of Sedan. By one o'clock on the early morning of the 13th he found it necessary to issue an Order of the Day:

'The time has come to fight to the end in the positions laid down by the Supreme Command. We no longer have any right to retreat.'

The ink was hardly dry on the signature when the Germans crossed the Meuse. On the 14th Corap's Army 'faded away'. On the 15th Prime Minister Reynaud telephoned Winston Churchill to say: 'We have lost the battle.' On the 16th the Military Governor of Paris advised the Government to evacuate the capital. On the 17th Reynaud sent a signal to General Maxime Weygand at Beirut instructing him to come at once to Paris. By the 18th the Armies of the North were moving back to the line of the River Scheldt and in the south the panzer divisions were 30 miles from Amiens. At eight o'clock on the morning of May 19th General Gamelin issued 'Personal and Secret Instructions No. 12'. He did not wish to interfere in the conduct of the battle, he gave his approval to all the arrangements which had been made. He felt that something should be done about maintaining the link between the Eastern Armies and the Armies of the North, and something else 'if necessary' about forcing the road to the Somme. There were other points, but these are the important ones. It was a directive, if it was anything at all – it was not a plan.

Early in the afternoon of that grim Sunday General Weygand arrived in Paris. Reynaud at once offered him the appointment of Supreme Commander in all theatres of operations, of the ground, sea and air forces. The reign of Gamelin was over.

In the strange circumstances of those desperate days a timetable is again perhaps the clearest way of outlining the progress of General Weygand. It will be remembered that he was summoned on the 17th. (The Germans were advancing on Cambrai and St Quentin.) Beirut is approximately 2,000 miles from Paris as an aeroplane flies. It is not explained why it took two full days in the fantastic urgencies of the moment for him to reach Paris. On the 19th he was offered the command 'in the early afternoon'. He announced that he would have to consult Gamelin and Georges, and he did not accept until the evening. (The panzer divisions had reached Péronne and occupied the line of the Canal du Nord as far as Marquion.) In the course of that evening Georges said: 'I should like to explain the situation to you.' And Weygand answered promptly: 'No, to-morrow.' Reynaud comments:[1]

'But Weygand had more urgent cares. He spent the best part of the daytime of the 20th in paying visits. Mandel was one of those he hurried off to see, as I learned later from Mandel himself.'

Allowing for Reynaud's bias, it remains a fact that no positive action was taken in Weygand's name on this critical day. (The German tanks hurtled across the last remaining stretch of France to the sea at Abbeville.)

When Georges finally had an opportunity of outlining things to him on the 20th, Weygand announced at once that it was necessary for him to go to the spot to judge the situation for himself. So began what Weygand called his 'Odyssey'. It is in the details of this extraordinary journey that much of Weygand's ignorance of fact and his total failure to grasp reality first and most clearly show themselves, and it is desirable to give its progress with some particularity.

It began with the decision of his staff to send his road transport to Abbeville, where the General was to join it by train. The transport arrived to find Abbeville in flames and the Germans entering. Weygand apparently had not appreciated this possibility, nor was he informed of it. Alternative arrangements were made, and at dawn of the 21st he flew instead to an airfield close to Béthune where he understood Billotte's headquarters to be. The airfield, when he arrived there, had been abandoned. Instead of driving the 12 miles or so to see Billotte at Béthune, he flew to Calais, which was about twice as far from the intended meeting place at Ypres. At Calais he located by accident General Champon, and arrangements were completed to meet the King of the Belgians at Ypres at three o'clock. Generals Billotte and Fagalde were summoned to attend. No signal appears to have been sent to

[1] *In the Thick of the Fight* by Paul Reynaud.

(and certainly no signal was received by) General Gort, who awaited a summons all day at his Command Post.

The meeting divided itself into three phases. In the first Weygand discussed future strategy with the King. He wanted him to agree to a retirement to the Yser to cover an attack to the south, which was to be carried out by the British Expeditionary Force and the French First Army in conjunction. An attack by the new armies, which Weygand was forming to the south, would be synchronised with this. The Belgian account of the affair says bluntly:

'It appeared from this interview that no well-defined plan for resistance existed, and that the Supreme Commander was not aware of the situation.'

In the course of the discussion, however, Weygand was informed by the Belgians that Abbeville was now in enemy hands and that the Armies of the North were finally cut off.

During a brief adjournment Billotte and Fagalde arrived.

In the second phase of the meeting Weygand was informed of the state of the French First Army. According to the Belgian account he agreed that the condition of the Belgian Army would make it difficult to withdraw to the Yser but suggested that if Belgian divisions could be substituted for certain British ones in the existing line, it would still be possible to mount an attack.

'It was, therefore,' says the Belgian account, 'necessary to invite Lord Gort to join the conference. But he could not arrive before 7 pm.'

At 5.30 pm Weygand announced that it was essential for him to return to Paris. Without seeing Gort, without hearing from him of the state of his army or explaining to him his intentions, without having seen anything of the situation 'on the spot' except from the remote viewpoints of Calais and Ypres, Weygand left urgently for Dunkirk. It had been decided that a return journey by air was impossible owing to enemy air attack, though the account of the French officer commanding the Calais airfield fails to record these attacks and aircraft continued to fly to and fro until the 23rd. Instead Weygand embarked in the torpedo-boat *Flore*, did not get to Cherbourg until the following morning and finally reached Paris by train at ten o'clock. *Flore* was capable of 30 knots. If Weygand had had any real sense of urgency, a simple message to Dover would have arranged for an aircraft to be at his disposal at the nearest Kentish airfield. He could have been back in Paris not later than ten o'clock the same night. If for reasons of pride or policy he had not chosen to use English facilities, he could still have landed at Dieppe – rather less than half the sea distance to Cherbourg – and travelled by train to Paris – rather less than half the rail journey. The whole affair, in fact, was a grotesque waste of time, and its accomplishment virtually nil. (While it was happening the Germans advanced to Montreuil and to the outskirts of Arras, and then – as Weygand, feeling self-consciously like Odysseus, steamed into Paris – began the attack towards Boulogne.)

At noon, at a meeting with Reynaud and Churchill, he explained, 'brisk, buoyant and incisive in spite of a night of travel', the 'Weygand Plan'. The Belgian Army would withdraw to the Yser. The British Army and the French forces in the north would attack 'as soon as possible, and in any case by tomorrow, 23rd', in the direction of Bapaume and Cambrai with eight divisions. The new French armies of the south, which were 'progressing towards Amiens, will advance northwards to meet the British divisions'.

This sounds more impressive than Gamelin's last effort. In actual content it was precisely the same. Only the positive details of the size of the force and the date differentiate it from Instruction No. 12. Neither it nor the Instruction were, in fact, practicable. No clear 'plan' emerged, and three days of Weygand's authority had been used up. The sands were almost out.

What were the realities of the situation on May 22nd? At the risk of some repetition it is desirable to restate them. The Belgian Army, exhausted, with its ammunition running low and its morale weakening, was engaged over a 60-mile front and had declared its inability to retire farther than the Lys. The BEF was fighting against a slowly increasing weight of infantry along the whole of its eastern front, while at the same time Gort was striving to build a wholly new front of fantastic length to the west against the left hook of the German armour. The French First Army was declining in supplies, in ammunition, and in morale with every moment. The German panzer divisions, far from presenting a naked flank, had turned to the north along the whole of the area from Valenciennes to the sea.

The withdrawal of eight divisions at this moment would have so thinned the line that Bock, with his mass of infantry, must have swept virtually unhindered to the beaches. But if by some miracle eight divisions could have been concentrated, they would have had to thrust, without armour and with ammunition supplies for a maximum of three days of battle, into a hornets' nest of ten armoured divisions and anything up to ten infantry divisions.

The Weygand Plan was military nonsense. Only the absolute breakdown of the French Command – of the French military mind – prevented that fact from being recognised at once.

Did Weygand himself recognise it? The screaming fury of his denunciations on May 24th of the withdrawal of Frankforce from Arras would seem to indicate an urgent, indeed a desperate search for an excuse and for a scapegoat. The reasons for the abandonment of Arras were dealt with earlier in this volume; it is not necessary to recapitulate them. It is only necessary to recognise in his accusations, first, against Gort and, then, against the British Government, and in his misleading of Churchill and Eden as to the 'recapture of Péronne, Albert and Amiens', a demonstrable dishonesty.

At midday on May 25th Weygand received a report on the state of Blanchard's army from a senior staff officer, Major Fauvelle. Fauvelle had left Blanchard's Headquarters at noon the previous day. His instructions were to inform Weygand that:

'. . . there was no longer any hope of Blanchard's being able to carry out the offensive that Weygand had ordered. The First Army had, in actual fact, only three divisions left which were in a fit state to fight. These only had a day's artillery ammunition in addition to that in the boxes of the batteries, and a day's provisions.'

Did anything happen in the twelve hours between the withdrawal from Arras and Major Fauvelle's departure to alter the condition of the First Army? Had anything happened – over and above the normal deterioration of three days of fighting – since the Ypres meeting? Billotte at that meeting had told Weygand that the First Army was barely capable of defending itself. Its new commander had now made a detailed statement – that is all. Weygand must have been aware of the facts, yet he told Reynaud and Churchill that the First Army would provide five divisions of the eight that his 'plan' demanded. If he were not aware, he stands condemned by every standard of the knowledge and the judgement necessary to a supreme commander. If he were aware, he stands condemned in common honesty.

The last paragraph of the minutes of the meeting says:

'General Weygand sent Major Fauvelle to General Blanchard and telephoned to him that, in the difficult situation in which he was placed, and of which we were fully aware, General Blanchard was the sole judge of the decisions which were to be taken and that the honour of the Army was in his hands.'

To put it vulgarly, on May 25th General Weygand 'passed the buck'. Thereafter his decisions have only an indirect importance in the history of Dunkirk.

On the evening of this same day the front-line generals took matters into their own hands. Gort's decision to abandon the attack to the south ended the phase of unreality. At midnight Blanchard agreed with relief to the abandonment and on the following morning he told Gort that he had already decided that the situation on both flanks made it necessary to withdraw.

'After an hour's discussion,' said Gort, 'we arrived at a joint plan for the withdrawal of the main bodies behind the line of the River Lys.'

It was on his return from this meeting with Blanchard that Gort was given the first of the telegrams from London which authorised the evacuation. Matters had passed for ever out of Weygand's hands.

It is difficult to find in the conduct of the northern campaign from May 19th until the end of the evacuation one concrete consequence of Weygand's assumption of command. It is all but impossible to distinguish a point where the advance was stopped – or even slowed – because the Supreme Commander ordered it. Yet in fairness to Weygand it must be stressed that he inherited an all but impossible situation. On the evening of the 19th, when he took over the Supreme Command, the front was already shattered. By the end of that day he must have discovered that no reserves existed with which to repair the breach. His inheritance was impotence.

Could he have done more than he did?

History is full of 'ifs'. If he had reached Paris on the 18th . . . if he had decided at once to take over the Command . . . if he had formulated a plan immediately . . . if he had issued practical orders for its instant execution . . . The answer to the question lies perhaps in Rundstedt's analysis of the Arras counter-attack on May 21st.

'For a short time it was feared that our armoured divisions would be cut off before the infantry divisions could come up to support them.'

The implication of that statement is that until the afternoon of the 21st the armoured attack was certainly vulnerable. It is probable that it was still vulnerable on the 22nd. It may have been so on the 23rd, but after that the opportunity was gone. Weygand had four days in which he could have exerted his influence on the course of history. He failed.

His defenders have suggested that he was using the Armies of the North to draw off forces which otherwise would be used against the slender line that he was endeavouring to establish along the Somme. If the Armies of the North were, in reality, holding up sufficient of the German strength to affect the issue, such a policy could be justified. But Weygand knew the strength and the inevitable fate of the armies of the Somme at least as early as the 25th when he suggested that his Government should consider the desirability of asking for an armistice. In fact, the German divisions which attacked and broke the line of the Somme on June 5th had either taken no part in the Dunkirk fighting or had long been withdrawn from the area and regrouped for the attack to the south.

Not until May 29th did he make up his mind to give the order for the First Army to evacuate. Weygand's epitaph must be: 'He threw time away.' Beside that fatal weakness his lesser failures are unimportant.

Under Weygand the next level of command was filled by General Georges. Considered the most brilliant general in the French Army, Georges had an international reputation. He was the 'fighting commander', commanding – under the policy level at which, first, Gamelin and, then, Weygand stood – the whole of the Armies of the North-East from the North Sea coast to the Swiss frontier. Those who were at his headquarters during the first fatal days say that he was cool, calm and unruffled. Coolness clearly is not enough. It is palpably obvious that Georges suffered, as did all the French generals, from a complete inability to adjust himself to the timing of the German thrusts. There is no evidence that he ever thought quickly enough to forestall a single important move by Rundstedt's spearheads or that he thought with sufficient calculation to interfere effectively with Rundstedt's follow-up. He was a sick man long before the campaign ended, but sickness is not an excuse in generals. The history of Georges' conduct of his campaign must be negative because it is wholly impossible to find anything positive in it.

The third level of command was occupied by General

Billotte. Theoretically the senior general on the north-eastern front (the front involved in Plan D) and formally appointed co-ordinator of the three Allied armies immediately after the beginning of operations, Billotte was completely inadequate to the situation. After the first penetration of the First Army front when it was in position between Wavre and Namur, he seems to have developed a habit of indecision which affected every detail of the conduct of the First Army and, in consequence, of the Allied armies thereafter. He is justly condemned by the British official historian.

His death immediately after the Ypres conference left Blanchard, who had not been at the Ypres conference and did not know 'Weygand's mind', to fill his position without any official intimation of the fact for three vital days. Blanchard appears to have done his best, but by that time the situation was beyond all possible mending.

It would be absurd to suggest that all French generals were incapable, just as it would be absurd to suggest that all lacked decision or courage. De la Laurencie by his independent action in bringing his corps back to Dunkirk, de Gaulle in his repeated attempts to bring about armoured intervention in the south, both made determined and courageous efforts to stop the rot. There were others. But the condemnation of the French General Staff and the core of senior officers was written savagely by the French Government itself. By the evening of May 26th sixteen French generals had been dismissed on the grounds that they had failed in their duty. No comment is needed.

Morale depends to a considerable extent upon Command. Qualification is made because in France it also depended upon a complex of political factors. There was a degree of Communist influence, there was a degree of Fascist influence, there was a degree of mistrust that had been inculcated by a succession of weak Governments and at atmosphere of political futility. As early as May 14th General Huntziger telephoned General Georges to say:

'. . . that certain of his troops were not holding out, that men were to be seen leaving block-houses with their arms raised, and that he had given orders for them to be fired on.'

On the 16th Lieutenant-Colonel Guillaut reported of Corap's Army:

'The disorder of this Army is beyond description. Its troops are falling back on all sides . . . It no longer knows even where its divisions are. The situation is worse than anything we could have imagined.'

The subject is distasteful. To multiply instances would serve no useful purpose. It will be remembered only that in the last hours at Dunkirk 40,000 leaderless men rose out of the cellars.

What of the other French Services?

The French Air Force began the war with 549 fighters of which a quarter were obsolescent, 186 bombers of which all but eleven were classed as obsolescent, and 377 reconnaissance and observation aircraft of which 316 were obsolescent. By May 10th the position had improved: there were now 700 fighters, 175 bombers and 400 reconnaissance planes. The proportion of modern planes had also improved, but the fighters had a speed inferiority of approximately 50 miles an hour. The organisation and the disposition of the available aircraft were faulty and as a whole the role of the French Air Force was ineffective. Its pilots fought bravely and were destroyed. Its bombers were totally unsuitable for army co-operation. The French Navy, however, had squadrons of what were virtually dive-bombers. These were sent inland in the earliest phase of the operations, and one-half of their effective strength was shot down in a very gallant attempt to destroy the bridges across the Oise. At the same time naval fighters took over the air defence of Paris. In the end, however, the main burden of the air fell upon the RAF.

The French naval story is an uneven one. On the part of the ships which took their share in the evacuation it is brilliant. Their courage and their endurance matches anything upon the British side. Their loss was grievous. But they came late to the battle, and for that the responsibility lies again with the High Command.

The French authorities, it will be remembered, began to consider the possibility of evacuation on May 19th at precisely the same time as the British. The efforts to organise a supply system have been described. Despite the worsening situation no positive action with regard to evacuation was taken until the meeting of Saturday, May 25th, when Major Fauvelle, after detailing the state of the First Army, stated that 'the British Army seemed to be preparing for its re-embarkation'. Weygand promptly requested Admiral Darlan to send his Chief of Operations, Captain Auphan, to Britain for information. It is in accordance with all the delays and hesitations of this time that Captain Auphan did not arrive at Dover until the morning of Monday, May 27th. Writing in 1956, Admiral Auphan said:

'It was not difficult for us to ascertain, from preparations already made, that the British were getting ready to begin immediately the evacuation of their expeditionary corps through the Straits. There was no doubt that this decision, taken by them some days previously, had been imposed irrevocably. They had told us nothing about it in spite of the confidential liaison which we had at all times; and this secrecy, when it was known in Paris, contributed greatly to making relations between the two governments bitter at a particularly tragic moment in the common war.'[1]

Admiral Auphan is mistaken in a number of particulars. The British were not 'getting ready to begin'; they had already begun the previous evening. The decision had not been taken 'some days previously' but on the day before, and it had not been kept secret from the French – Reynaud had been informed of it by Winston Churchill at the meetings at the Admiralty·in London on the Sunday afternoon. The Prime Minister, recording this on the 27th, said:

'I had informed M. Reynaud the day before that the policy was to evacuate the British Expeditionary Force, and had requested him to issue corresponding orders.'

Eden in his signal to Gort on the afternoon of Sunday, the 26th, said:

'. . . M. Reynaud communicating General Weygand and latter will no doubt issue orders in this sense forthwith . . .'

' Weygand, as in every major crisis of the campaign, delayed his orders. Captain Auphan had received no instructions at the time of his departure. He wrote:

'On the spot, without delay, I took the necessary measures for the requisitioning of everything afloat in the French channel ports, small boats and average sized, even fishing vessels. About 250 units joined (unfortunately several days late with respect to the British) the powerful force which the latter had already brought together.'

French estimates as to the number of ships which took part vary considerably. Reynaud said that '300 French war and merchant ships, and 200 other craft' took part. A day-by-day analysis of the liftings by Jacques Mordal mentions approximately 230 ship movements, the largest number of ships sail-

[1] US Naval Institute Proceedings, June 1956.

ing on any one day being the sixty-three which crossed in the final all-out effort of June 3rd. Some of the ships involved made as many as five trips to Dover and a large number of others made four, three or at least two. The total number of French vessels, therefore, which actually reached Dunkirk is very much smaller than the French political estimates.

As the result of Captain Auphan's energetic action the requisitioning of suitable small ships and craft, which had already been initiated by naval parties, was accelerated. Rear-Admiral Landriau was designated as the commander of the flotilla of the Pas de Calais and sailed for Dover in the sloop *Savorgnan de Brazza*. The embarkation of wounded was already in progress, and on May 28th the evacuation of French 'specialists' began. Finally, on May 29th General Weygand at last issued his orders for the evacuation of 'as many of the French First Army as possible'. It was three days late.

As with the Royal Navy, much of the burden and very much of the loss was sustained by the destroyers. Of Captain Portzamparc's 2nd Flotilla (nine ships of which were put under Admiral Abrial's orders) four were sunk and the remaining five damaged. Their loss was a serious one, not only to France but to the general story of the evacuation.

Torpedo-boats of the *'Pomone'* class also did extraodinarily well, *Bourrasque*, for example, carrying back almost 800 men on one passage. The five dispatch boats of the *'Elan'* class were also admirably handled, and the decision to withdraw these ships from the operation to cover the return of evacuated troops to France through Southampton was ill-judged. Their absence was felt heavily in the last days.

The four French cross-Channel steamers *Côte d'Argent*, *Côte d'Azur*, *Newhaven* and *Rouen* rendered valuable service, though *Côte d'Azur* was sunk early in the operation.

The number of French troops lifted by French vessels is in dispute. In the Ramsay dispatch the total is given as 20,525 men disembarked in the United Kingdom, with an unknown number transported direct to French ports. This figure does less than justice to the French effort. It gives the liftings for the 27th and and the 28th May as nil and begins with 655 men on the 29th. On the first two days 900 wounded were actually brought across, and on the 28th some 2,500 'specialists' were embarked in French store ships. The French figures disagree with those recorded in Admiral Ramsay's dispatch for almost every day. They differ also for classes of ship. The three cross-Channel steamers, for example, are credited with lifting 12,000 men as against the figure in the English records of 7,454. In addition a large proportion of the Belgian trawlers which took part in the operation were manned by French naval crews, and their liftings should, therefore, be added to the French total. Altogether, according to M. Mordal, the French Navy, together with its merchant ships and fishing vessels, evacuated 48,474 men, of whom 3,936 were taken directly to French ports. It is not necessary to challenge this figure. In the circumstances of the time no estimate can be wholly accurate. The work of the French ships was valiant and self-sacrificing, and no man who went to Dunkirk will question their claim.

Could the French Navy have done more?

Had the Command made up its mind earlier and decided on its course of action there is no doubt that it could have taken a very much larger part in the operations, and in this connection the character and temper of Darlan have been canvassed. Darlan operated in accordance with the directives and instructions which he received from Weygand, who, it will be remembered, had on the 19th been made Supreme Commander of all French forces. Whether his preparations would have been completed earlier had he operated on his own it is impossible to say. His delays and indecisions follow precisely the same pattern as the general delays of the French Command at this period.

It has been suggested that owing to the greater distance from Dunkirk of the French ports which remained out of enemy hands and the responsibilities of the French western naval forces for the escort of convoys across the Biscay area, the French were at a disadvantage with regard to the British in the number of ships and small craft which they could produce. The claim is a doubtful one. The French had the resources of Dieppe, Le Havre, Cherbourg and Brest on which to draw, together with the smaller Brittany ports, and they had also the whole complex of the Seine. The difficulty does not appear to have lain in the number of ships available so much as in the speed and efficiency with which they were directed into action.

When the ships reached the area of Dunkirk they were handled well and resolutely. The principal criticism – in fact almost the only criticism that can be directed against the French naval effort – must be that it was too small and too late.

CHAPTER XIX

The British Achievement

*This much is certain, he that commands the sea is
at great liberty and may take as much or as little of
the war as he will, whereas those that be strongest
by land are many times nevertheless in great straits.*
                                        SIR FRANCIS BACON

THE STRENGTH and quality of the British Expeditionary
Force in 1939 was the inevitable consequence of the
variable policies of British Governments between 1918 and
1938. Like the French Army it was wholly inadequate for
modern war. It would, however, be unwise to draw too close a
parallel with the state of the French forces. The one constant
factor in British policy in the period between the wars was the
desire for disarmament. Not until the crisis of Munich – and
not with any real urgency even then – was rearmament placed
squarely before the people of Britain. Up to April 1938,
British policy in the event of war with Germany was, in a
nutshell, that the Navy and the Air Force would provide for
the offshore defence of the United Kingdom while the Army
would cover the coasts and be available for protecting colonial
areas. It was a twentieth-century version of Bacon's principle:
    '. . . he that commands the sea . . . may take as much or as
little of the war as he will'.
    There is a certain similarity here with French policy. France
concentrated on a defensive force which would hold her
frontier and behind which forces for offensive war could be
built up after the outbreak of hostilities. Britain decided to
build up her forces in the same way behind her Navy and her
Air Force. Basically it was the policy that had been followed
from 1870 onwards, and it was scarcely modified after the
First World War even to allow for the advent of the aeroplane.
Against the scale and type of the German attack the French
policy was impracticable. Was it possible for Britain? The
answer lies in the four years between Dunkirk and the invasion

of Normandy. Throughout those years, against a closer and more immediate threat than had been anticipated, the Royal Air Force and the Royal Navy were able to maintain the defence of Britain.

After April 1938, policy moved by degrees towards direct aid to France: a two-divisional force at first; then, in April of 1939 a force of two corps; and, finally, with the introduction of conscription at the end of that month, an understanding as to a rapid build-up. These decisions were political, taken because of the necessity to sustain the alliance with France. Following normal practice they were taken with – though not upon – military advice. Lord Gort had been appointed Chief of the Imperial General Staff in 1937, and the advice as to the size and shape of the force was, therefore, largely his, though the influence of the Secretary of State for War, Mr Hore-Belisha, the limitations placed on development by the Treasury, and advice from experts outside the Army played their part. The policy, however, was the Cabinet's, and any direct comparison between Gort and Gamelin in this period is pointless.

There has been much criticism as to the state of readiness of the force that crossed to France. It lacked certain essential items of equipment, certain essential arms, certain essential training. These deficiencies are sufficiently obvious in all the records of the time. But the blame, if there be blame, lies not with Gort as CIGS nor with the general direction of the Army, nor perhaps even with successive British Governments, but with the British electorate, which for twenty years refused to face the possibility of another war.

The heaviest criticism in detail lies in the failure to provide a proper armoured component for the expeditionary force. Basically British Army thinking in the period between the wars was as inadequate as that of the French with regard to the employment of armour. Though the ideas of a small number of independent thinkers, led largely by Captain Liddell Hart, had produced a theory of tank warfare – a theory upon which the Germans had extensively drawn – until the beginning of this phase of rearmament official British military thinking still considered the tank in the light of an infantry support weapon. It is important, therefore, to recall that it was during Gort's tenure of office as CIGS that the creation of the first two armoured divisions was embarked upon, though the earliest experiments towards an armoured division began in 1934. The first of these divisions was still far from ready at the outbreak of war. It is necessary to stress the fact that less than five months was available between the Cabinet decision which set the size of the British Expeditionary Force, and the sailing of the first transports. The plain truth is that it was impossible in the time to produce the necessary *matériel*. Neither the Ministry of Supply nor the armament industry was yet geared to war.

Despite these things 152,000 men, 21,000 vehicles and 120,000 tons of stores and ammunition were shipped to France by September 27th. That achievement is, in the main, Gort's. As CIGS he was responsible for Plan W 4, which provided both the outline and the detail for its accomplishment. Gort was fully cognisant of the deficiencies of the expeditionary force, but it was his responsibility to implement the political policy of his Government in so far as it was humanly practicable. He made it practicable.

He sailed with the force as Commander-in-Chief. At this point it is necessary to reconsider the background of Gort's Commands. As was outlined earlier, his promotion as Chief of the Imperial General Staff was outside the normal succession. He was comparatively young for the post, his detractors said that he was unready for it, he had never commanded a large force either in war or in peace, and he was promoted over the heads of men older than himself and senior to him on the Army List. At the time of his promotion a section of the Army had expected Sir John Dill to succeed to the post. It was further believed that General Alan Brooke, Dill's favourite pupil, would in turn succeed his master.

The consequences of such a promotion in time of peace are unpredictable. There appears to be ample evidence of faction in the higher levels of the Army in the two years which preceded the war. It was Gort's especial misfortune that the consequences pursued him into war. It will be remembered in addition that the veteran General Ironside had confidently believed that he would receive the appointment of Commander-in-Chief of the Expeditionary Force. Indeed it is claimed that he was informed verbally that he would be appointed. Instead he was made CIGS in Gort's place. The reason for this was, in part, political, since Hore-Belisha and Gort had found it increasingly difficult to co-operate. Ironside is reported to have said subsequently:

'I should never have been sent there. I told Hore-Belisha at the time. I had never been at the War Office, didn't know a thing about it. I should have refused the appointment. But who else was there?'

Sir John Dill was already appointed to the command of I Corps and General Brooke was appointed to command II Corps. Gort crossed to France with officers who had originally been passed over on his behalf, above him and below him.

Ironside's tenure of office was in accordance with his own views of his appointment. In April it was decided to strengthen the War Office team by recalling Dill from France and establishing him as Vice-Chief of the Imperial General Staff. Winston Churchill wrote:[1]

'There was a very strong feeling in the Cabinet and high military circles that the abilities and strategic knowledge of Sir John Dill . . . should find their full scope in his appointment as our principal Army adviser. No one could doubt that his professional standing was in many ways superior to that of Ironside.'

On May 25th Ironside, apparently aware of that feeling, generously 'volunteered the proposal that he should cease to be CIGS, but declared himself quite willing to command the British Home Forces'.

Brooke remained in France to continue his criticism of Gort and to enter his opinions in his diary.

Gort's position as Commander-in-Chief obviously was one of extreme delicacy. Essentially a man of great modesty, he seems to have allowed that delicacy to affect his relations, first, with Dill and, later, with Brooke to the extent that he was unwilling to discuss major problems of strategy with them. It is quite impossible on the evidence of the campaign as it was fought to accept Brooke's criticism that Gort

'. . . wandered about scratching the barks of the trees and you could never get him to come out and look at the wood as a whole.'

Gort's handling of the Western battle in particular shows a largeness of vision and a sense of timing which is wholly incompatible with Brooke's acid and petty remarks, and it seems probable that Gort out of courtesy and consideration sought to avoid acrimonious discussions with men older than and senior to himself.

It is very important to remember here that Gort's own hands, so far as major movements were concerned, were en-

[1] *Their Finest Hour* by Winston S. Churchill.

tirely tied. His position *vis-à-vis* the French Command was fixed, his place as an instrument of policy was fixed, and though he had an 'escape route' in the clause which permitted him to refer to the British Government if he considered that the expeditionary force was being endangered, it was very clearly a clause which could only be invoked when the danger was apparent.

Gort has been criticised in regard to the general strategy of the opening phase of the campaign and, in particular, for a failure to lodge objections to Plan D. Plan D was agreed upon at the highest levels. It is difficult to see how Gort could, in fact, have objected to it in principle. In 1940 the French High Command still carried the aura of perfectionism that, despite the historical evidence, had surrounded it since Napoleonic times. Gort met the French Command as a young general, abruptly promoted and commanding at the time the plan was agreed a small and relatively unimportant component of the general machinery for the defence of France. Even when Plan D was launched his force consisted only of ten divisions: it supplied no weight of armour, and the British contribution in the air was largely outside Gort's control. His voice in council was inevitably commensurate with his strength in the field. Strategy was in the hands of France, and France was in the hands of Gamelin.

None the less he did protest, and protest in the strongest possible terms, against the proposal that was made for an advance as far as the Albert Canal line. It is probably this refusal that gave rise to the most direct criticism that the French made of him in this preliminary phase. Reynaud in *In the Thick of the Fight* says:

'. . . the British, when they had agreed to a reasonable distribution on the Franco-Belgian frontier, demanded a disastrous one on the Belgian battle-front. They only consented, in fact, to hold an extremely small sector from Louvain to Wavre, protected by the flooding of the Dyle river.'

This is an expansion of a statement in Gamelin's autobiography *Servir* that Gort expressed 'reservations' when Georges asked him to extend the British front to the south of the River Dyle. It is evidence at third hand. There is no official record of such a disagreement. The main axis of the British advance to their position on the Dyle lay along the Tournai-Enghien road. To have occupied an extended area to the south they would have needed another road of approach.

The only alternative road was that through Mons, which was the main axis of advance for the French First Army. No discussion as to alternative roads took place and no surviving members of Gort's staff have any recollection of any disagreement over this point.

It is easiest to consider Gort's handling of the campaign by dividing it into four phases.

The first comprises the advance to the Dyle and the consolidation of the BEF on that position. It was carried out swiftly and efficiently, and the position was held against all enemy attack. In this brief statement is the justification both of Gort's staff work and the planning prior to May 10th, and of the training of the British Expeditionary Force during the nine months' respite. In detailing the staff for his Command Post he took forward with him General Mason-MacFarlane, his Director of Intelligence. It is held that this was responsible for Gort's subsequent lack of information as to events in his rear areas. The criticism is fair. Intelligence was canalised through rear GHQ at Arras, and the lack of a directing head at that point must have caused certain delays and failures. Yet Gort moved forward to an encounter battle in which he must have expected his vital information to come either from the area of his own front or from that of the Allies on his immediate flanks. Had the battle developed as the French in planning it believed would be the case, the rear areas would have been wholly unimportant. It was the unexpected collapse of the Ninth Army which made them vital.

The second phase begins with the retreat from the Dyle on May 16th. It is important to remember here that Gort was forced to send a senior officer to General Billotte's Headquarters before he could get formal orders for his withdrawal, for this signalises the beginnings of the French Command breakdown which was to affect the whole campaign thereafter. Throughout the opening stages of the retreat he received no further written orders from Billotte and he conducted his share of the movement, co-ordinating it with that of the French First Army on the right and with the Belgian Army on the left, in circumstances of considerable difficulty. The language differences, the normal problems of inter-allied working, were superimposed upon the different rates of movement which existed between the mechanised British Army and the foot soldiers and horse transport of the Belgians and of part of the French. The final movement of the co-ordinated retreat, the withdrawal to the line of the old frontier fortifications on the night of May 22nd, was initiated by Gort himself after a conference with his corps generals and agreed upon at the Ypres meeting. Despite Billotte's failure to effect co-ordination and despite all the contingent circumstances, then, the retreat was efficiently conducted, and Gort effected his purpose of bringing back his army unbroken to the frontier position.

The third phase overlaps this period. It begins, in fact, as early as May 17th. It is the phase of the establishment of the stop-gaps, the Special Forces, out of which Gort built up his line of defence for the Western battle. These forces, as was stated earlier, were criticised at the time. None of the critics, however, has yet put forward a reasonable alternative. Gort in those early days was making bricks without straw. Out of those bricks, militarily 'untidy' as they were, he made, first, the illusion of a counter-attack and, then, the illusion of a defensive line. The word 'illusion' is justified in both instances because Franklyn's force could never have hoped to break through to the south in the strength which was available to it, and the stop-gap forces along the Aa Canal could never have hoped to hold had the Germans attacked with their full weight; but in both cases the fact of their existence, coupled with the determination with which they held the positions that were allotted to them, were sufficient to create the belief in Rundstedt's mind that he would have to fight hard and sustain heavy loss if he continued the assault.

The results of that decision have been examined at length. They were sufficient to give Gort time to establish the more formal defence in the Western battle that was set up on May 24th. The seven days of this period afford a magnificent object lesson in the utilisation of small forces. The imagination and the prescience by which one stop point after another was chosen, the skill and ingenuity by which forces were assembled at the critical positions, and the determination with which these were held, combine to make one of the most tremendous chapters in the history of the British Army. Gort, fighting two battles simultaneously, had divided his staff to conduct them separately. General Pownall's co-ordination of these two halves was masterly, but the fundamental credit belongs to the Commander-in-Chief. A share of it, however, must unquestionably go to the staff training at Camberley, which ensured 'common thinking' and practice on the part of individual commanders and staffs.

The fourth phase of the campaign is that of the actual retreat to Dunkirk. It begins with Gort's decision at six o'clock on Saturday, May 25th, to abandon the Weygand Plan, and to use the troops earmarked for it to reinforce his left flank, where General Brooke commanded II Corps on the old frontier position. It is scarcely necessary to reiterate the courage, the clarity and the vital importance of that decision. It made possible the successful conduct of the Eastern battle and it made practicable the decision to withdraw to the Dunkirk perimeter. It was in every sense of the word independent, yet Gort informed the French of his decision at the earliest possible moment and on the following morning urged Blanchard to withdraw to the line of the River Lys. In any consideration of this last phase it is essential to remember that of a front of 128 miles held at this moment by the British and French armies 97 miles was held by British troops, and with the now inevitable collapse of the Belgians a further 25 miles would be added to that total. The withdrawal to the Lys, which was begun on Gort's insistence, was designed to shorten the perimeter of the British and French armies by 58 miles. It was after this meeting that Gort received from London his orders to evacuate the British Expeditionary Force.

The story of the final retreat into the Dunkirk perimeter has two sides even as the battle had two fronts. Almost as Blanchard and Gort reached their agreement on the withdrawal to the Lys, Bock on the eastern front put in the full weight of his attack on the Belgians and the British, and Hitler ordered the waiting armour on the western front to move forward once again. Gort's dispositions held both attacks. The story of the 2nd Division's battle for the Canal Line between St Venant and La Bassée is imperishable. In its centre the 4th Brigade, standing against the heaviest attack of armour, of artillery and of dive-bombers that was suffered by any British unit in the whole retreat, fought with a most desperate endeavour until it was destroyed. Its courage was matched by the defenders of Cassel, by the men who held out at Hazebrouck, Wormhoudt and Ledringhem, and at a dozen other points on the long western front. The measure of their courage and of their resistance was the final abandonment of the German armoured thrust on May 30th when Rundstedt withdrew the last elements of the panzer divisions to the south.

The main battle of the left flank began – so far as the British were concerned – on the morning of Sunday, May

26th. Once again the accuracy of Gort's timing is apparent. The 5th Division, moved over on to Brooke's flank following Gort's decision to abandon the Weygand Plan, took up its positions as the German artillery began to shell the area. It was a 'close run thing'. Gort had held on to the possibility of the attack to the south, as he was from every aspect both of duty and of expediency bound to do, to the very last possible moment, but he had not held on too late to cover his necessities.

The picture that has been presented to the world of this left flank battle is wholly unjustified. It was not an independent campaign fought as a personal triumph by General Brooke. It was an integrated part of a general defence scheme of immense magnitude. It was an important part – it can even be said that it was a vital part – but it was no more vital than the battle of the 2nd Division on the Canal. Twenty miles separated the Western from the Eastern battle. Had the Western battle broken on the 27th, the 28th or the 29th, Brooke must have been taken in rear and overwhelmed. In these final days of the retreat the Armies of the North were compressed into a shape that has distinct parallels with the traditional 'square'. The square was being attacked simultaneously on three sides. Had any side given, the whole must have gone. No side gave.

There remained, however, a gap, the gap between the left flank of Brooke's corps and the sea. The whole purpose of the left flank battle was to close that gap. Yet when on the morning of May 28th Bock's motorised reconnaissance formations reached the planned perimeter at the outskirts of Nieuport, Brooke was still not in a position to extend his flank into the area; and it is at this point that the last of the Special Forces, the last of Gort's stop-gaps, triumphed. The first German reconnaissance was driven off by the 12th Lancers, which Gort had wisely kept under GHQ orders. The main attack delivered later in the day was held by Adamforce, the improvised formation of engineers and artillery-men fighting as infantry, which stopped the Germans in the houses of Nieuport after they had crossed the main bridge, which the French had left unblown. It was the final example of Gort's prevision and sense of timing, and it held until Brooke on the evening of the following day was able to take up his allotted position on the perimeter line.

It is implicit in every major development of this phase that Gort maintained his grasp of the situation as a whole. With

274

great wisdom, he delegated a very high degree of authority to his corps commanders and to his Special Force commanders. The conditions of the retreat, the problems of communication, the congestion of the roads made direct control difficult and at times even impossible. He was justified in that delegation even if upon occasion the response was uneven. Of the three corps commanders, General Adam proved resilient, resourceful and energetic. The consolidation of the defence of the western area was largely his accomplishment and the defence of the Dunkirk perimeter was his achievement. General Barker's command appears to have been less satisfactory. General Brooke fought well through the first phases of the campaign and brilliantly through the battle of the left flank. That the importance of this battle has been overestimated and Brooke's share in the campaign, as a result, wholly overstated, does not detract from the intrinsic merit of II Corps' effort.

Of the junior generals, Franklyn, for his work, first before Arras, then in the defence of Arras, and finally against the main weight of Bock's thrust, deserves all the praise that has been given him – and perhaps considerably more. General Montgomery's employment of his division throughout, and his night march to the extreme left flank in particular, marked him out for high responsibilities. General Thorne, by his brilliant handling of the 48th Division, must share much of the glory of the defence of the perimeter. General Alexander's conduct of the 1st Division from the start was impeccable, and the honour of commanding the final stages of the evacuation of the British Expeditionary Force was justly his.

Morale, as was said earlier in connection with the French Army, is contingent upon Command. One of the minor but persistent myths of Dunkirk makes serious charges as to the morale of the BEF. In the early stages of the evacuation, and particularly in the first two days of the 'forlorn hope' phase, there was unquestionably disorder and indiscipline on the beaches. Boats were rushed; they were, as has been detailed, on occasion sunk under the weight of men or overturned in the surf. This was the period of the last of the 'useless mouths' and of the base troops, and of the small units that had been ordered to get back to Dunkirk under their own steam. Because in many cases officers remained behind to complete the work of clearance or had been drawn into the Special Forces, there was a lack of leaders and a lack of leadership. But this

275

was a temporary phase and at most it led only to local difficulties. The morale of the fighting army when it reached the beaches and the Mole matched the very highest traditions of the Service – it did more, it added to them.

There was, however, a defect in this phase. At no time did the Army set up a proper and permanent beach organisation of its own. It should have done so. In part this was due to a breakdown of the Provost Service. Each corps had its own beach officer, and magnificent work was accomplished by certain units (the 12th Lancers once again being in the forefront at La Panne), but in general the beach organisation was temporary and tended to fold up when the units which supplied it evacuated. A feeling appears to have existed in the Army that the Navy should have assumed complete control. This was not possible. The Navy was wholly unable to man all the ships and small craft which were necessary for the operation. Permanent beach parties should have been set up by the Army with naval liaison and naval signals, and they should have remained until the beaches were clear. Much misunderstanding between sea and shore would have been avoided had this been done.

This is a minor defect, however, to set in the balance against the conduct of the retreat as a whole and of the general handling of the evacuation. It is appropriate here to recapitulate the figures of this operation. 139,732 British troops were evacuated in the course of 'Dynamo', 139,097 French and Belgian troops were brought away. To these must be added 58,583 British evacuated before 'Dynamo' began and 814 Allied troops. Through the retreat and on the beaches the British Army lost 68,111 killed in action, missing, wounded or prisoner. It lost, in addition, 2,472 guns, 63,879 motor vehicles, and half a million tons of military stores and ammunition.

It is impossible to set up a profit and loss account in war. The sacrifice of the Dunkirk campaign was heavy. Set against the single fact that by the efforts of its commanders, its officers and its men the British Army came back unbroken to Britain, the loss was militarily acceptable.

Gort was well served by his commanders and well served by his men. The understanding that existed between him and them was always sufficient to the necessities of the hour. No clearer judgement of his capacity and of his accomplishment has been made than the summing-up of the conduct of the campaign in the official history of the war in France and Flanders.[1]

'In the fearful position in which his army was placed, with Allies on either flank whose support was crumbling hour by hour, he quickly perceived the probable outcome; he chose the course which alone offered any practical way to avoid disaster and allowed nothing to deflect him from it. All his major decisions were both wise and well-timed. His judgement, not only of what was needed at the time, but of what would be needed in the days ahead, was never at fault. He foresaw that, *if* the French could not quickly close the breach in their front, the Allied armies in the north would be contained by the enemy and would be forced to fall back to the coast and attempt evacuation. He saw when Arras must be held and when it must be given up. He realised the importance of the Canal Line in his rear, days before it was attacked, and by the show of opposition which he improvised there he bluffed the enemy into a pause which gave him time to build a more solid defence. He saw the danger of a break in the Ypres front in time to avert it. He initiated the organisation of the Dunkirk bridgehead and the planning of partial evacuation before ever the policy of general evacuation was accepted by his own Government or by the French. Indeed, his sense of timing is apparent throughout the campaign and neither Cabinet suggestion nor French exhortation could persuade him to attempt operations which he considered ill-timed or impracticable.'

To that may well be added the judgement of Major-General Sir John Kennedy, who for three years after Dunkirk was Director of Military Operations at the War Office.[2]

'I think now that the appointment of Gort to be Commander-in-Chief may be regarded as one of those strokes of great good luck which came our way more than once in the course of the war. Under any other commander, the Field Force might, for quite good reasons, have been manoeuvred differently, and in such a way as to be cut off from the sea when the French Army collapsed – a disaster from which it would have been difficult to recover.'

It seems hardly necessary to add further comment. The facts speak for themselves.

*   *   *

[1] *The War in France and Flanders* by Major L. F. Ellis.
[2] *The Business of War.*

The part played by the Royal Air Force in the Dunkirk campaign was subject at the time to strong criticism. It has ever since been subject to even stronger defence. It is therefore necessary to examine it with particular care.

The RAF frequently throughout its short career has been accused of endeavouring to 'fight its own war'. The accusation was repeated in France in 1940. The RAF in the years before the war concentrated both its resources and its thinking on its two major divisions – Fighter Command and Bomber Command. The theory of the possibilities of the bomber offensive occupied almost the whole of the offensive strategic thinking of the Service.

It is not necessary here to explore at length the long quarrels among the three Services before the war. Delays due to faults on both sides found the Royal Navy without adequate aircraft at the outbreak of war, but it is doubtful if this circumstance played any material part in the evacuation. With the Army the result of pre-war manoeuvrings and indecisions was more immediate and the results in the Dunkirk campaign more apparent. Because of the concentration on the bomber offensive and the fighter defensive theories the scale and quality of air co-operation provided for the Army in Flanders was inadequate, but it must not be thought that the RAF was wholly or even principally to blame for this. As was noted earlier, no Army policy for an expeditionary force in a European war existed at all until 1938 nor were the Army's requirements clear until late in 1939. Neither the Army nor the RAF before May 1940 appears at any time seriously to have considered war in terms of the German doctrine of close support, dive-bomber co-operation and instant response to ground requests. It is probably fair to say that the initiative should have come from the Army and that successive Army Councils failed in their duty of thinking ahead.

There are other factors in the situation but this broad outline will serve. As a result of it the British Air Force in France in May 1940 was inadequate both in numbers and in quality to the tasks which it was to be asked to perform. It had been created in January of that year, under Air Marshal A. S. Barratt, out of the original Air Component which had been devised for Army co-operation and the Advanced Striking Force which had been stationed in France as an extension of Bomber Command. The amalgamation appears to have had little effect on the general efficiency of the organisation. The thinking of the Command was not attuned to the doctrine of 'close support', and communications between Army and RAF were intolerably slow and wholly unsuited to the circumstances which developed. Moreover, the Army considered that the commander of the Air Component, Air Vice-Marshal C. H. B. Blount, and his staff failed to accommodate themselves to the requirements of a rapidly changing and deteriorating situation.

There was a basic difference between British and French air policy. Briefly, Britain adhered to a policy of home defence for the greater part of her available fighter strength, and strategic bombing of selected targets deep in Germany. The French, who because of their weakness were unable to contemplate the same possibilities, considered that all bombers should be used for the purpose of bombing enemy communications and concentrations.

Against these forces and this divided conception the great strength of the German Air Force was devoted with an entire singleness of purpose to the immediate tactical demands of the blitzkrieg.

On May 10th the British Army moved forward to its position on the Dyle unharassed by enemy aircraft. Some credit was taken for that circumstance by the Air Component, but in actual fact the Luftwaffe was almost wholly involved in direct co-operation with the German attack. To the north Air Fleet 2 was dropping parachutists, landing glider troops, providing protection for them and giving bombardment support. In the south Air Fleet 3 was landing airborne troops and providing the maximum of air cover over the advancing panzers together with the maximum of air bombardment in advance and in support of them. There was almost literally nothing to spare to harass the columns that were wheeling over the open Flanders plain, nor was it the intention of the High Command to harass them. As has been said, the German Command was perfectly content that the Northern Group of Armies should be met on improvised positions at the end of outstretched lines of communication rather than on the prepared positions and dumps of the Franco-Belgian frontier.

It was realised at once that the number of fighters available to the British Air Component was inadequate, and on the first day of the campaign two additional squadrons were flown over from England to be followed by thirty-two more aircraft three days later.

If the task of the fighters of the Air Component above the

advancing Expeditionary Force, however, was relatively unimportant, the task of the bombers from the first day of the attack was bitter and dangerous. On May 10th four waves of eight Battle bombers each were sent in to attack the German armoured thrust, covered by fighters. Thirteen were shot down, the remaining nineteen were damaged. On the following day eight Battles attacked an enemy column close to the German frontier. Only one returned, badly damaged. On May 12th the vital Maastricht bridge was attacked by volunteers. Five bombers went in covered by fighters. One returned.

These instances show at once the imperishable gallantry of the air crews involved and the complete unsuitability both of the aircraft and of the tactics used. The whole conception of attack and defence, the whole strength, was totally inadequate against the strength and purpose of the German attack. On May 14th in a long series of strikes mainly directed against bridges, 56 per cent of the bombers engaged were lost. The heroism of those attacks is incomparable. It is doubtful, however, if they inflicted any significant delay upon the German plan. By May 15th daylight bombing was cut down to an absolute minimum and the Advanced Striking Force switched to night bombing in the Sedan area. It was almost wholly ineffective. Britain had already lost 248 aircraft shot down or damaged and useless when at midnight on May 15th the more northerly units of the Advanced Air Striking Force were compelled to move back to airfields farther south, their bases already imperilled by the German advance.

On May 16th, 17th and 18th, as the BEF fell back from the Dyle, the bombers of the Air Striking Force were out of action and unable to assist the British Army. By May 19th the Air Component was also falling back fast: its rear headquarters had moved to Boulogne, its operational control was working under conditions of the greatest difficulty, its reconnaissance function had almost broken down, and it was virtually impossible to implement requests for strikes. By the afternoon of the 19th a considerable part of the Component was withdrawn to England; the remainder was concentrated well to the south. When on that day General Gort reviewed his three alternatives, it was in the light of the knowledge that he was without air support, and that what cover the British Army had thereafter would have to be flown from England. The limitations of that cover were set out for Gort in information he received through Colonel (now General) Festing.

In the week preceding Operation 'Dynamo' air cover over Dunkirk, and over the long pocket that stretched for 70 miles south-east from Dunkirk into France and over the waters of the approaches to Dunkirk, was provided by Fighter Command from the Kentish airfields. A glance at the map will make clear the implications of this. The closest of the Kentish airfields was more than 50 miles from Dunkirk. The short range of the fighters of the day offered little fighting time over Dunkirk and progressively less time over the routes by which enemy bombers and fighters had to approach the target area. Simultaneously, the Belgians and French were clamouring for air support, and in London the Air Council and the Cabinet had to decide the relative merits of the three sets of demands and balance them against the possibility of the defeat of France and the consequential necessity to defend England itself against the whole weight of the German Air Force.

Patrols were made at the start approximately at squadron strength and at frequent intervals. On May 26th, for example, there were twenty-two patrols and on the 27th twenty-three. On the 28th British losses forced Fighter Command to a new policy and eleven patrols only were flown – though at almost double or even treble the strength of the previous days. Thereafter the number of patrols dropped steadily from nine to eight and, after June 1st when daylight evacuation stopped, to four. There were thus prolonged periods when there were no friendly aircraft in the area. As the Luftwaffe was operating from Belgian and French airfields considerably closer to the perimeter than the Kentish bases, the possibilities of coming in to the attack immediately after the end of a strong British patrol were obvious. This was particularly apparent on June 1st. The major attacks, which caused very heavy loss to shipping on this day, occurred in the intervals between the sweeps.

Could more patrols have been flown? The Army historian accepts broadly the RAF contention that the patrols were the limit of the effective effort of the available airfields and aircraft. The naval historian accepts the Air Ministry's comment on Admiral Ramsay's dispatch that 'it was not to be expected that all air action would be visible from points on the coast', and by implication criticises Ramsay's adverse comment. It is left to the Air Force's own historian,[1] after examining the different views on the matter, to say:

[1] *The Defence of the United Kingdom* by Basil Collier.

'Even so, a daily average of about 300 sorties at a period of crisis may seem less than might have been expected from a force some six or seven hundred aircraft strong.'

It is true, as he also points out, that numerical strength is not the sole criterion. None the less it would have been physically possible, in view of the strength in modern fighters possessed both by the front-line squadrons and by the training areas, and reserve, to have mounted a very much larger effort from the number of airfields available in south-eastern England within reasonable range of the Dunkirk beaches.

Why, then, was this not done? The answer has two aspects. The official explanation is that the Air Council considered the defence of the United Kingdom to be the primary responsibility of Fighter Command. It appears to have interpreted that responsibility in narrow terms.

The first and most critical factor in the defence of the United Kingdom in the last week of May was the position of the British Expeditionary Force. On its successful withdrawal depended the building up of the armies for the future prosecution of the war. The BEF included – it is necessary to state this once again – the greater proportion of the professional strength of the British Army. Without it there would have been no cadres for the new armies, no body of trained non-commissioned officers, no tried commanders.

It is difficult to define in precise terms the air defence of a country, but it would seem to have as a starting point the destruction of the enemy's air force. If this is accepted, it becomes difficult to reconcile the RAF's apparent reluctance to make a maximum effort over the period of the evacuation with the claims it made for the results of the air fighting at the time. They are crystallised in Winston Churchill's speech in the House of Commons on June 4th.

'Wars are not won by evacuations. But there was a victory inside this deliverance, which should be noted. It was gained by the Air Force . . . This was a great trial of strength between the British and German Air Forces . . . We got the Army away; and they have paid four-fold for any losses which they have inflicted . . . All of our types and all our pilots have been vindicated as superior to what they have at present to face.'

If in fact qualitative superiority was established, if in fact Fighter Command was destroying four German aircraft for the loss of every one of its own, Dunkirk would appear to have been a highly profitable point at which to begin the air defence of Britain.

What are the figures?

Fighter Command lost 106 aircraft during the period of the evacuation. Mr Churchill (presumably briefed by the RAF) and M. Reynaud in Paris both gave the enemy loss as four to one. Were 424 German aircraft destroyed?

The first official claims issued by the Air Ministry totalled 390.

A more careful analysis of these claims made when the immediate heat of the battle was over resulted in a reduction of the total to 262.

A meticulous examination of the captured German records after the war showed that the total German loss for the period in question *on all parts of the front* was 156 aircraft.

Nineteen of these were known to have been destroyed in fighting over other parts of the front and five were lost to other causes. The Dunkirk total was thereby reduced to 132.

Of this total a proportion must be allowed to the anti-aircraft units both with the retreating armies and in the Dunkirk perimeter, the French Navy credits its ships with a small number, and the Royal Navy formally claims 35.

It is difficult to read into these figures any justification for the widely repeated declaration that Fighter Command established qualitative superiority over Dunkirk. It is true that qualitative superiority does not necessarily rest upon a profit and loss account. Factors such as the numbers involved on either side are of importance. None the less, even here there appears to have been a certain misjudgement. The RAF at this period estimated the German first line strength for the attack in the west as 1,500 fighters and well over 2,000 bombers. In fact, at the height of the offensive the Luftwaffe had about 1,200 fighters and about 1,600 bombers. These forces were divided into two air fleets, and it was Air Fleet 2, Kesselring's northern force, that was in the first phase entrusted with the destruction of the Armies of the North and the attack on Dunkirk. Kesselring's force at that time had been reduced by the transfer of VIII Air Group to Air Fleet 3. It had been engaged for sixteen days in ceaseless operations in support of the German Army, and according to Kesselring himself: 'These operations exhausted our men and material, and reduced our strength to 30–50 per cent.' When later in the battle Air Fleet 3 was partly utilised, its strength was also considerably diminished.

It is certain, then, that the German strength available over Dunkirk during the period of the withdrawal was not at any time as great as it was believed to be at Fighter Command Headquarters. The tactical advantage gained by the Germans by their rapid occupation of abandoned airfields in Belgium and Northern France, however, unquestionably enabled Kesselring to put a remarkably high proportion of his force into the air at selected moments. That proportion appears to have been consistently greater than the proportion of Fighter Command's resources which RAF policy permitted. The inevitable consequence was the outnumbering of the patrols over the area, and much of the disparity of loss would seem to be directly attributable to this fact.

There is an additional factor which must be considered in this connection. The area over Dunkirk and beyond it was outside the effective range of the radar equipment then in use. In a very great measure this probably explains why the qualitative superiority which obtained during the Battle of Britain did not, in fact, obtain during the Dunkirk fighting. None of these things in any way affects the personal gallantry and the self-sacrifice of the individual fighter pilots and of the squadrons which strove to cover the armada of the evacuation. Tributes are frequent in many eye-witness accounts of the time. If criticisms are more frequent, it was because policy dictated the scale of the effort. One thing is certain. If it had not been for the vigour and bravery of those who were sent across, the loss must have been infinitely greater than it was.

*   *   *

One of the most important elements in the genius of the Royal Navy is its capacity for the unorthodox. The records carry ample proof. The campaign against the Armada was unorthodox, so was Nelson's attack at Trafalgar. Heligoland, Zeebrugge, Narvik, and St Nazaire in recent times all represent departures from the strict norm of the 'Fighting Instructions'. But in all the register of shifts and stratagems in the history of the Service it is difficult to find an adequate measure for the nine days campaign of Dunkirk, nor is it easy to discover a just parallel for its cool abandonment of the rules and its calculated acceptance of the risks. It is not the least among the paradoxes of Dunkirk that Bertram Ramsay was an orthodox admiral.

The position of the Royal Navy at the outbreak of war was

considerably more satisfactory than that of the Army in relation to its probable task, but there were certain weaknesses which showed themselves clearly in the course of the first phase of the sea battle. The Navy had put most of its available funds into two channels of construction. On the one hand, to counter the heavy German ships from the '*Deutschland*' class to the '*Bismarcks*', together with what was known of the Z-Plan, there was a considerable battleship programme: five ships of the '*King George V*' class and four of the '*Lion*' class. To implement the far-sighted ideas of the advocates of air power in conjunction with surface ships there was at the same time a heavy aircraft-carrier programme: *Ark Royal*, three ships of the '*Illustrious*' class and three ships of the '*Indomitable*' class.

This heavy-ship programme absorbed the greater part of the money set aside for new construction, and the direct consequence was that the Navy began the war seriously deficient in a number of classes of smaller ships. There was a second reason for this. The development of the Asdic anti-submarine instrument in the years between the wars had been welcomed on insufficient evidence as the solution to the submarine problem. There is very little doubt that successive Boards of Admiralty placed too much reliance on the potential of the Asdic instrument and in consequence paid too little attention to the development of anti-submarine vessels. As a result of these two things, then, the Navy began the war with 100 destroyers for Fleet purposes and 101 destroyers and sloops for the defence of the convoy routes. The number was wholly inadequate. There was a further weakness. With the big ships anti-aircraft defence had been brought to a level of some efficiency: with the smaller ships it had been neglected. Whole classes of modern destroyers possessed no anti-aircraft armament at all, nor was their main armament capable of elevating sufficiently to deal with aircraft at bombing angles. These ships had to be withdrawn progressively from service to have ancient anti-aircraft guns from reserve welded to improvised positions. Certain of the older classes of destroyers, however, had been or were in process of being converted to anti-aircraft ships at the outbreak of war.

The inadequacy of the British destroyer flotillas has already been explained in detail. It will be remembered that out of 202 destroyers at the outbreak of war the Royal Navy had already lost fourteen and had a very large proportion of the remainder in dockyard hands. Moreover, the Home Fleet flotillas were heavily engaged in the last stages of the Norwegian campaign, and, finally, the Boulogne evacuation had sunk or put out of action all except one of the regular Dover flotilla.

It is unnecessary to make a direct comparison between the attitudes of mind of the Air Council and of the Board of Admiralty during this period, yet there is an important parallel. The Navy's responsibility for the defence of the United Kingdom was twofold: it had to provide surface ships against possible future invasion, and it had to ensure the continued safety of the convoy routes. In both these fields the destroyer flotillas were of the utmost importance. The continued existence of the United Kingdom depended on the safety of the convoys. In theory Britain could be destroyed as surely by starvation as by direct attack. It was with this salutary consideration in mind that the Admiralty reached its successive decisions with regard to the reinforcement of Admiral Ramsay's command. No fewer than forty destroyers were in due course placed under his control. That represented the entire strength of the three home bases of the south coast and of the east coast, as well as a number of ships from the Home Fleet. It was again with this consideration in its mind that the Admiralty withdrew the modern destroyers on May 29th, and it is by this that its decision to send them back into the fray on Ramsay's appeal must be measured.

It was upon the destroyers, together with the cross-Channel steamers, that Admiral Ramsay based his preparations. The progress and timing of the 'Dynamo' plan has already been given in some detail. It is enough here to recall that the work progressed under the dramatic circumstances of the German breakthrough and the capture of the Channel ports. The facilities available for its execution diminished while the plans were being drawn up from four major ferry ports, with all their equipment and berthing accommodation, to the single wooden plankway of the East Mole at Dunkirk and the open beaches from there to La Panne. It was drafted while the very small staff of the Dover Command was stretched almost to the limit of its capacity by the demands, first, of the evacuation of Holland and, then, of Boulogne and of Calais. That it was completed in time and adjusted in accordance with the swift and terrible changes of the hour is in itself a naval masterpiece.

In general terms the plan provided for the dispatch in a

steady flow of two ships every four hours. These were to be drawn from the sixteen cross-Channel steamers on hand in the Dover area, supplemented by the destroyers that had already been sent to make good the losses of the previous week, and by smaller vessels. They were to use the harbour so long as it remained possible or, alternatively, were to pick up their men from the open beaches, utilising such small craft as were available together with ships' boats.

This plan foundered, as has been shown. The anxiety in London which led to the signal to Ramsay to try to lift 45,000 men before evacuation became impossible, was unjustified – though it would be a bold man who would say that it was unjustifiable. The measures that Gort had taken to cover his flank against the collapse of the Belgians proved sufficient. The Monday morning came with the Belgians still fighting, Brooke's front remained unbroken, the preparatory moves for the withdrawal to the Lys had taken place, and at a conference at Cassel the defence of the perimeter of Dunkirk had been agreed with the French by General Adam.

In the early afternoon Captain Tennant crossed to take up the position of Senior Naval Officer at Dunkirk. His first signal, it will be remembered, declared that embarkation would be possible only from the beaches east of the harbour. It was followed at eight o'clock by the signal which asked for all available craft as 'evacuation tomorrow night is problematical'. There followed a further report from two unidentified officers from GHQ which suggested that the Germans might succeed in cutting off the BEF from Dunkirk.

As a result of these signals Dover redoubled its efforts. All available ships were sent across – the destroyers to the La Panne area, the personnel ships to the nearer beaches – and all question of maintaining a time-table on the lines of the original plan went by the board. At the same time the shelling from the Calais area entered strongly into the situation. A number of ships were turned back by this on the first evening, and preparations were at once put in hand to sweep the new route which was subsequently to be called Route Y, and to begin the sweeping of a third alternative route, Route X.

Out of the welter of confusion and uncertainty engendered by this brusque change of plan Ramsay received one heartening signal – Tennant's message that it was possible to berth ships at the East Mole. On the basis of that fact Ramsay began at once to reconstruct his plan. Simultaneously the full importance of small craft upon the beaches became apparent.

Perhaps the most enduring of all the Dunkirk myths is the belief – widely held not only in England but elsewhere – that the evacuation was carried out by the spontaneous action of innumerable small craft sailing independently under the influence of an enormous enthusiasm from the ports of south-eastern England to the rescue of the Army. The part played by the little ships is beyond praise, it has added a new chapter to the sea story of Britain; but it was a controlled enthusiasm, an organised movement. The Small Vessels Pool at the Admiralty, the Ministry of Shipping, the boat yards and yacht clubs and harbour authorities from Poole to Lowestoft all played their part in it, and the boats that were commandeered or that volunteered were canalised through a highly organised series of routes to Margate and Ramsgate and Dover for the actual crossing.

It is in this aspect of the operation that Ramsay's genius comes to its highest peak, for out of inchoate enthusiasms and widely dispersed units he created, shaped and maintained the armada of deliverance. He was magnificently supported by his subordinates: Admiral Somerville, who alternated with him as his deputy and whose energy and brilliant handling of human material played a vital part in the control; Captain Morgan, who, as Chief of Staff, held together the Dynamo Room; Captain Phillimore and Captain Wharton, who directed the fantastic work of the small boats from Ramsgate; Admiral Wake-Walker, who commanded afloat in the long channels off the Dunkirk beaches; Captain Tennant, who through the nine days, as Senior Naval Officer, was the focal point of the evacuation in Dunkirk itself; and Commander Clouston, who made of the post of pier-master of the Dunkirk mole a command as glorious as that of any ship in history and who died in the last hours of splendour. These and a host of men – the captains of the destroyers, the masters of the cross-Channel steamers, the skippers of the coasters, the fishermen, the yachtsmen, the retired admirals, the laundry van drivers, the lifeboat men, the Civil Servants, the tug-boat men, the cockle-boat men, the garage hands, the clerks, the innumerable, infinitely varied volunteers from every section, every facet of British life – these made possible the miracle of Dunkirk.

They were backed by astonishing efforts on the shore. The work of the women at Sheerness and Margate, at Ramsgate and Dover and Folkestone, who met the returning troops with hot tea and food, who provided the postcards for them to tell their families of their safe arrival, who handed out cigarettes and found clothing and blankets for survivors, was indefatigable. The efforts of the small harbour staffs, reinforced by local volunteers, the achievements of doctors and nurses and VADs, of air raid wardens and police was everywhere equal to the need. And the accomplishment of the Southern Railway in moving a third of a million men swiftly from the vulnerable harbour areas was invaluable.

It would be incorrect, however, to suggest that everything was perfect in the record of Dunkirk. There were, as has been seen, boats whose skippers and crews refused to take them over on the grounds that they were unsuitable to the conditions; there were ships that turned back. As the evacuation progressed and exhaustion began to tell on officers and men alike, there were individual failures, there were ships that did not sail – there was even one that left the area against orders. Yet these things were small, hardly to be discerned in the tremendous vigour and sweep of the movements. Against the triumphant fact that 338,226 men were brought safely back to England they have no significance except inasmuch as they serve to light the courage and sacrifice of those who went.

The price of admiralty was, as always, heavy. Six destroyers, eight personnel ships, a sloop, five minesweepers, seventeen trawlers, a hospital ship and 188 lesser vessels and small craft were sunk and an equal number damaged out of the 693 British ships which took part in the operation.

It is given to few men to command a miracle. It was so given to Bertram Home Ramsay, and the frail iron balcony that juts from the embrasure of the old casemate in the Dover cliff was the quarter-deck from which he commanded one of the great campaigns in the sea story of Britain.

CHAPTER XX

The Three Men of Dunkirk

. . . and think foul scorn that Parma or Spain, or any prince of Europe should dare to invade the borders of my realm.

Queen Elizabeth at Tilbury, 1588

THE RETREAT to Dunkirk 'will ever be regarded as a brilliant episode in British military annals'.[1] Lord Gort foresaw its necessity, devised its plan and controlled its execution. Admiral Ramsay at Dover built out of the scattered units of the Royal Navy, the Merchant Service, and the small craft the armada of the evacuation and fired it with his genius. What would have happened if these two men had failed?

Perhaps it will never be possible to arrive at an absolute answer to that question.

General Brooke, writing as Lord Alanbrooke in the years after his long and brilliant service as Chief of the Imperial General Staff, said:[2]

'Had the BEF not returned to this country, it is hard to see how the Army could have recovered from this blow. The reconstitution of our land forces would have been so delayed as to endanger the whole course of the war.'

But it would not have been a matter of armies alone. Modern war is an affair of peoples. If Dunkirk had failed, a quarter of a million men would have been severed at one blow from the life of Britain. Nations have withstood greater shocks, but it would be folly to pretend that before May 1940 Britain was wholly committed to the war. Disarmament, pacifism, the Peace Pledge Union, even Communism, between the wars had sapped at the national will to fight. It has been fashionable to condemn politicians for appeasement. Appeasement, in some measure at least, was a political expression of the will of the people. For proof of that it is necessary only

[1] *Their Finest Hour* by Winston S. Churchill.
[2] *The Turn of the Tide* by Arthur Bryant.

290

to remember the tumult of the night of the Munich agreement.

The nine months of the first phase of the war scarcely hardened that will. Inept propaganda and consistent underestimation of the enemy had built up optimism to a point where absolute defeat must have had, as with France, dangerous psychological connotations.

It seems inconceivable now that Winston Churchill could have been broken. None the less, it was possible; his Government might, in fact, have broken from within – there were still appeasers in its ranks. The combination of the shock to the electorate of the loss of a quarter of a million sons, fathers, friends, with the defeat of Norway, Holland, Belgium, and Britain's one strong ally France, and the political weakness of certain sections of Parliament, might have forced acceptance of a carefully calculated German offer of peace.

Consider Churchill's record as Prime Minister up to May 26th:

He had succeeded to office at the crisis of the Norwegian disasters, and they continued.

The day he went to Downing Street the Belgian front was shattered.

On the third day the French front broke and Corap's Ninth Army 'faded away'.

On the sixth day the BEF began the long retreat.

On the tenth day it was fighting for survival.

Sixteen days after he kissed hands on taking office he authorised the evacuation of Dunkirk.

These things were not of his begetting, they were his grim inheritance; but they could have weighed against him in the scales of politics. Grimly he foresaw their danger and he began early to prepare his barricades. On May 17th, one week after taking office, he asked for an examination of 'the problems which would arise if it were necessary to withdraw the BEF from France'. Deliberately he selected Neville Chamberlain to carry out the examination.

Ten days later he put the question to the Chiefs of Staff:[1]

'In the event of France being unable to continue the war and the Belgian Army being forced to capitulate after assisting the British Expeditionary Force to reach the coast . . . what are the prospects of our continuing the war alone?'

The answers to that question are a harsh analysis of Britain's chances. As long as the Air Force remained in being, the

[1] *Their Finest Hour.*

Chiefs of Staff felt that the Air Force and the Navy in conjunction could stave off invasion. If Germany gained complete air superiority, the Navy could hold out alone, but only for a time. If the Navy failed, the Army (remember the question postulated the return of the BEF) could not alone prevent it.

Could Germany gain air superiority?

Day attack on the aircraft industry, said the Chiefs of Staff, could be held. No guarantees were possible against night bombing; if the Germans pressed home night attacks, they were 'likely to achieve such material and moral damage within the industrial area concerned as to bring all work to a standstill'.

There was a last paragraph in which the Chiefs of Staff paid tribute to the morale of the civil population. It is hard to believe that it was more than a sop to the faith, the optimism, and the belligerence of the Prime Minister. For the rest, the answer reads perilously like an admission of defeat.

On Tuesday, May 28th, in Parliament Churchill warned the nation. 'The House,' he said, 'should prepare itself for hard and heavy tidings . . .'

These words are perhaps the real starting point of one of the great adventures in leadership in human history. Up to this day it is possible to criticise Churchill's exercise of office at certain points: he misappreciated the position in the battle of France in its early stages; he allowed himself to be misinformed; he accepted bad advice; for a time he mistrusted Gort; he permitted the French to infect him, at least for a little, with their own unrealism.

Now he outfaced disaster. That afternoon he called together the twenty-four Ministers of Cabinet rank who were not in the War Cabinet. In plain, blunt terms he told them the facts, explained the balance of probabilities, and then, without underlining, without emphasis, he said:

'Of course, whatever happens at Dunkirk, we shall fight on.'

Westminster is not emotional – it makes something of a parade of that fact – but at those quiet words there was a demonstration that can have had few parallels since the eighteenth century. Men shouted, men cheered, men leapt from their seats to run to Churchill and pat him on the back.

The Dunkirk Spirit is in itself one of the last myths of Dunkirk. Like the other myths it has something of truth behind it; but the Dunkirk Spirit was not a vast incandescent flame of self-sacrifice and high endeavour that swept the country in a night. Like the flow of the little ships, it was something that awoke spontaneously but that had to be guided, encouraged, supported – like a small red heart of embers that must be blown upon.

The production statistics of the time seem an unlikely source of confirmation, yet they make remarkable reading. Deliveries of tanks that were vital to the very beginnings of defence rose very slowly through June, July and August to an average of a little over 120 a month. Deliveries of field guns rose from forty-two a month in May and June to sixty in July and seventy-two in August. Deliveries of fighter air-craft showed on paper a swift increase, but it was achieved departmentally at the risk of mortgaging the future. Real production rose in parallel with tanks and guns.

The embers glowed, but they were still embers.

Churchill blew on them.

The great speeches of the time in the House of Commons and out of it, his handling of his colleagues, his encourage-ment of the war leaders, his sense of urgency, his patriotism, his burning, blazing faith in Britain, blew a flame from the embers – a flame that was to temper the nation to sacrifices undreamed of, to victories unimagined.

There were three men of Dunkirk – Gort, Ramsay and Churchill.

No words in all this time, few in British history, sound so like a trumpet call as the speech that Winston Churchill made when Dunkirk was over and the waters were at last at rest.

'. . . we shall defend our Island, whatever the cost may be. We shall fight on the beaches, we shall fight on the landing-grounds, we shall fight in the fields and in the streets, we shall fight in the hills; we shall never surrender; and even if, which I do not for a moment believe, this Island or a large part of it were subjugated and starving, then our Empire beyond the seas, armed and guarded by the British Fleet, would carry on the struggle, until, in God's good time, the New World, with all its power and might, steps forth to the rescue and the liberation of the Old.'

APPENDIX A

List of Ships which took part in Operation 'Dynamo'

PART I: BRITISH SHIPS
Asterisk (*) denotes ships sunk

AA CRUISER
Calcutta

DESTROYERS

Anthony	Intrepid	Venomous
*Basilisk	Ivanhoe	Verity
Codrington	Jaguar	Vimy
Esk	Javelin	Vivacious
Express	*Keith	*Wakeful
Gallant	Mackay	Whitehall
*Grafton	Malcolm	Whitshed
*Grenade	Montrose	Winchelsea
Greyhound	Sabre	Windsor
Harvester	Saladin	Wolfhound
*Havant	Scimitar	Wolsey
Icarus	Shikari	Worcester
Impulsive	Vanquisher	(23 damaged)

SLOOP
Bideford (damaged)

CORVETTES

Guillemot	Mallard	Sheldrake
Kingfisher	Shearwater	Widgeon
		(1 damaged)

GUNBOATS
Locust   *Mosquito

MINESWEEPERS

Albury	*Devonia	Emperor of India
*Brighton Belle	Duchess of Fife	Fitzroy
Brighton Queen	Dundalk	Glenavon

295

MINESWEEPERS (contd.)

Glengower
Gossamer
*Gracie Fields
Halcyon
Hebe
Kellett
Leda
Lydd
Marmion
Medway Queen

Niger
Oriole
Pangbourne
Plinlimmon
Portsdown
Princess Elizabeth
Queen of Thanet
Ross
Salamander
Saltash

Sandown
Sharpshooter
*Skipjack
Snaefell
Speedwell
Sutton
*Waverley
Westward Ho
Whippingham
(4 damaged)

MINESWEEPING CRAFT

Alcmaria
Arley
Botanic
Brock
*Calvi
Clythness
Chico (E.S.)
*Comfort
Conidaw
Dorienta
Feasible
Fidget
Fisher Boy
Fyldea
Genius
Gula
*Gulzar
Inverforth
Jacketa
Jackeve
Jeannie Mackintosh

John and Nora
John Cattling
Lord Barham
*Lord Cavan
Lord Collingwood
Lord Grey
Lord Hood
Lord Inchcape
Lord Keith
Lord Melchett
Lord Rodney
Lord St Vincent
Mare
Maretta
*Nautilus
Olivae
Our Bairns
Overfalls
*Polly Johnson
Reed

Relonzo
Renascent
Restrivo
Rewga
Rig
Sarah Hyde
Sargasso
Saturn
Silver Dawn
Starlight Rays
Stella Rigel
Strathelliott
Strive
Swift Wing
Taransay
*Thomas Bartlett
Thomsons
Three Kings
Tweenways
Unicity

ANTI-SUBMARINE TRAWLERS

*Argyllshire
*Blackburn Rovers
Cape Argona
Cayton Wyke
Grimsby Town
Kingston Alalite
Kingston Andalusite

Kingston Olivine
Lady Philomena
Olvina
St Achilleus
Saon
Spurs

*Stella Dorado
*Thuringia
Topaze
*Westella
Wolves
(2 damaged)

THAMES SPECIAL SERVICE SHIPS

*Crested Eagle
Golden Eagle
Royal Eagle

MA/SBs, MTBs, Etc.

DC Motor-boat (ex *Excellent*)	MA/SB 10	MTB 68
	MTB 16	ML 100
MA/SB 6	MTB 22	MTB 102
MA/SB 7	MTB 67	MTB 107

Dover Flare-Burning Drifters

*Boy Roy	Golden Sunbeam	Shipmates
Eileen Emma	Lord Howard	The Boys
Forecast	Lord Howe	Torbay II
Gervais Rentoul	Midas	Ut Prosim
Girl Gladys	Netsukis	Yorkshire Lass
*Girl Pamela	*Paxton	Young Mun
Golden Gift		

Portsmouth A/P Yachts

Ahola	Caryanda	Noneta
Anlah	Eila II	Seriola
Ankh	Lahloo	Thele
Bounty	Marsayru	

Miscellaneous HM Ships
(small craft)

ALC 5
ALC 15
ALC 16
ALC 17
Alouette II (Echo Sounding Yacht)
*Amulree (Harbour Defence Patrol Craft)
Aronia (Yacht)
Ben and Lucy (Drifter)
Bluebird (MB)
Bystander (Echo Sounding Yacht)
Caleta (Harbour Defence Patrol Craft)
Chrystobel II (Harbour Defence Patrol Craft)
Dolphin's motor boat
Evelyn Rose (Trawler)
Excellent's A/A motor-boat
Gava (Trawler)
Glala (Harbour Defence Patrol Craft)

Grey Mist (DAN-laying Vessel)
*Grive (FAA Yacht)
Kindred Star (Drifter)
*King Orry (Armed Boarding Vessel)
Llanthony (Examination Service Vessel)
Lormont (Armed Boarding Vessel)
Monarda (Drifter)
Mona's Isle (Armed Boarding Vessel)
St Olaves (Rescue Tug)
Turret (A/S Yacht)
Thrifty (Drifter)
V 4 (Vernon's pinnace)
Vella (Armed Trawler)
Vernon I
Viviana (A/S Trawler)
 (1 damaged)

DUTCH SKOOTS
(Commissioned with Naval Crews)

Abel Tasman
Aegir
Alice
Amazone
Antje
Atlantic
Bart
Bornrif
Brandaris
Caribia
Delta
Demok I
Deneb
Despatch II
Doggersbank

Fredanja
Frisco
Gorecht
Hebe
Hilda
Hondsrug
Horst (abandoned)
Java
Jutland
Kaapfalgia
Lena
Oranje
Orange Yreeswijh
Pacific

Pascholl
Patria
Princess Juliana
Reiger
Rika
Ruja
San Antonio
Sursum Corda
Tilly
Tiny
Tung
Twente
Vrede
Zeus

PERSONNEL AND HOSPITAL SHIPS

Archangel
Autocarrier
Ben-My-Chree
Biarritz
Canterbury
Clan MacAlister
Côte d'Argent[1]
*Côte d'Azur[1]
Dinard (Hospital)
Dorrien Rose (Store Ship)
*Fenella
Foam Queen
Isle of Guernsey (Hospital)
Isle of Thanet (Hospital)
Killarney
King George V
Lady of Mann
Levenwood (Store Ship)
Lochgarry
*Lorina
Maid of Orleans
Malines
Manxmaid
Manxman

*Mona's Queen
Newhaven[1]
Nephrite (Store Ship)
Ngaroma
*Normannia
Paris (Hospital)
Prague
Princess Maud
Queen of the Channel
Roebuck
Rouen[1]
Royal Daffodil
Royal Sovereign
St Andrew (Hospital)
St David (Hospital)
St Helier
St Julien
St Seiriol
*Scotia
Tynwald
Worthing (Hospital)
Whitstable
(13 damaged)

[1] French vessels working with British personnel ships

MERCHANT VESSELS

*Abukir
Beal
Bullfinch
Clewbay
Corinia
*Firth Fisher
Gateshead
Hythe
Kitty
Lowick

Sandhill
Scottish Co-operator
*Sequacity
Sodality
Spinel
Westown
Williamstown
*Worthtown
Yewdale
Yewglen

TUGS

Betty
Cervia
Challenge
Contest
Crested Cock
Doria
Empire Henchman
Fabia
Fairplay I
Foremost 22
Foremost 87

Fossa
Gondia
Hibernia
Java
Kenia
Lady Brassey
Ocean Cock
Persia
Racia
Simla
Sun

Sun III
Sun IV
Sun V
Sun VII
Sun VIII
Sun X
Sun XI
Sun XII
Sun XV
Tanga
Vincia

SMALL CRAFT

Ace
Ada Mary
Adeline
Advance
Adventuress
Agnes Cross (Life-
    boat)
Aid
*Albatross
Aljanor
Aloa-Oc
Aloha
Alouette
Amity
Andora
Andora II (RAF
    Launch)
*Anee (Wherry)
Anne
Anthony
Antoinette

Aqua Belle
Ashingdon
Athola
Auntie Gus
Aura
Balquhain.
Barbara
Barbill II
Basildon
Bat
Beal
Bee
Belfast
Bessie
Betty
*Beverley
Bhurana
*Black Arrow
Black Java
Blackpool
Blue Bird (1)

Blue Bird (2)
*Boat (16 feet)
*Bobeli
*Bonnibell
Bonny Heather
Bou Saada
Bournemouth
    Lifeboat
Boy Billy
Boy Bruce
Boy Fred
B.P. One
Breadwinner
Brenart
Britannia IV
*Britannic
Brywyn
Bullfinch
*Bull Pup
Burgonia
Burton

Cabby
Cachalot
Cairngorm
Camellia
Canvey Queen
*Carama (15-foot punt)
Caraid
Carmen
Caronia
Caversham
Cecille
Cervantes
Chamois
Chantecler
Charlotte
Chriscraft (25 feet)
*Clara Belle (Wherry)
Claude (Water Boat)
*Commodore
Constant Nymph
Cora-Ann
Cordelia
Cornelia
Corsair
Count Dracula
Court Belle II
Creole
Cruiser
Curlew
*Cyb
Dab II
Dandy
Daphne
Dawn
Deenar
Defender
Desel II
Desiree
Devilfish
Dhoon (Trawler)
Diamond
Diana Mary
Diante

Dianthus
*Dinky (10-foot boat)
DLG
Dolphin
Dogger Bank
Doreen
Dorian
*Doris (Wherry)
*Dreadnought II
*Dreadnought III
Duchess of York
Duke
*Dumplin
Dwarf
D 1
D 4
D 7 } (Harbour Launches)
D 9
D 16
DC 715
DG 694
DG 950
Eastbourne Belle
Eastbourne Lifeboat
*Eastbourne Queen
*Edina (Wherry)
Edna
Edward & Mary
Edward Nissen
*Edwina
Elaine
Elizabeth Green
Ella
Elvin
EMED (Motor Lifeboat)
*Empress
*Enchantress
Encourage
Endeavour
Enterprise
Eothen
Erica
ERV
Eskburn

Esperanza
Ethel Ellen
Ethel Maud
*Ex-Service Dinghy
Fair Breeze (Drifter)
Fairwind
Faith
Falcon II
Favourite SM 225
Fawley (Gosport Ferry)
Fedelma II
Felicity
Ferry King (Gosport Ferry)
Ferry Nymph
Fervent
Fishbourne (IOW Ferry)
Firefly
Fleet Wing
Floss Hilda
Folkestone Belle
Formidable
Formosa
Fortuna
Forty Two
Fram
Francis (99B)
Frightened Lady
FW 23 (Lighter)
Galleon's Reach (Hopper)
Gavine
Gay Crusader
Gay Fly
Gay Venture
Gertrude
Gipsy King
Girl Nancy
Girl Vine
Glenway (Barge)
Glitter II
Golden Lily
Golden Spray

*Golden Spray II
Goliath
Gondolier King
Gondolier Queen
Gondolier III
Good Hope
Good Luck
Gourka
Grace
Grace Darling IV
Grace Darling
    (E 36)
Grappler (Lighter)
Greater London
    Lifeboat
*Green Eagle
Greta
Gwenny
Haig (WD Craft)
Halfway
Handy Billie
*Hanora
Hastaway
Hastings Lifeboat
Hawfinch
*Hazard
Heather Bell LN
    101
Henry Harris
Hilda
Hilfranor
His Majesty
Holland
Hopper 26
Hound
Hurlingham
Idaho
Imshi
Industry
Inspiration II
Iolanthe
Iota
*Iote
Irma
Irenic
*Island Queen

Jacinta (Trawler)
James 67 (Hopper
    Barge)
Jane Hannah
Janis
Jeff
Jetsam
Jockett II
Johanna (Eel Boat)
Jong
Jordan
Karina
Kayell
Kestrel R 7
King
King Fisher
Kingsgate
Kingwood
Kintail
Kitcat
Kitty
Kongoni
Lady Cable
Lady Haig
Lady Isabelle
Lady Kay
Lady Nancy
Lady Rita
*Lady Rosebery
Lady Sheila
Lady Southborough
    (Hopper Barge)
Lamouette
Lansdowne
*Lark
Laroc
Latona
Laudania
Laurel Leaf
Lavinia
Lazy Days
Leach's Romance
Leading Star
Leila 4
Lent Lily
*Letitia (1)

Letitia (2)
Liebestraum
Lijns
*Little Ann
Little Admiral
    LN 85
Little Mayflower
Little O' Lady
Lorna Doone
Lotus
Louisiana
Lurline
Lydie Suzanne
Madame
    Pompadour
*Madame Sans Gêne
*Maid of Honour
*Ma Joie
Major
Malden
*Malden Annie
Malvina
Marasole
Marchioness
Mare Nostrum
Margaret Mary
*Margherita
Marina
Marlborough (WD
    Craft)
Marquis (Tug)
Marsayru
Mary
Mary Irene
Mary Jane
Mary Rose
*Mary Spearing
Mary Spearing II
Massey Shaw (Fire
    Float)
Mata Hari
Matilda
Matoya
Mayflower
May Queen SM 270
Mayspear

SMALL CRAFT (contd.)

Meander
'Medora (Wherry)
Mermaiden
Mersey
MFH
Michael Stevens
Millicent D. Leach
Mimosa
*Minikoi
Minnedosa
Minoru II
Minotaur
Minx
*Miranda No. 58
 boat
Miss Ming
Miss Modesty
Mizpah
ML 108
Moiena
Monarch
*Montague (Whaler)
Moss Rose
Motor-boat (36 feet)
Motor-boat (30 feet)
Motor-boat 42
Motor-boat 27B
Motor-boat 43
 RAF
Motor-boat 101
 RAF
Motor-boat 102
 RAF
*Motor-boat 243
 RAF
Motor-boat 270
 RAF
Motor-boat 275
 RAF
ML 8 (WD Craft)
MTB M2
Mousme
Murius
Mutt
Naiad Errant
Nancy Belle

Nanette II
Narcissa
Nautilus A
Nelson (Motor-
 boat)
*Nemo IV
Newhaven Lifeboat
New Prince of
 Wales
*New White Heather
New Windsor Castle
Nin
Nirvana
No Name II
Norwich Belle
No. 4
No. 101 } (Hopper
No. 102 } Barges)
Ocean Breeze
Offemia
Olivia
Omega
Ona II
Oratava RX 45
Orellana
Orient Line Motor-
 boat
Oulton Belle
Our Lizzie
Our Maggie
Palmerston
Pandora
Papillon
Papkura
Pauleter
Pearl
*Peggy IV
Pellag II
Petra
Pigeon (WD
 Craft)
Pioneer
Polly
Pride of Folkestone
Prima (Tug)
Prince

Prince of Wales
Princess
Princess Freda
Princess Lily
*Princess Maud
Providence
Provider R 19
Pudge
Queen
Queen Alexandra
Queen Boadicea
Queen Boadicea II
*Queen of England
Queen's Channel
 (Hopper Barge)
Queensland
Quicksilver
QJ & J
Quisiana
Quest
Ramsgate Lifeboat
Rapide
Rayon
Reda
Reliance
Remembrance
*Renown
Resolute
Ricas
*Roberta
Robert Cliff
Robina Tenant
Rocinante
*Rosabelle
Rosa Wood and
 Phyllis Lund
Rose
Rose LN 19
Roselyne
Rose Marie
Rowan (Smack)
Royal Thames
Rummy II
Ryegate II
St Abbs
St Clears

302

*St Fagan
St Olaf
St Patrick
Sally Forth
Salvage Launch
Sandown
Santosy
Sarah & Emily
Satyr
Saviour
Scene Shifter
Schedar
*Sea Falcon
Sea Foam
Seagull
Seagull LN 203
Sea Hawk
Sea Roamer
Seasalter
Seaschool
Sea Swallow
Seine
Seymour Castle
*Shamrock
Shannon
Sheldrake
Sherfield (Motor-
   barge)
Shunesta
Silicia (Coaster)
Silver Foam
*Silver Queen
   (Motor-boat)
Silver Spray
Silver Spray LI 230
Silvery Breeze
Sinbad II
Singapore I
Singapore II
Skylark (1)
Skylark (2)
Skylark I
Skylark II
*Skylark II SM 281
*Skylark III
*Skylark III SM 391

Skylark IV SM 5
Skylark VI
Skylark IX
Skylark X
Small Viking
Smiling Through
Smolt
Smuggler
Snow Bunting
Sonia
Southend Britannia
Southern Queen
*Southern Queen
   PL 17
South Ray
Speedwell
Spinaway
Spindrift
Sprite (Harbour
   Launch)
Starfish
Stonehaven
Suffolk's Rose
Sultan
Summer Maid
Sundowner
*Sunshine R 13
Surrey
Swallow
Sylvia
Tankerton Towers
Tarpon
Tenias
Thark
*Thetis
Three Brothers
3270
Thurn
Thyforsa
Thyme
Thyra
Tigris I
Tom Hill
Trillene
Triton
Tony LN 40

Tortoise
Triton
Two Rivers
Two Sisters
Unique
Usanco
Valerie
Vanguard
*Vanitee
Vedettes
Venture
Vera
Victoria
*Viewfinder
Viking
*Viking III
Viscount
Volante R 110
Volo
Waiakei II
Walmer Castle
Walton and Frinton
   Lifeboat
Wanda
Warrior (1)
Warrior (2)
Wave Queen
Welcome
Wessex (Lighter)
Westall
West Cove
Westerley
Westgrove
Westward
Weymouth Queen
White Bear
White Lady
White Orchid
Whitewater
White Wing
   (Motor-boat)
*Willie & Alice
Windsong
Wings of the
   Morning
Winmabet

Winston	W 24 (Hopper	YC 63 ⎫
Wolfe	Barge)	YC 71 ⎬ (Lighters)
(WD Craft)	X 95 ⎫	YC 72 ⎭
Wolsey	X 134 ⎬ (Lighters)	*Yola*
Wootton (IOW	X 209 ⎭	
Ferry)		

PART II: FOREIGN WARSHIPS

POLISH

Blyskawica

FRENCH

Amiens	*Diligente*	*Mistral*
Amiral Mouchez	*Epervier*	MTB 24
Arras	*Flore*	*Simoun*
Belfort	*Foudroyant*	*Siroco*
Bouclier	*Impetueuse*	T 112
Bourrasque	*Incomprise*	T 113
Branlebas	*Leopard*	T 143
Cyclone	*Marceau*	

DUTCH

Netherland Motor-boat M 74

PART III: FOREIGN SHIPS, OTHER THAN WARSHIPS

Abel Dewulf
Ambleve (Belgian Launch)
André Louis
André Marcel
Angele
Arras
Ausa
A 5 (Belgian Patrol Craft)
A 73 (Belgian Patrol Craft)
AD 389
Barbara Auguste
Belge
Bernadette de Lisieux
Besta (Dutch)
Bordeaux
Caporal Pungest
Chalutier
Chantecler (Dutch Eel Boat)
Chasse Rave

Chasseur
Chasseur 7th
Chasseur Marrie
Cods Cenade
Commandant Delage
Constant Leopold
Cor Jesu (Belgian Trawler
  O 227)
Cul de France
Dame Franche
Denis Papin
Drifter 145 (Belgian)
Duperre (French Trawler)
Dutch Daffil
Dutch MVM
Emile Deschamps
Emile Lastus
Emile Louise

304

*Escaut (Belgian Launch)
Fransah
Gamboul
Gaston River
Gativois
Georges Edouard (Belgian
   Trawler O 86)
Gilda
Guido Gazelle (Belgian
   Trawler O 225)
Hdaya
H 51 (Belgian Trawler)
H 75 (Belgian Trawler)
Ingenieur Cachin
Jean Bart
Jean Ribault
Jeune France
Jonge Jan (Belgian Trawler
   O 200)
La Cere
Louise Marie
Lucien Gaigy
Lutter
Mana Elena
*Maréchal Foch (Belgian
   Trawler)
Meuse (Belgian Launch O 274)

Monique
Moya
M 2 (French Trawler)
Normanville
N 53 (Barge)
Onder Ons
O 87 ⎫
O 92 ⎬ (Belgian Trawlers)
O 318 ⎭
Patrie (French Trawler)
*Pierre Marie (French Drifter)
Pinette
President Buars
Puisse Marie
Reine de Flots
Sambre (Belgian Launch)
Sarzik
*Semois (Belgian Launch)
Sideres Louise
Surcouf de Guesclin
Thérèse Louise
VP 19 (French Barge)
Watonprise
*Yser (Belgian Launch)
Z 25 ⎫
Z 26 ⎬ (Belgian Trawlers)
Z 40 ⎭

Air Support

No. 11 GROUP FIGHTER PATROL – DUNKIRK AREA HISTORY

Date	Patrols	Total flying hours daily	Enemy aircraft assessed as destroyed
26th May	22	480	20
27th May	23	536	38
28th May	11	576	23
29th May	9	674	65
30th May	9	704	—
31st May	8	490	38
1st June	8	558	43
2nd June	4	231	35
3rd June	4	339	—
4th June	3	234	—
Totals	101	4,822	262

Notes

(1) It will be observed that the number of patrols decreased from May 27th onwards, whilst there was an increase in the daily flying hours. This is due to the fact that the fighters were employed in increasingly bigger patrols as the enemy air opposition increased.

(2) Operation 'Dynamo' suffered most from enemy air effort on May 29th and on June 1st, after which latter date the combination of enemy air attack and shore artillery fire led to the suspension of the operation by day.

(3) The question of the assessment of enemy aircraft destroyed is examined fully in Chapter XIX.

SUMMARY OF AIRCRAFT DATA CONCERNING RN

Enemy Aircraft Destroyed by Ships' Fire off Dunkirk
(between 0300/May 27th and 2000/June 1st)

27th May	.	.	.	.	4
28th May	.	.	.	.	3
29th May	.	.	.	.	4
30th May	.	.	.	.	Nil*
31st May	.	.	.	.	11
1st June	.	.	.	.	13

Total 35

In addition over the same period 21 others were heavily damaged by ships' fire and seen in distress but not definitely seen to crash.

* On May 30th flying conditions were bad and few enemy aircraft operated. After June 1st evacuation proceeded only between evening dusk and dawn.

Index I

CRAFT TAKING PART IN OPERATIONS OR MENTIONED INCIDENTALLY

Listing names only; for classifications and mentions of nationality, damage sustained, etc., see 'Dynamo' list, pages 294–304, and refer to names. These two lists are not interchangeable. B=Belgian, D=Dutch, F=French, P=Polish.

Index II

GENERAL

Aa Canal, 17, 49, 235, 239
Abbeville, strategic importance of, 37, 43
Abrial, Admiral (*Amiral Nord*), 13, 33, 66, 73, 74, 77, 95, 96, 97, 115, 165, 263; Alexander's first consultation with, 186; at June 1 meeting, 199; at June 3 meeting, 227; embarks for England, 233; and the lost destroyers, 264
Adam, General, 46, 95, 96, 107, 123, 159, 167; assessment of, 274; at Cassel 'perimeter' conference, 287
Ailwyn-Jones, Capt, 163
Air forces: French, 261; German 'Luftwaffe', 305; failure of G. at Dunkirk analysed, 241–2; G., help of, for Rundstedt, 241; main attacks of, June 1, 188 seqq.; mining operations of G., 243–4; RAF, 17, 139, 197, 198, 277–83; summary, 305–6.
Alanbrooke, Lord, *see* Brooke, General
Aldis, Capt T., 130, 170
Aldrich, H., 155, 192
Alexander, Maj.-Gen. the Hon. H. R. L. G. Alexander, 166, 186, 187, 199, 206, 223, 275–6; May 31 command of, 187; assessment of, 276
Allied and German strength, May 16, 36
Anduse-Faru, Commandant, 220
Anti-Tank Regiment, 69th, 73
Antwerp: blocking of, 57; demolition, 33, 34
Anzac forces (War I), 15–16

Ardennes drive (German), 25, 28; *and see Fall Gelb*
Arnim, General von, 16
Arras, British counter-attack at, 44–8; and failure of Plan Yellow, 239; Weygand and, 50
Atkins, J. E., 175
Auphan, Capt, 103, 115; allegations made by (*re* evacuation decision), 262; contribution of, 263

Backhouse, Admiral Sir Roger, 32
Bacon, quoted, 266
Barker, General, 46, 275
Barnard, Col H. T. B., 217
Barratt, Air Marshal A. S., 278
Barrell, Allan, 151
Barthélémy, General, 227, 234, 235
Bartlett, Sir Basil, 116
Baxter, Capt, 162, 171, 193–4
Battle of Left Flank assessed, 84–5, 123 seqq., 273–4; false conclusions drawn from, 90; *see* Eastern battle
Bedfordshires and Hertfordshires, 144
BEF, embarkation of, 20; numbers of, 20, 268; ports of landing, 30; question of evacuating, dating of, 42, 46, 47, 55–7, 58, 71, 87, 98–9, 111, 258, 262; supply re-organization, May 15, 31, 64–6; wartime strength of, 266–8; in France by June 5, 212–24
Belgium: accuses Gort, 38, 120–4, 140; army of defeated, 98; assessment of May 28 defeat

312